a

SAÏD THE FISHERMAN

SAÏD THE FISHERMAN

BY

MARMADUKE PICKTHALL

FOURTH EDITION

NEW YORK

M'CLURE, PHILLIPS & CO

1904

PART I

THE BOOK OF HIS LUCK

"There were some of them who made a covenant with God : Verily,
if He gives us of His abundance, we will give alms and become righteous
people."—ALCORAN.

SAÏD THE FISHERMAN

I

THE house of Saïd the fisherman nestled among the sand-hills of the seashore at a long stone's throw from the town, in whose shadow it lay at sunset. Within, it was a single room, very dirty, the abode of many aged smells; without, a squat cube with walls of stone and roof of mud sun-baked and rolled to a seemly flatness. Hard by was a fig-tree, the nearest to the sea in all that coast. Here, in a crotch of the branches, Saïd would place his mattress in the stifling summer nights and snore two deep bass notes in peace and coolness, while his wife trumpeted a treble from her couch upon the housetop. Here, when the day's work was done, he would squat in the shade, drawing leisurely at his narghileh, with the sound of bubbling water to cool him at every puff.

He was not a great fisherman, such as is to be found in Europe, with a sailing-boat of his own, who will go far out to sea with his nets. If there were any such in all the coasts of Arabistan, Saïd had never heard of them. Sometimes he would row out in a friend's boat to a little distance from the shore and drop his nets, a great circle of bobbing cork and driftwood to mark their whereabouts. But mostly he would go to some river-mouth or promontory where flat-topped rocks stretched far into the sea, promising safe foot-hold. And there, mother-naked, save for a huge turban, he would paddle and flounder all day long with his cast-net, sometimes alone, sometimes with several comrades.

At times, when the catch had been good, he would go into the city with a crate of fish and take his stand in the market-

A

place, in a corner which from long use he had come to call his own. There he would cry in a loud voice, beseeching Allah to put a craving for fish into the hearts of the passers-by. And Allah often lent a kindly ear to his prayer, for he seldom went home but with an empty basket.

It was one evening as he was wending homeward, dragging his empty basket with him across the sand, that the first gust of misfortune struck him.

The sun drew near to his setting, though as yet the sky was innocent of red. Shadows lengthened eastwards across the sand, of the colour of a periwinkle flower. A number of dogs were lying replete about the body of a dead donkey at the edge of the ripples, panting drowsily with their tongues out. They blinked at him as he passed, and their bellies heaved uneasily. They were too full to snarl. A sense of well-being was upon him. He stopped to draw forth a little bag from the girdle of his robe. It contained the gains of the day. He let go the empty basket and squatted down upon the sand, telling out the money piece by piece into his lap. His eyes gloated over the pile.

He held the fingers of his left hand wide apart and touched them one by one with the forefinger of his right. His brows puckered with the effort to reckon how much he could afford to lay by in that hole in the floor of his house which held his savings.

So far as he could count, it needed but one more day like this to make up the price of the coffee-house he had it in his mind to buy. Then he would leave the fishing business to Abdullah, his friend and partner, and customers would know him thenceforth as Saïd Effendi. That was but the first step in the path of his ambition. Presently he would be a Bey—an Emir, perhaps. He would lie all day upon a cushioned couch, smoking from a narghileh of rare workmanship. And when Abdullah came to beg him to buy fish, he would seize him by both ears and spit in his face.

Of a sudden the sound of loud shouting broke upon his reverie.

"Oäh! Oäh! Look to thyself, son of a dog!"

He was aware of two horsemen galloping madly down upon him from a gap in the sandhills—Turkish officers of the garrison by their uniform. They were close upon him. He leapt

to his feet and sprang aside just in time to save himself from
being knocked down and trampled under their horses' hoofs.
He heard them laugh aloud and curse him as they sped by,
blinding him for the moment in a cloud of sand.

"May their house be destroyed!" he snarled, looking after
them and showing his fangs like a dog that is angry. Then
he remembered the money which had been in his lap when
their shouts startled him, and there was no longer any room
for anger in his heart.

A wild light of hope and fear in his eyes, he flung himself
full length upon the ground and fell to groping and sifting
with trembling hands. But the wild rush of the horses had
played the whirlwind with the sand, scattering it hither and
thither and dinting it deep with hoof-prints. After many
minutes of burrowing and seeking he had found only two
small copper coins; and already the sun was sinking behind
the city and its headland, whose shadow was within a hand's-
breadth of him. A long train of camels passed him going
towards the gate, the drivers cheerful at sight of their journey's
end.

"What seekest thou, young man?" cried one of them as
he passed the fisherman.

Saïd raised himself to a kneeling posture and spread his
hands over his eyes.

"Away, scoffer!" he cried sternly. "Who art thou that
thou shouldst question a pious man at his prayers?" Then,
after an interval of meditation, he prostrated himself so that
his forehead touched the sand and forthwith resumed his
search, earnestly beseeching Allah to guide his fingers aright
and to keep all prying strangers at a distance.

The shadow was now upon him. All the west was a blaze
of red gold, so that every roof, every dome, every palm tree
upon the sky-line stood outlined clear and black. It was time
to give over this frantic groping and clutching which gave such
meagre results. He sat up and, squatting on his heels, began
a more orderly and less haphazard search, taking one handful
of sand at a time, sifting it between his fingers and laying it on
one side upon a heap. After more than an hour's experience
of this process he had recovered some twenty small coins,
amounting perhaps to a fifth part of the sum he had lost.

Night fell: the stars shone out, blackening the bulk of the

dead ass, a few paces distant, which the dogs, reinforced by
stray comrades from the city, were beginning to worry anew.
The ripples, breaking in luminous foam upon the beach,
murmured sadly in his ears.   Hunger began to get hold of
him.   Hasneh would be wondering what had happened, and
that savoury mess of lentils and oil would be baked to a
cinder.   Why should he not go home, eat and drink, and
return to his search later on?   It was not likely that the sand
would be again disturbed that night. He could come back early
in the morning and collect the rest of his scattered fortune.
His basket would mark the exact spot.

So thinking, he rose and went homewards.   A faint light
streamed from the door and window of his dwelling.   Hasneh
was in there with the lentils.   His heart warmed at the
thought, making the neighbouring void colder and more empty
by contrast.   As he drew near to the house a sound of wailing grew in his ears—such wailing as he had heard at funerals
of the rich, where mourners were well paid for it.

His first thought was of the lentils, that they were spoilt.
His next, not without relief, that someone was dead within
the house.   But there was no one to die except Hasneh herself, and she it was who was wailing, as he had sometimes
heard her scold, in a shrill cadence.   His desire to learn the
truth lent wings to his feet.   In a few long strides he gained
the threshold.

His woman lay stretched upon the floor within—a heap of
clothes from which those ghastly moans and howls proceeded,
mingled with curses on some unknown being of the male sex.
For a moment Saïd stood frozen in the doorway.   Then the
sight of something black and shrivelled in a pan upon the
brazier sent angry blood coursing through every vein in his
body.   That something had once been a savoury mess of
lentils baked in oil, the lust of which had drawn him from his
search among the sand.   He sprang to a corner of the room,
seized a great staff which leaned against the wall, and fell to
belabouring the woman with all the strength of his arm.   Her
droning wail changed all at once to a lively shriek.   She leapt
to her feet and closed with him, trying vainly to wrest the
stick from his hand.

"May Allah cut short thy life!" she cried.   "What have
I done to deserve this of thee?"

"The lentils are spoilt!" retorted Saïd, furiously, wrenching his arm free of her and bringing the stick down heavily on her back. "May thy house be destroyed!"

"Madman!" she screamed. "Thou speakest of lentils when an enemy has robbed thee, ruined thee! Look!"

She pointed to a hole in the floor which had been hidden by her body when Saïd entered. Little mounds of fresh sand on the brink of it showed that hands had lately been at work there.

As Saïd's eyes followed the line of her forefinger his jaw fell and the anger died out of his face. His stick clattered on the ground. Some thief had found out the place where his treasure was hidden, had come in his absence and unearthed the savings of ten long years.

He peered into the hole to assure himself that it was quite empty. Not a single para had been let fall or overlooked by the miscreant. His eyes became dull and filmy as those of a blind man. His face grew livid as the face of a corpse. He fell back against the wall of the room.

Supposing that the shock of her news had killed him, Hasneh began to wail anew, beating her breast and plucking at her robe to tear it. Her voice revived Saïd somewhat.

"Be silent," he muttered — "thou thief! Thou alone wast in the secret of the hiding-place."

"Thy life is my life; thy fortune, my fortune," replied the woman, with indignation. "If thou prosperest, I prosper; and I have a part in thy loss. Listen now to the truth, nor judge me hastily unheard.

"Having prepared the lentils, I sat awaiting thy return, when my heart became sad within me. And I thought, if I uncover the hiding-place and fill my eyes with the sight of that which is good to see, there is no sin. So I took the piece of a broken vessel and scraped until the heap of coins was laid bare to mine eyes. So my heart had peace.

"And as I sat gazing upon my husband's wealth which is mine, the voice of Abdullah called from without: 'Behold the great fish, the giant of the deep, whose back is like Lebanon and his fins as the winnowing fans of Allah, with which he makes the winds to blow and stirs the sea to madness! It is Saïd who has brought it to land. It lies by the white stone where

the nets of Saïd are spread out to dry.   Run, O Hasneh, and
thou shalt see that which no woman has ever seen.'

"At that I gathered up my raiment and ran out of the
house, expecting to find Abdullah; but I found no man.   I
went all about the house, but I found not Abdullah nor any
other.   Then I trembled and fear came upon me.   But the
news of the great fish drew me onward, until I came to the
white stone and found it lonely as ever and the sea-fowl undisturbed upon it.   Then I knew that an evil spirit had cried
in the voice of Abdullah to lead me astray.   So I ran back
with all speed along the shore.   When I came to the house
the hole was as thou seest it and all the money gone."

Her last words were almost drowned in a flood of tears.

Saïd trembled and cold sweat stood in pearls upon his
forehead.

"An evil spirit has done this," he murmured hoarsely.
"Oh, that my enemy had been a man!"

He fell to bemoaning his fate, cursing the day that he was
born, and calling upon Allah to have mercy upon his faithful
servant.   The house that had been rifled by an evil spirit
seemed dreadful and unfamiliar.   The night which wrapped
it about was filled with hideous faces, which glowered at him
and mocked him through door and lattice.   At length he
exclaimed: "Abide here, Hasneh, and keep watch.   If thou
hearest a voice or seest any evil sight, cry aloud upon the
name of Allah and thou shalt be safe."

With that he stepped out into the night, and, girding up
his robe, sped across the sand to the city, black on the starlight, where a few scattered lights shone faintly.

II

CLOSE to the gate which is called the sea-gate, by which one goes down to the shore, there was a house, or rather hovel, built against the wall. This was the dwelling-place of Abdullah, Saïd's bosom friend and partner. Abdullah himself was sitting in the doorway, smoking his narghileh, when Saïd came upon him. He was a fat man, with small bright eyes which were seldom at rest. Within the house a wick, floating in a saucer of grease, threw a fitful light upon the four walls, upon a couch whereon his wife lay huddled, a baby at her breast, upon the disorderly litter of the floor. At sight of his friend Abdullah started to his feet. His eyes were shifty to right and left, as though seeking some way of escape.

"May thy night be happy," he faltered.

"May thy night be happy and blessed," replied Saïd, keeping the rule which bids every man return a compliment with interest. Then with a frantic gesture, "I am ruined! An evil spirit is my ill-wisher. My money—all that I had saved these many years—has been stolen. Oh, that a man had been the thief!"

Saïd's hands clutched murderously at the air and clenched, showing how he would have dealt with a mortal foe.

Abdullah's composure returned to him at these words. His face was almost cheerful as he exclaimed, "Merciful Allah!"

"Listen, Abdullah," pursued the other. "In my way homeward from the market I sat down to count over the price of the fish I had sold, when—whizz!—came two horsemen out of the air, and would have ridden over me had not Allah put it into my mind to jump aside. They laughed as they galloped by. They had the faces of jin—you know them!—eyes set slantwise, ears long and leaf-shaped like the ears of a pig.

7

Then I found that all the money I had been counting was
scattered in the sand.   After long seeking I recovered but a
few coins of small value.   It grew dark.   A train of camels
came along the shore.   Each camel was as big as a house,
with a hump like the dome of a mosque.   One of the drivers
looked at me and asked me what I did.   His eyes were two
flames.   They seemed to burn through to my heart.   But I
prayed to Allah and he vanished, the camels with him.   I
went home, hungry and thirsty, to supper; but I found my wife
cast down upon the floor, weeping, and the lentils quite spoilt.

"Then she told me what had happened.   As she sat in the
house a voice cried to her, for there was a great fish like a
mountain lying on the shore by the white stone.   She stepped
out, but saw no man.   She went to the stone, but there was
no fish great or small.   When she returned to the house she
found a hole in the floor at the place where my treasure was
hidden.   All the money was clean gone.   Oh, that my enemy
had been a man!"

"Said she aught of the voice which tempted her?" asked
Abdullah, with a hint of anxiety.   His form was outlined in
shadow upon the faint light which streamed from the doorway, so that Saïd could not see his face.

"Yes—a strange thing—she says that the voice was as thy
voice, O father of Azìz."

"There is no doubt that some devil has robbed thee," said
Abdullah, quickly.   "Allah be my witness, I have not left my
house since noon by reason of a pain in my belly.   Is it not
true, Nesibeh?"

The woman thus appealed to rose from her couch and
came shuffling to the door.   "Yes, it is true, by Allah," she
averred.   "He has been very ill.   I feared he was at the gate
of death.   But, praise to Allah, the pain has left his belly and
he is now in health again.   An afrìt has robbed thee and has
beguiled thy woman with the voice of Abdullah."

"I am ruined!   What can I do?" Saïd cried in a frenzy
of despair.   "Thou, O Abdullah, art known in all the city for
a wise man.   Counsel me, I entreat thee!"

Abdullah's face assumed the stolid expression supposed,
by the muleteers and camel-drivers whose oracle he was, to
betoken wisdom.   His eyes became intent upon the inwards
of a fish which adorned the ground near his feet.   He sucked

long and steadily at the mouthpiece of his narghileh, causing the water in the bowl to bubble convulsively and the charcoal in the cup above to give forth a lurid glow. Then he took the tube from his mouth, cleared his throat, spat solemnly, and said,—

"A devil has a spite against thee—that is known. He has entered thy house once, he will enter it again. It is likely that he is of those who haunt the waste places of the shore, perhaps the very same who dwells in the ruined shrine among the sandhills. It were well for thee to take thy staff and thy woman and go into some far country—into Masr or into the sunset-land which lies beyond. So thou shalt have peace, being far from the enemy."

"What a mind!" exclaimed his wife, with hands raised in admiration. "He speaks like a prophet. The mind of Abdullah is not as the mind of other men. He is a devil!"

"Tush, be silent, woman!" said the sage, indulgently.

Saïd squatted down at the threshold beside his friend. He put a hand to his forehead and remained thus thoughtful for some time. Then he said, "Thy advice is good. To-morrow, at the rising of the sun, I shall depart. But thinkest thou in truth that the evil spirit will not follow me?"

"The jin have their homes like men," replied Abdullah, sententiously. "They love to spend their lives in one place. In another city thou shalt surely live undisturbed."

"But I have no money," Saïd moaned. "Without wealth I shall find no place in a strange land."

Abdullah shook his head sadly.

"I am a poor man," he said, "but all that I have is thine. Go, Nesibeh, see how much money there is in the house."

The woman left the doorway and shuffled across the room to the couch where her baby slept. She felt under the coverings and drew forth a small box, which jingled as she shook it.

Raising the lid,—

"Alas!" she moaned. "It is a bad day with Abdullah. There are but a few baras."

"It is a shame to ask my brother to accept so little!" exclaimed her husband.

"A little is much to one who has nothing," whispered Saïd, eagerly. "Give me but the few baras that are there and may Allah increase thy wealth!"

Nesibeh turned the box upside down over the palm of her hand, and a number of small coins fell from it. Saïd's brown fingers closed on them like an eagle's claws. Then he rose to take leave.

"In thy grace, I depart," he said. "May Allah prosper thee, O father of Azîz."

"My peace go with thee," said Abdullah, his voice broken with grief.

Saïd strode away, sad at heart, his mind busy with plans for the future. Hope was all but dead within him, for he had eaten nothing since sunrise. Alone once more and in the darkness, fear fell upon him with renewed strength. All the night was full of ghastly faces, of fiery eyes that glowered upon him. Strange shapes flitted among the sandhills. The sea burned with a pallid light. A fitful moaning was in the air. Pausing for a moment, he fancied the night an endless procession of weird forms—a multitude which moved glidingly, silently, as one man. It filled him with a strange new horror, which yet seemed half familiar, as something remembered from a dream. Well-known sounds, such as the hooting of an owl, the bark of a dog from the city, or the howl of a jackal from some landward garden, were separate terrors.

He had not made many steps from the door of his friend's house ere the fear of the Unknown which lurks in darkness took hold of him. He girded up his loins and ran across the sand as fast as his brawny legs would carry him. He looked neither to the right nor left till he reached his house. On the threshold a savoury smell attacked his nostrils and hope suddenly revived. Hasneh stood with her back towards him, leaning over the brazier, from which light steam arose enveloping her and filling the house with that peculiarly hopeful smell. "Allah is just!" murmured Saïd, licking his lips.

III

IT was the coolest hour of all the twenty-four when Saïd
the fisherman climbed down from his nest in the fig-tree.
In spite of the troubles and fears of the evening before
he had slept soundly and was refreshed. The eastern sky
was whitening to the dawn, and a wave-line of distant
mountains was grey and cloudlike upon it. Darkness still
lingered on sea and land, but it was a darkness of the earth
rather than of the heavens.

From a jar within the threshold of the house he took a
little water and went through the form of ablution. Then,
facing south, he knelt and fell prostrate several times, thumbs
fast behind his ears and hands spread across his eyes as an
open book.

As he walked along the shore to the place where he had
left his basket overnight, the cry of the first awakened sea-
bird hailed the dawn. The little city with its dome and
minarets grew white before him against a sky still dark and
studded with stars. A man came down from the sea-gate
riding upon an ass. Then came another man with two
camels. The folk of the city were astir and going every man
about his business.

The place was just as he left it, save that the carcase of
the donkey had been dragged a few yards to landward by the
hungry tearing of the dogs, and the backbone was now laid
bare. He flung himself face downward on the sand and fell
at once to his groping and sifting.

The stars shone dead in the west, then vanished altogether.
Rosy light stole over land and sea, mantling on the white
buildings of the city like the shame in a young girl's cheek.
Then the sun flashed forth above the distant hills and all
things had colours of their own once more.

The rays struck warm on Saïd's back as he lay prone

beside his basket. Their touch cheered him like a friend's hand. He set to work hopefully with the result that, in half an hour, he had recovered many coins, amounting to within a few paras of the sum lost.

By that time there were many people on the beach, some entering, some leaving the city. It was unsafe to prolong the search lest someone, guessing his task, should fall upon him and rob him. He got up, therefore, and walked homeward, trailing his basket along with him.

Hasneh stood in the doorway looking out for him. A donkey, burdened with two sacks, was tethered to a low-bending branch of the fig-tree. He smiled approval as he slipped off his shoes at the door. She had been stretched upon the roof when he set out and snoring loudly. He had been gone but a little while, yet here was the ass laden with all in the house that was worth carrying, and the morning's meal of bread and curds ready to be eaten.

His fast fairly broken, Saïd went out to the fig-tree to see that the girths were firm which held the sacks to the body of the ass. The sunlight danced on the little waves as they pushed shoreward, and made pearls of the dewdrops which yet hung in the shade of some feathery tamarisks behind the house. The sky was a great blue dome over sea and land. His heart turned sick with the thought of quitting the well-known scene, with its familiar voices, to sojourn among strangers in a strange country. Why need he go? The terrors of the night before had no weight with him now. They had faded with the darkness and the stars.

Doubtless his loss was great and hard to bear; but others had suffered worse things. The evil spirit which had robbed him might not return again; and if it did he had but to write the name of Allah upon the doorposts, then upon the shutters of the window, and his house would be safe. He stretched out his hand to loose the burden from the donkey's back.

"May thy day be happy, O Saïd," came a complacent voice from behind him. Turning, he stood face to face with Abdullah, his partner. "Thou art to depart—not so? I am come to see if I can serve thee in the work of packing and lading."

"My mind is changed. Perhaps I go not," rejoined Saïd, moodily.

"What is this?" exclaimed the other, seeming horror-stricken. "Thou art mad to stay after all that has befallen thee here."

"What matter! The like or worse may befall me in a strange land. I will stay in the place where I was born, wherein is my father's grave."

Once more Saïd put forth his hand to unload the ass, but Abdullah caught his arm.

"I advise thee to thy advantage," he whispered angrily. "We spoke last night of devils. What are they? Their power is only in the night. There are who have power to harm thee both by night and day." He sank his voice as if fearing lest a bird of the air might carry his words to high places. "The Basha has heard of thy wealth which thou pretendest to have lost. Men have told him how thou dost grope in the sand. Remember the fate of Ali ebn Mahmud, who was said to have a treasure hidden in his garden, how they beat and tortured him so that he died!"

Saïd's jaw fell. "Is this true?" he faltered.

"True, by Allah!" replied the other, his face anxious, his little eyes keenly watchful of his friend's countenance. "Am I a liar?"

A wild light of terror flamed in Saïd's orbs. He strode to the door of the house and shouted to Hasneh to make ready for the start. Then he returned and, untying the rope which bound the ass to the tree, bestrode the already laden beast. At the same moment his woman appeared from the house, a great bundle upon her head.

"Allah be with thee!" he cried, striking the ass with his staff, so that it started forward at a shambling trot.

"But what of thy nets, of thy house, of thy fig-tree?" cried Abdullah, wringing his hands.

"Take them—all that I have!" shouted Saïd, without looking back. He was sitting on the hindquarters of the donkey, flourishing a rope which served for bridle, his long brown legs stretched along the sacks, his feet erect beside the beast's ears. His whole frame jolted with the trotting of his steed. The woman ran behind with one arm raised to keep her bundle from falling.

"Whither away?" shouted Abdullah.

"To Es-Shâm — to Baghdad — to India! — far away!

What matter, so that I be out of his reach.   May all his race perish !"

Abdullah stood looking after the fugitives until they were lost to sight among the sandhills.   Then he took a cigarette from somewhere in the depths of his trousers, lighted it and squatted down in the shade of the fig-tree now his own.

IV

A S for Saïd, he urged his steed across the sand as fast as
the weight on its back and the looseness of the ground
would allow. His arm rose and fell continually with a
backward sweep, and the hindmost part of the donkey rang •
wooden to the thwack of his stick. A constant growl of
curses rolled upwards from his throat. Hasneh, her bosom
heaving, her breath coming and going in short pants, struggled
to keep up with him.

As they proceeded the soil became firmer under foot;
creeping branches of the wild vine, rank grasses and sundry
big-leafed plants, bound the sand together. Soon they came
into a road with a hedge of prickly pear on either side, fencing
an orange garden. Through gaps in the hedge golden globes
shone amid dark foliage with here and there a spray of white
blossom. The air was cloyed with a fragrance from which
the hum of bees seemed inseparable. A gate by the wayside
stood open. Within were two men busy packing a great heap
of oranges into square wooden boxes. Saïd shouted a salutation as he sped by, and in return they pelted him with the
fruit—a dozen at least—which Hasneh stayed to gather up
into the bosom of her robe. The scarlet flowers of a
pomegranate tree flamed among the leafage on their right
hand.

A little while and the gardens were left behind. The wide
plain rolled in smooth waves before them, away to the foot
of the mountains, with a shimmer of grey olives in the
distance.

At the end of an hour, during the whole of which Saïd
ceased not for a minute from beating his donkey, they drew
near to a village which stood upon a hill, three fine palm-
trees tapering skyward from among its squat dwellings of sun-

15

baked mud. Here the fisherman proposed to rest awhile till the heat of the day should be passed. Hasneh praised Allah for the respite.

As they entered the narrow pathway, choked with offal, which ran between the hovels, a man's voice called to them from a doorway,—

"Deign to enter, O Saïd! Honour my house with thy presence."

The speaker came forth and bowed low, holding a hand to his forehead. He was a huge, loutish fellow, who had seen thirty summers and more. He had a bushy black beard, and big brown eyes of rare stupidity. His long garment and his turban had grown old upon him. He came sometimes to the market to sell the produce of his field. Saïd had seen him there and spoken with him more than once. He was called Muhammed abu Hassan, and bore the reputation of a good-tempered, lazy fellow.

The fisherman, nothing loth, alighted, and having touched the hand of his host in salutation, proceeded to tie up his ass to the doorpost. That done, he slipped off his shoes and allowed himself to be ushered into the house. Hasneh squatted down humbly at the threshold of the door.

Their host set to work to kindle some charcoal upon a stone in one corner of the room, grumbling all the while because his woman was not there to do it for him. She was at work in the tobacco-fields, it appeared, with others of the village.

Somehow—it must have been by magic, or the laden ass tethered outside may have had something to do with it—it soon became known in all the village that a stranger had arrived from the city and was the guest of Muhammed abu Hassan. Men dropped in, one by one, feigned surprise at sight of Saïd and of each other, and squatted down with their backs to the wall.

"What news?" was the first question of a newcomer after the proper civilities had been exchanged.

To which Saïd replied, in every case, "There is nothing new to-day."

"It is said that there will be war between the Turks and the Franks?" said an old man, reverend and very dirty, in a tone three parts of assertion, one part of inquiry.

"I have heard nothing of it," Saïd answered, rolling a cigarette between thumb and forefinger.

"Allah grant that there be no war!" cried an aged sheykh, with face wrinkled as a withered olive, in a quavering voice. "I remember, when the last war was, they sent suddenly and seized every horse, mule and donkey in our village for the soldiers to ride. Only a horse and two asses were restored to us when all was over. And after two days the horse died."

There broke forth a chorus of guttural curses upon wars and soldiers.

At last the business of grinding and stewing the coffee was accomplished. Two small cups were passed round the circle from hand to hand, Muhammed filling and refilling them until all had partaken. Even Hasneh, sitting patient and submissive on the door-sill, was not forgotten in the end.

"Whither goest thou?" asked Muhammed of his guest, when at last he had leisure for conversation.

"To Damashc-ush-Shâm," replied Saïd, and hesitated. He dared not tell the true reason of his leaving home, lest he should forfeit the esteem of his hearers. A man who bewails his misfortunes before strangers is a fool and rightly despised; but he who exalts himself is sure of honour. He added,—

"I go to Es-Shâm, to the house of my brother, who is dead. He was a great man and rich. Moreover, his woman was barren. I go to claim the inheritance."

The murmur of congratulation which this fiction called forth had scarcely died away when a clatter of hoofs rang through the village. Faint shouts and cries came from the distant field where the women were at work.

"The soldiers! The soldiers are upon us!" cried Hasneh from her post at the threshold.

Every man sprang to his feet and rushed to the door, Saïd with the rest. Five Turkish soldiers and a young officer rode at a foot's pace up the narrow path between the hovels. Remembering the words which Abdullah had spoken that morning, Saïd's teeth chattered. Doubtless the Pasha was informed of his flight and these men had been sent to take him.

"Where is the house of the sheykh of the village?" cried the officer as he rode by.

B

A score of turbaned heads were bowed, a score of brown hands saluted, and a score of voices proffered directions in divers tones of self-abasement. Saïd was reassured. Had the officer been looking for him he would not surely have asked for the house of the sheykh. The next moment his heart sank again and a cry of dismay broke from his lips. One of the troopers, in passing, bent down, and severing the cord by which the donkey was tethered with one stroke of a knife, caught the end deftly as it fell, and rode on, leading with him all that remained of Saïd's worldly goods. With a shriek of rage and despair, the wretched man broke through the crowd and sprang forth into the blinding sunlight. A few fierce bounds and he had overtaken the plunderer. He strove to wrest the rope from his grasp.

"Stay! Stay!" he cried. "Let me but take off the sacks! It is all that I have!"

For answer he received a blow on the wrist which forced him to quit hold.

"Pig!" cried the soldier, angrily. "The Sultàn has need of thy beast for his soldiers; and I that am his soldier have need of those sacks for myself. Dost understand? Let go, son of a dog!"

Saïd, baffled in his design upon the rope, was now struggling frantically to wrench the sacks from the donkey's back.

The cavalcade had come to a standstill before the house of the sheykh, and the other soldiers looked on good-humouredly, laughing now at their comrade, now at the fisherman, with perfect impartiality. Their laughter stung the plunderer to frenzy. He unslung the carbine from his back, and, leaning over the saddle-bow, dealt a vicious blow at Saïd's head with the butt of it. The daylight swam blood-red before the fisherman's eyes. His head seemed to dilate and there was a singing in his ears. He fell forward, senseless, upon the ground.

V

WHEN Saïd again became conscious of his surroundings
he was in the house of Muhammed abu Hassan, lying
on a couch. Hasneh and another woman were bending
over him. The latter drew her veil hastily across her face as
his eyes blinked at her in bewilderment. Hasneh uttered a
cry of delight.

Saïd looked about him wondering. Sullen, scowling faces
filled the doorway, blotting out the sunlight. A sound of
muttered oaths was in the room. Of a sudden he remembered
all that had befallen him and staggered to his feet.

"I am ruined!" he cried. "They have taken my donkey
—all that I have. May Allah cut short their lives."

Responsive curses came from the group in the doorway,
and Muhammed replied,—

"We are sad for thee, effendi. The journey to Es-Shâm
is long and wearisome for one that goes on foot. Yet art thou
more happy than we. Thou wilt have the inheritance of
thy brother who is dead. Thou wilt have wealth wherewith
to buy horses and asses, as many as thou needest. But they
have taken all that was ours. Curse their father! Of all our
beasts there remain but a camel, and a mule which is on the
point of dying."

Saïd's hand was pressed to his forehead. His face had
the inward look of one reviewing things past. At length he
asked eagerly, "What is the hour?"

"It is near the third hour since noon," replied Muhammed
after a brief glance at the shadow of his dwelling.

The fisherman turned to his woman. "Ready, O
Hasneh?" he asked.

"Ready," was the meek rejoinder.

"But thou art yet weak from the blow which the soldier—
burn his house!—gave thee," Muhammed, as host, was bound

19

to protest. "My house is thy house. Rest here till evening.
The first hours of night are pleasant for travelling."

But Saïd, remembering the words of Abdullah, was
resolute. Pursuers might come upon him at any time. With
profusion of thanks to Muhammed for his kindness he took
up his staff and set out once more. Hasneh followed, her
bundle poised upon her head.

They passed out from the village down a steep slope, where
big red anemones shone amid ragged grass, across a stony
wady with a trickle of water among the pebbles, and entered
a grove of olive trees. Here Saïd lay down in the shade. He
was still dizzy from the stunning blow he had received, and
the strength seemed to run out of his legs. He complained
bitterly of thirst; whereupon Hasneh produced those
oranges which had been thrown at them in the morning from the bosom of her robe. Having devoured
two of them, Saïd wiped his dripping mouth upon his
sleeve and felt refreshed. He was preparing to resume
his way when the sound of a man's voice close at hand
stayed him.

"Praise be to Allah, who has placed such fools in the
world! I asked for bread, and he gave me meat as well.
And when I had finished eating he gave me money for my
journey. A madman—may Allah reward him!"

The sun through the leafage cast a chequer-work of golden
light and blue shadow upon the ground. The speaker came
towards them, walking slowly between the gnarled trunks,
with eyes upturned. It was a hale old man of sixty years or
more, tall and upright. His body was clad in a loose robe,
whose colour had once been blue, reaching to a little below
the knee. His bare feet and shins were grey with dust.
Upon his head was a battered and tasselless fez, with a dirty
rag wound round it by way of turban. Happening to let his
eyes fall a minute from their heavenly contemplation, he
became aware of the presence of fellow-creatures and his
whole demeanour changed in a second. His form seemed to
shrivel and grow less. His head sank down upon his breast,
his eyes writhed upward so that only the whites of them were
visible, and his whole body was distorted to a semblance of
the last agony.

Stretching forth a trembling hand he besought the pity of

his hearers for a poor old wretch who found himself alone and without money in a strange land.

"Allah will give to you!" he whined. "For the love of Allah, help me or I die! . . . O Lord! . . . Allah will give to you! . . . By the Coràn, I am at the gate of death! . . . Allah will give to you! . . . My sons were killed by the Bedawin; my daughters were ravished before my eyes! . . . Allah is bountiful! . . . O Lord! . . . I myself have a hand that is withered! . . . O Lord! . . . My house was destroyed by an earthquake; a thief came in the night and stole my mare from me! . . . Allah will give to you! . . . My children were slain before my eyes! . . . O Lord! . . ."

It is likely that he would have gone on whining in this strain for an hour or more had not Saïd broken in,—

"Allah will give to thee! I am poor even as thou art. I, too, have been robbed and my house brought to ruin. I, too, was once a rich man, having flocks and herds, houses and vineyards, ay, and the half of a city belonging to me. And now there is no difference between me and thee. Allah will give to thee; I have nothing."

In a twinkling the old beggar resumed his natural shape. His head rose, his body straightened, the pupils of his eyes came again into sight.

"Is it true?" he said in a friendly tone, squatting down in the shade beside the fisherman. "Then I tell thee thou art happy. All to gain; nothing to lose. There is no trade like ours. All the day long we cringe, we flatter, we weep and none can resist us. And afterwards, when the evening is come, we laugh and are merry, with eating and drinking, with music and women. Behold, I love thee, for thy likeness to my son, Mansûr, who forsook me. I feel as a father toward thee. Is it a long time that ruin is upon thee?"

"But a few hours, O, my uncle," replied Saïd, bitterly.

The old rascal threw up his hands and cast his sly eyes skyward.

"Ah, it is sad at the first, and thou art downhearted—it is natural. But after a few days—a week—a month, thou wilt not envy the greatest in the land."

Saïd was not pleased to have his misfortunes thus lightly treated as part of the common lot of mankind. He made haste to explain.

"With another man it would have been a small thing.
He would have lost a camel, or perhaps a house. But as for
me, I was a great man—the greatest in all the city. Men ran
to kiss my robe as I walked abroad. I had camels and
horses, asses and mules, more than a man can count in an
hour. It is no common loss that makes me sad."

"I suffer with thee," said the beggar, with a reminiscent
shake of his head. "I also was lord of great wealth. In
those days men knew me by the name of Mustafa Bek.
Now I am only Mustafa, the old beggar. Allah is
greatest !"

But Saïd was not to be outdone.

"But yesterday men kissed the ground between my feet,"
he said, with a shake of the head the counterpart of the
other's. "I was called the Emîr Saïd, and none dared
come near me save with forehead to the earth. Allah is
greatest !"

"I had twenty men whose only pleasure was to do my
bidding," said the beggar in his turn, "and the beauty of my
three wives made the fair ones of Paradise jealous."

"All the men of the city were as slaves before me," said
Saïd ; "and if I had a desire towards any girl, I had but to
command her father and she was given to me."

"And how wast thou deprived of all this?" asked his
rival, curiously. "Such things do not fade away like stars at
the sun's rising. By Allah, they do not go out like a lamp for
a puff of wind."

"My city was by the seashore," faltered Saïd, after a
moment's hesitation. "Last evening, at the hour of sunset,
the waters rose and swallowed up all that was mine. I
and this woman alone remain alive of all that were in the city."

The beggar rose to his feet with a laugh.

"Thou hast yet much to learn, O Emîr," he said scornfully,
yet with a certain indulgence. "The sea rises not once in a
hundred years, and then all the world knows of it. Yesterday,
at the hour of sunset, I stood by the shore and beheld the
sea calm and undisturbed as usual. Thou hast much to
learn, my son."

"May thy house be destroyed !" muttered Saïd, grinding
his teeth with mortification. "How far is it to the next
village, old man ?"

"Perhaps an hour—maybe an hour and a half—Allah knows!—perhaps two hours."

"Who was that of whom thou wast speaking at the first?" asked Saïd with some eagerness. "He gave thee meat, thou wast saying, and money for thy journey. Doubtless it is some great one whose house is open to poor wayfarers?"

"I spoke but of a Frank who passed me in the way," said the old man, with a chuckle at the recollection. "He was dressed all in black, and rode upon a fine horse. I knew him for one of those who preach to the Christians and would have all men believe in three gods. I saw him a long way off and, when he drew near, I flung myself down in the way, swearing horribly, and crying out that Allah had forsaken me. Thereat he got down from his horse and tried to comfort me with soft speaking and hard words from the book of his religion. But I cursed the louder and let him know that I was very hungry; whereupon he drew out a paper from his saddlebags, wherein was bread and meat, which he gave to me."

"When I had made an end of eating I began to weep and told him a grievous tale of how my house had been burned and all my children killed by Turkish soldiers. This I said knowing that a Frank loves always to hear evil of the Turks. He wept with me as he listened. He gave me money—as much as a man could earn by the labour of a week. Then he mounted and rode away, his face sad from the tale which I had told him. May Allah reward the unbelieving fool!"

"Y'Allah! Let us depart at once," cried Saïd, eagerly. "Perhaps we may overtake him before the night."

"Did I not tell thee that he rides upon a horse, and that a fine one?" said the beggar. "Thou can'st never hope to overtake him. He told me that he was going two days' journey on the way to Es-Shâm, to the place where he dwells. Whither goest thou?"

"To Es-Shâm," cried Said, gleefully. "I will visit him and tell the tale of my great loss. Allah be with thee!"

Saïd set forward through the olive grove at a great pace, Hasneh shuffled after him with her usual docility—the good beast of burden, ready to stand or go on at her master's word. As for the beggar, he stood looking after them until they were lost to sight among the tree trunks. He chuckled often as he went his way, repeating the word "Emîr" with scornful emphasis.

Sunset fires were blazing high in the west when Saïd and Hasneh drew near to the village of which the beggar had told them. It was a small place, built of stone, crowning the utmost slope of the mountain seaward. To reach it they had to climb a pebbly road, which wound upwards serpent-wise among terraces of fig and olive trees. At the entering in of the village grew a giant sycamore, about whose trunk the elders of the place were squatting in solemn conclave, smoking. Saïd saluted them politely as they drew near.

"What news?" asked a reverend sheykh, who seemed the head man of the place.

"There is war," replied Saïd, with a low obeisance. "Soldiers scour the country for horses and mules. I know it well, alas! for they have taken my mare—curse their fathers!—a thoroughbred worth fifty Turkish pounds, by Allah!—and I am forced to pursue my journey on foot."

"Allah restore her to thee," rejoined the sheykh, fervently. "We guessed that all was not well in the land, for this afternoon, as my son was ploughing on the hillside yonder, he beheld a company of soldiers ride across the plain, and many beasts of burden with them. Thanks be to Allah, we are warned in time. Ere the rising of the sun all our cattle shall be in a safe place among the hills, save a few that are sick, which they can take if it please them."

Saïd, seeking tidings of the missionary, was told that he had ridden through the place about the third hour after noon, and must be sleeping at Beyt Ammeh, a mountain village four hours distant.

"Is there a guest chamber in this village where I and my woman may pass the night?" asked Saïd, in some anxiety.

"Thy news is timely and thou art welcome," replied the sheykh. "My house is thy house. Deign to follow me."

With that he rose and led the way to a house which was larger by a room than other houses of the village. This room was built on the roof and had the appearance of a tower when seen from a distance. Within, it was a small chamber, softly carpeted, with a cushioned divan running round the walls, destined for the lodging of guests of distinction. Saïd would never have been admitted to its precincts but for that fabulous mare of his worth fifty Turkish pounds.

Here, having partaken of a feast such as he had seldom enjoyed, he spent the night, a pale sky flaked with stars watching his slumbers through open door and lattice.

VI

IN the morning Saïd rose early, and having breakfasted and taken leave of his host, set forth with Hasneh in the cool twilight and started to climb the steep path which twisted among olive trees up from the village. At the top he paused for a last look at the plain he was leaving. Away to the southwest a little promontory jutted into the sea. White buildings, a dome and two slender minarets were just discernible upon it in the pale light which comes before the sun. That was the city of his birth, and there, somewhere on the yellow rim of the bay, was his own little house with the fig-tree beside it from which he had seen the sun rise morning after morning, year after year. From where he now stood he could trace his whole course of the previous day. There, midway in the plain, on the crest of a wave of green, was the village where his donkey had been taken from him, where he had been stunned by that blow of the soldier's carbine of which the very memory brought pain. He knew it from the other villages dotting the landscape by the three tall-palm trees tapering above its hovels, like rich plumes in a ragamuffin's cap. There was the olive grove where he had spoken with the old beggar. And here, two hundred feet below, at the foot of a terraced slope so steep that it seemed easy to throw a stone down on to the roof of the sheykh's house, was the village he had just left. His eyes ranged over the prospect, to return always to that white town upon the headland which was his birthplace. The sun rose upon the sea and the skirts of the plain, though the shadow of the mountains still darkened the near villages. Standing at the doorway of his home he would have been in the sunlight now. The thought gripped him by the throat. A sob from Hasneh told that her mind was straying in the same direction. Saïd's voice was hoarse as he set forward once more, bidding her follow him.

26

The path dipped rapidly to the brink of a rocky gorge, and naked hills closed in upon them as they descended. To Saïd it seemed as if a door had slammed behind him, shutting off the past. His heart sickened for a while.

But the fresh air of the spring morning would not brook despair. In spite of himself hope came uppermost as he made his way along the rugged mountain side. The beggar's words kept ringing in his ears: All to gain, nothing to lose! He could rob a man now without fear of reprisal. He had all the world before him, and bright, keen wits, undulled by the least rust of conscience, for a sword against his fellow-man. He had nothing to lose, unless——

A thought, which was almost a wish, flitted through his brain. He turned his head and let his eyes rest for a minute upon the form of Hasneh plodding patiently beneath her burden.

The shadows dwindled with every minute. The dew on the ground rose in steam wherever the sun's rays touched it. For long they trudged on in a land of mountains barren and rocky. Overhead the deep blue sky paled about a blinding sun. Not a tree was to be seen. The distance swam before them in streams of heat. The sound of Hasneh's breathing was like the panting of a dog at his heels. In the shade of a great rock they sat down to rest. All around them, between the boulders, anemones held out scarlet cups to the sun. Small pink flowers filled the crannies of the rocks. Here and there, from its clump of dark-green leaves, a tall spear of asphodel stood up, bristling with buds. Saïd eyed the scene with disgust as he mopped his forehead with one hand.

"By the Coràn, it is hot to-day," he muttered. "And there is no water until we come to Beyt Ammeh."

Hasneh thrust a hand into her bosom and drew forth the few oranges which were left. Saïd seized one and devoured it greedily. A second went the same way. By the time his thirst was slaked but one remained, which Hasneh, despite the craving of her dry lips and throat, put back within her robe.

They set forward once more and had not made many steps before a man met them, asleep on the hump of a camel. Saïd called to him to know the way; whereat he awoke with a start, lost balance, and fell heavily on the stones by the wayside. He staggered to his feet, blood streaming from a wound in his forehead. Cursing bitterly, he caught up a big stone and hurled it at Saïd, who dodged it narrowly and, without waiting for further provocation, rushed on his assailant and closed with him. Hasneh shrieked loudly for help, wakening vain echoes. The camel, nose in air, chewed the cud placidly, as a wise man smokes his pipe, with a downward, supercilious glance at the fighters.

Victory did not hang long in the balance. Saïd was a tall man, lean and wiry, while his opponent was short and hampered with fat. The fisherman forced him backward until he tripped on a boulder and fell. Then he set foot on the belly of the fallen one and raised his staff to strike at the face of his enemy. Fury blazed in his eyes.

"Stay! may thy religion be destroyed!" panted the camel-driver in a rapture of fear. "What am I to thee that thou shouldst slay me? Thou art a devil to cause me to fall and then to destroy me! May thy father perish! Strike not; I am no enemy of thine! I never beheld thee till this hour!"

Saïd lowered his stick, but his brow was still clouded and his posture threatening.

"Take away thy foot!" gasped the other. "What have I done that thou dost so ill-treat me? All that I have is thine, only spare my life!"

Saïd did not budge.

"A man's life is worth much," he said thoughtfully. "How much wilt thou give me?"

"May thy whole race perish! I will give thee all that I have—ten piastres."

"Not enough." Saïd's foot pressed more heavily upon the mound of flesh.

"Twenty—thirty piastres!" shrieked the man.

"Not enough."

"A Turkish pound! . . . By Allah, it is all that I have. And it is my master's money, not my own. Alas for me, I am ruined!"

Saïd withdrew his foot.

"Rise not until thou hast paid the ransom or I will slay thee," he said savagely.

The man loosened his garment, showing a linen bag which hung by a string from his neck. Slipping the cord over his head he flung the bag to Saïd with a curse. The fisherman examined the contents in a kind of dotage, then nodded to the hostage.

"It is well," he said. "Go in peace. And another time, when thou fallest by chance from thy camel, throw no stones at those who stand by lest a worse thing befall thee."

Calling to Hasneh, he strode on his way with a light heart, leaving the camel-driver to digest the gall of his loss as best he might. They had gone some twenty paces when a noise of mighty cursing filled the air behind them. At the same moment a great stone came whizzing within a foot of Saïd's head. Another struck Hasneh on the back, causing her to stagger and fall forward. Saïd girded up his loins and ran until he was beyond the utmost range of any missile. Then he got upon a rock and began to revile his assailant in a loud voice, using his hand as a trumpet. He watched the wretched man climb upon his camel again and heard the scream of rage and hate with which he turned to shake a fist at his plunderer. The fisherman laughed aloud and ceased not from insulting his enemy until a shoulder of the mountain hid camel and rider from sight.

Hasneh had struggled to her feet by this time and was making her way towards him, stumbling, one arm hugging her bundle, the other outstretched, like one walking in the dark. He cried to her to know if she were hurt. Her answer was in the negative, but faintly and without conviction. Saïd waited until she was within a few yards of him and then pursued his way, chuckling over his own cleverness in turning what had once seemed a misadventure to good account. The linen bag nestled lovingly to his chest, seeming to recognise a worthier owner.

All to gain, nothing to lose. . . .

He could no longer apply the words strictly to himself. Nevertheless, they rang hopefully in his ears, seeming to tell him that the sum he had just acquired was but an earnest of the wealth in store for him.

The sun was almost at the zenith when they came in sight of the village of Beyt Ammeh ; for the great heat oppressed them and they walked slowly, taking frequent rests. The squat, flat-roofed houses were hardly to be made out at a distance, so little did they differ in form and colour from the

surrounding rocks.   Only a few ragged fig-trees and a thank-
less striving after cultivation in the immediate neighbourhood
told of a dwelling-place of man.

On the outskirts of the village, just below the ringed
threshing-floors, a spring gushed out beneath a ruinous arch
by the wayside.   Flat-topped stones had been placed in the
shadow to serve as seats to wayfarers.   Here Saïd stopped,
and after a long, refreshing drink proceeded to bathe his
head, hands and feet.   Hasneh sank down upon a stone with
hand pressed to her side, waiting patiently until her lord
should have done with the water.   Then she rose, took one
step forward, staggered, and, with hands outstretched to the
fountain, fell heavily upon her face.

For full three minutes Saïd stared down at her blankly.
Such behaviour was quite beyond the cycle of his experience.
At last he bethought him of the cold water and began to dash
it over her wildly with both hands.

Then, as she did not move, he concluded her dead
and sat down to try and get used to the notion.   He was
engaged thus, staring at the lifeless form of the woman at his
feet, when a shadow darkened the ground before him.   At the
same moment a quavering voice asked to know what was the
matter.   Lost in reflection, Saïd had not heard the patter of
feet drawing near.

Alarmed by the suddenness of the apparition, he leapt up
with a curse.   An old woman stood before him, bent almost
double beneath a heavy burden.   Her head nodded, her
limbs quaked with palsy.   Her jaw working like a camel's,
she repeated the question in a shriller tone as Saïd stared at
her with wide-open eyes.

" It is my woman who is dead," said the fisherman, ruefully, pointing to the ground.

" How dost thou know that she is dead ? " asked the old
hag, in scorn.   " As I came out from the village I saw her
fall, and would have run to help her but that I am very old
and feeble.   But I watched thee.   Thou hast done nothing
more than throw a little water upon her clothes.   Turn her
over, madman, so that she lies upon her back."

Something in the manner of the old woman daunted Saïd
and made him ashamed.   He had not done much to revive
Hasneh, it was true ; but then, he had supposed her dead,

and none but a fool would wantonly waste his time in trying to bring a dead woman back to life. He had now little doubt that she lived, thanks to the old woman's scornful suggestions. In his heart he cursed the crone for breaking in upon him just when he had brought his mind to a peaceful contemplation of his wife's dead body. Yet he obeyed her, and, lifting Hasneh in his arms, laid her down again, face uppermost.

"Now, sprinkle water upon her lips!"

Saïd obeyed a second time, with the result that after a little while Hasneh opened her eyes.

"Take her up and bear her to the village! Thou hast no more mind than a donkey!" piped the hag, in shrillest scorn, seeing him stand purposeless.

The shame Saïd felt at having his actions ordered by a woman found vent in a hearty curse on her, her religion and all her belongings. Nevertheless, he did as he was bidden, and taking Hasneh in his arms entered the village, grumbling at every step.

At the threshold of one of the hovels, on the edge of the sunlight, sat a woman grinding at a small handmill. Saïd called to her that his wife had fallen sick and needed rest. She rose at once from her business to bid him enter and welcome. The darkness of the room within was refreshing after the scorching glare of noon. A man rose from a squalid couch against the wall and greeted Saïd in a sleepy voice. He waved a hand to the dirty mattress he had quitted, and then to the woman in the fisherman's arms.

"May Allah increase thy wealth!" murmured Saïd, laying down his burden upon the bed.

"Leave a woman to the care of a woman," said the man of the house, beckoning him to the doorway. "This woman of mine will tend her and, after a little, we will drink some coffee."

Saïd squatted down beside his host, just within the shadow of the room. The outlook was of stony hills whitening under the burning noonday sky, and in the foreground the low mud roofs of the village in broken terraces.

"Whence comest thou?" asked the lord of the house, after a silence spent in the rolling and lighting of cigarettes. Saïd told him the name of the village where he had passed the night.

"Didst thou meet any man by the way?" he asked with sudden interest. "My brother—his name is Farùn—set out this morning on the road to the plain. He is a short man and very fat. He rides upon a camel laden with stone. Hast seen him?"

"Yes, I saw him," replied Saïd, thoughtfully, as one recalling a picture to his mind. "He was sitting by the wayside and blood streamed from a wound in his head. His camel strayed browsing at a little distance. He told me that robbers had fallen suddenly upon him in the way. They had taken all that he had of money. They had beaten him with a stick and stoned him. I helped him to bind up his wound and gave him of my money—all that I could spare. Then I saw him mount upon his camel and ride away. He bade me tell his brother what had befallen him when I should reach this village. The sickness of my woman had ousted it from my mind till now."

"Now, may Allah requite thee, for thou art a good man and bountiful!" said the other, with eyes and hands upraised. "I hold thee as my near kinsman for this kindness done to my brother. My house is thy house. Rest here to-night, I pray thee. To-morrow, about the third hour, my brother will return. Abide with us till then that he may thank thee once again. By Allah, I think he would slay me were I to suffer thee to go thy way unfeasted. Stay at least till the evening. Seeing the mishap which has befallen him it may well be he will return ere night. By the Coràn, it is lucky that the robbers did not take his camel also!"

"I cannot stay," said Saïd, hurriedly. "My brother is dead in Damashc-esh-Shâm and I go to claim the inheritance. I must hasten on my way."

"If not for thine own sake, for the sake of thy woman abide here till evening," urged the host.

Saïd appeared wrapt in thought for some minutes. His face was moody with knitted brows. Of a sudden it brightened.

"For myself, I cannot stay," he said. "But it were well for my woman that she should rest a while till the sickness leave her. . . "

His eyes looked eager inquiry at the other.

"She is welcome and more than welcome!" cried the host, without hesitation.

"May Allah increase thy wealth!" murmured Saïd, fervently, making a low salaam. "When I come to the city I will send to fetch her, and thy reward shall be very great. Think not because thou seest me poorly clad that thou art showing kindness to a beggar. My brother was rich and I go to claim the inheritance."

He glanced furtively towards the couch, in fear lest Hasneh should have heard anything of his speech. But her eyes were closed, and her bosom's rise and fall was of one in a peaceful sleep, gentle and even. Her robe hung open at the neck, showing something round and yellow nestling in the soft brown hollow between her breasts. It was the orange which she had forborne to eat that morning. The sight of it in the bosom of the sleeping woman warmed Saïd's heart to something like pity. It was an appeal to his good nature, the stronger for being voiceless. For a moment his purpose was shaken.

"All to gain: nothing to lose!"

His heart hardened as he recalled the words of the old beggar. There was a glint of steel in his eyes as he turned them once more upon his host.

"It is past noon," he said. "In thy grace I depart. Take care of the woman belonging to me and thy reward shall be great. May thy wealth increase!"

"My peace with thee!" said the man, staring at him with amazement. "But stay at least until thou hast drunk coffee with us. See! it is almost ready."

Saïd dared not break the law of hospitality. He waited, fidgety, and ill at ease like one sitting upon a red-hot iron. He shifted his seat continually, and his eyes kept veering round to where Hasneh lay asleep, yet never looked at her. When at length a tiny cup of coffee was put into his hand he flung his head back and swallowed the whole contents at a gulp. Then he pressed both hands to his chest and his whole body writhed. He had forgotten in his haste to drink and be gone that the stuff was scalding hot. Tears streamed from his eyes, sweat stood in great beads on his forehead as he set down the empty cup and rose to take his leave.

"Thou art a fire-eater, by Allah!" cried the lord of the house, staring aghast at him, cup in hand. "Why art thou in so great a hurry? A minute or two will not

C

rob thee of thy inheritance, and the heat of the day is not yet past."

But Saïd was more eager than ever to be off. Glancing fearfully in the direction of the bed he had seen Hasneh open her eyes and stare vacantly about her.

"Take all care of her, and may Allah prosper thee!" he muttered hurriedly, crossing the threshold and dodging behind the doorpost. "After a week I shall send to thee. Allah requite thee, O father of kindness!"

He set off at a great pace, spurred by the thought that Hasneh might discover the trick played on her and come running after him.

VII

A T the village where he passed the night, a village half-way
down a mountain side, terraced and fledged with olive-
trees, which looked over a wide stretch of flat country, Saïd
gleaned tidings of the missionary of whom he hoped so much.
The man in black had ridden through the place before noon
and was gone to his house in the plain, an hour's journey
beyond. His heart was light when he set out in the morning.
Far away across the plain, mountains—the hugest he had ever
seen—were dreamy in the mists of early dawn. A white gleam
of snow among their summits was new to him, and would have
held his eyes but for the nearer charms of a red-roofed house
in the plain below, where a blessed fool dwelt and a man
could have money for the asking. Thanks to the hospitality
of the villagers, the Turkish pound was still untouched in the
linen bag upon his chest. With what he hoped to obtain from
the preacher he would enter the great city in triumph instead
of beggary.

The sun was already hot upon the plain when he reached
the house of the Frank. A tall negro, clad in a flowing robe of
yellow and white, finely striped, with a clean white turban
bound about his scarlet fez, was sweeping the doorstep with a
broom. Saïd wished him a happy day, and sitting down upon
his heels—for the ground was dewy—disposed himself for a
chat. But the negro was gruff. All Saïd's compliments were
returned as curtly as the barest politeness would allow, and
his leading questions answered by an "Allah knows!" and a
shrug of the shoulders far from satisfying.

Finding that there was nothing to be gained by flattering
the surly doorkeeper, the fisherman changed his tone. Rising
to his feet, he cried, in a loud voice, meant to sound like
thunder, "Go, tell thy master that I wish to speak with him!"

35

The negro paused in his sweeping to look at him and laughed, showing two rows of dazzlingly white teeth.

"My master sleeps," he said. "Thou knowest little of the ways of a Frank if thou thoughtest to speak with him at this hour."

"At what hour will he awake?" asked Saïd in the same lofty tone.

"Allah knows!" replied the negro, with a shrug, going on with his sweeping.

Saïd squatted down once more upon his heels.

"I wait here till he is ready!"

The negro grinned angrily and indicated the vastness of the horizon by a flourish of his broom.

"Walk!" he said grimly.

Saïd seemed not to understand.

"Walk!" repeated the negro, fiercely, rushing upon him with broom upraised.

With a scared curse Saïd scrambled to his feet and bounded away, swift as a gazelle in fear of the hunter. The negro stood looking after him, his broom still threatening, until the flutter of a blue robe and the twinkle of brown legs were lost to sight among the knotted trunks of an olive grove.

As soon as he thought himself safe Saïd flung himself upon the ground, panting for breath. A pair of doves fluttered somewhere among the branches, cooing sadly over a lost paradise. The sunlight made its way here and there through the leafage in bars of golden haze. A sound, made up of the barking of a dog, the cries of children and the musical clink of a hammer on iron, told him that there was a village somewhere in the depths of the wood. The grating song of the cicadas, that waxed and waned in his throbbing ears, seemed the live spirit of the sunlight stirring in the shade. Warm breaths, the sweet steam from dew-drenched plants and moistened earth, rustled the leaves and silvered them faintly.

"May his father perish!" muttered Saïd between his clenched teeth—a sign that his breath was returning.

A little later, when he had ceased panting, he crept to the edge of the sunshine. Keeping his body hid behind the wide-spread trunk of an ancient olive he peeped forth.

At a stone's throw the house of the missionary rose sheer amid a waste of rank grass and thistles traversed by a bridle-path. Beyond rose the mountain side, filmy in a bluish heat-mist. Half-way up Saïd descried the place where he had slept, a cluster of low buildings of the same hue as the neighbouring rocks, seeming as natural a growth as they.

The negro had left the doorway ere this, and was gone out of sight to some other place where was need of his broom. But Saïd dared not yet step forth into the open, an impression of the black man's strength of limb and the broom's menace being fresh upon him. He watched and waited.

Soon there were signs of a stirring to life within the house. The shutters of an upper window were closed against the sun by an arm thrust out for the purpose. At the same time a man's head was seen for a moment. Then a little boy with thin brown legs came out of the olive wood, passing close to Saïd but without seeing him. He must have come from the village near at hand for he carried a big pitcher of milk easily and without fatigue. He passed round a corner of the house, and shortly returned swinging the empty pitcher. Windows were opened. A shrill Arab chant in a woman's voice came from some lower room. How many servants had this accursed unbeliever? Saïd wondered.

Presently, just as he was thinking of trying his luck once more, the negro being nowhere to be seen, a tall Frank, clad all in black save his arms, which were in white sleeves, appeared in the gloom of the doorway and shouted, "Cassim!"

Saïd had taken a step forward, with intent to rush across the intervening space and fling himself at the blessed madman's feet, when the reappearance of his enemy made him shrink back. The man in black seemed to be giving an order, to which the negro bowed assent. Then Saïd saw the Frank re-enter the house, while the servant ran round to the back of the building.

The coast was clear once more. But the second coming of the negro to thwart him had made Saïd cautious. Choosing what he deemed the wise man's part, he watched still and waited. But after a few minutes the negro returned, leading a handsome grey stallion by the bridle, when Saïd had the vexation of seeing the missionary mount and ride away. His parting charge to the black servant, shouted as the restive horse broke into a canter, reached Saïd's ears distinctly through the still, sounding air.

"I return at sundown, O Cassim! Tell the people there will be no school to-day!"

The negro stood awhile looking after the horseman. Then he turned and, going about his business, passed once more out of sight.

Saïd flung himself down in the deep shadow behind his tree trunk, calling down every ill he could think of upon the Frank and all his race. The tall negro also was not forgotten in that all-embracing curse, nor his father, nor his grandfather; not so much as an aunt or a cousin was left out. Then, feeling better, he began to sound the depths of his disappointment.

From the time of his meeting with the old beggar he had looked to the bounty of the Frankish missionary as a traveller in the waste looks forward to the place of waters. He snarled as he thought that he might have gained his end and gone rejoicing on his way but for the selfish devil that kept the door, who guarded the well for his own use. Now he must leave the place as he had come, with only a single Turkish pound in the linen bag against his chest. It was nothing beside what he had hoped to get from the mad preacher of unbelief. He had no mind to stay there till nightfall on the slender chance of eluding the watchfulness of the negro and winning the ear of his master. The city called him with a siren's voice. There, in the vast bustling hive, were wondrous chances for a young man and a strong who had nothing to lose. There were women fairer and sweeter than Hasneh—young girls, perhaps, pure as lily buds, who would tremble and wax faint at a kiss. He licked his lips softly.

A sound of footsteps close at hand startled him out of a languorous dream. It was the negro, who, unobserved of Saïd, had crossed the open space of sunlight and was threading his way among the gnarled trunks of the grove, a large basket on his arm. He passed within twelve paces of the fisherman, but without perceiving him, so still he lay.

Then a thought came to Saïd. Now that the enemy was gone what was to hinder him from entering the house and viewing for himself the splendour which must assuredly reign within? From all he had seen and heard during his long watch it was unlikely that the unbeliever had more than one manservant. There would be none but women in the house;

and if one of them should surprise him and ask what he did there, he had only to tell her of his wish to speak with the Frank, her master. He stole from his lair and stepped out into the sunlight.

The silence of the place, with all those windows gazing so fixedly at him, was a little daunting at first, so that he advanced warily. It seemed as if a shout must come from the open door, which looked so like a mouth. But when he had made a few paces unchallenged courage returned to him. The Arab chant he had before heard came faintly from some room at the back. But for that, and a great cat blinking to sleep on a window-sill, the place seemed desolate.

Slipping off his shoes on the doorstep he passed swiftly into the cool gloom within. There was a sort of hall, wide and lofty, having two windows, one on either side of the entrance. Upon a table in the midst of it lay the remains of a feast—broken bread and meat, a plate of oranges and a bowl half empty of curds, besides a great cup and saucer and two white jugs of an outlandish fashion. Facing him, beyond the table, were two doors, both shut, from behind one of which the sounds of chanting seemed to proceed. He stole past the table, his bare feet making no noise on the stone pavement or the matting which was over part of it. There was a stairway in a recess to the right. He mounted swiftly and stealthily.

At the top an open door attracted him. It showed a room with a bed in it and soft rugs upon the floor. Saïd went straight to the bed and fell to examining its framework, sitting on his heels and exclaiming, "Ma sh'Allah !" under his breath. It was almost like a table standing on six iron legs; but four of the legs reached above it as well as below, and each of the four was crowned with a little knob, like an orange, of some burnished yellow metal he took for gold. A wonderful thing ! It was long ere he could tear himself away from the marvel.

The room was cool and pleasant, shaded from the sun, which beat on that side of the house, by the shutters of the window, which were closed. Upon a small table there was a mirror. He saw his counterpart for a minute without recognition. Then he grinned, and scanned the face in the glass with complacency. From a peg beside the door hung a long garment of brown stuff, soft as wool, yet thick and strong as if it had been of camel's hair. It was braided with red at the collar and on the sleeves, and a red cord dangled from a loop in the middle, ending in two red tassels. Above it, on a nail, was a scarlet fez, of the high shape worn by Turks and great ones.

Saïd took off his own cap and the encircling turban which old ties of dirt and perspiration had made of one piece with it. The back of his shaven head, thus laid bare, was reflected in the looking-glass, the ears standing out from it huge and grotesque as those of a jinni. He eyed his ancient headdress with disgust. The round tarbûsh, shaped like the half of a pomegranate, with its clumsy tassel which had once been blue, appeared a sorry thing indeed as he looked from it to the new scarlet of that other cap. His raiment, too, was old and stained, in need of a cloak to hide its shortcomings. Taking down the brown robe from the wall he turned it about and about, seeking the holes for the arms. Then he slipped into it and, setting the scarlet fez upon his head, went back to the mirror.

He noticed a fault. The fez, being used to cover a thick crop of hair, was too large for his shorn poll. His ears alone prevented it from putting out the light of his countenance. He cast about for a remedy. There was upon the table a small white cloth or kerchief of finest linen. This he made to serve his turn by twisting it tight round cap and forehead as a turban. That done, he grinned freely and examined other objects upon the table. Among them was a picture of a girl, clad indecently after the manner of the Franks. Saïd eyed it closely, wondering what purpose it could serve. Then he remembered that the Franks are but idolaters, who worship pictures and other forbidden things of their own making. "It is his god, by Allah!" he muttered, turning away with a gesture of disdain. Before leaving the room he cast his discarded headgear upon the bed with a parting curse on its religion.

VIII

AS Saïd was making his way downstairs, with less of caution than he had observed in his ascent (the joy of his new finery had elated him beyond all prudence), a door was opened in the hall below and a woman came out. Beholding him she drew her veil hastily across the lower part of her face. Her eyes were bright and her movements had the grace of youth.

"Who art thou? What dost thou here?" she cried shrilly. "The khawajah is on a journey and Cassim is gone to the village. I am alone in the house, the old woman, my mother, being ill. If perchance thou hast an errand to my master I can give word to him on his return."

Of a sudden her voice rose to anger.

"Allah, pardon! Where gottest thou that cloak? Thief that thou art! It is the robe of my lord, which hangs always in his own chamber. O Cassim, there is a thief in the house! A thief! O Cassim, a thief!"

She ran screaming to the outer door and opened her mouth wide towards the olive grove, crying always, "O Cassim! O Cassim! A thief! a thief!"

Saïd rushed on her and pinioned her arms.

He tried to fling her to the ground, but she struggled like a mad thing, and at length, bending swiftly, with the yell of a wild beast, bit the fisherman's hand so that he cried out with pain. Need to look at the wound made him loose his hold, whereupon she broke away and fled within the house, barring a door behind her.

Saïd frowned at the marks of her teeth in his flesh, from which the blood began to ooze. He put the place to his mouth and sucked it—an act which prevented a storm of curses. And even as he was tending his wound in such a

manner as Nature prompted, the screams of the woman broke
out anew, as of one in a frenzy,—

"O Cassim! Help! a thief! O Cassim! O Cassim!"

This time there came an answering shout from the olive
grove.

Turning, he beheld the negro running towards the house
as fast as his long black legs could carry him. Saïd snatched
up his slippers from the doorstep. With the spring of a
hunted animal he leapt out into the sunlight, and gathering
up his new robe, sped away from house and olive trees, out
into the wide plain, where hot air swam along the distance in
liquid mist.

Once he turned to look back. The negro had set down
his basket and was pursuing at a steady trot which meant
business. Saïd fled on, but with slackened pace. He had
need to husband his breath, for the race was like to be a long
one. Panting, sweating from every pore, he stumbled across
a wady where a little freshet of water tinkled among boulders
from pool to pool. Brushing through the belt of oleanders
on the further bank, he ran on across the bare land, trampling
rank grass, thistles and creeping plants.

But the negro had long legs. Saïd learnt, by the growing
beat of footfalls in his ears, that he was losing ground. Soon
he could hear also the hard breathing of his pursuer. He
made a spirt, though his heart was near to breaking, it thumped
so against his ribs.

"Allah is merciful!" He had almost fallen into a deep
hole, overgrown with weeds at the mouth—a disused cistern,
it might be. He had lengthened his stride only just in time.
A piteous shriek came from behind him. He turned to glance
back, still running. The black was nowhere to be seen. He
dropped to the ground, pressing his hand on his heart.
"Praise to Allah!" he gasped, and then lay still, panting.

The sun beat hotly upon him there in the open plain.
He longed for some patch of shade, were it but of a shrub,
enough to shelter his head and face. Only a few paces
distant a lonely carub-tree of great size spread its gnarled
boughs and glossy dark foliage over a rough pavement—a pious
foundation for the repose of travellers. Saïd dragged himself
thither and lay a great while with eyes closed.

"Praise be to Allah!" he exclaimed again, when breath

had quite returned. Then he bethought him of the black
man and that the hole might be of no great depth after all.
He rose and went to the place.

While he was searching among weeds and dwarf shrubs
for the mouth of the pit he saw a black hand come up out
of the ground and clutch the stalk of a big blue thistle. Then
he regretted bitterly that he had flung away his staff lest it
should prove a hindrance in running. For want of it he took
a jagged stone in his hand and beat viciously with it upon
the bony parts of the fingers. The desired yell at once
reached his ears, and the hand was nimble as a lizard to slip
back into its hole. Then Saïd, lying flat upon his stomach,
wriggled forward until he could look down into the prison.
There was his enemy standing upright in a narrow place like
a well, but dry to all appearance. By stretching down his
arm he could almost have touched the negro's white turban.
Cassim glared up at him with white eyes of hate. Saïd could
hear him grind his teeth for rage of helplessness.

He looked forth over the wide brown plain with faint
blue mountains everywhere along the skyline, and back to
where the house of the Frank at the foot of the hill was like
a tiny white box shut tight with a high red lid.

Then peering again into the hole, he laughed aloud.

"Is it cool down there, O son of a pig?" he inquired.
"By Allah, thou art well housed and I envy thee. Up here
I am roasting in the noon-day, whilst thou, within arm's
length of me, dost enjoy the cool of night. There is a road
not far from thy dwelling, O foul scion of a race of swine;
also a great tree where travellers may rest in the shade. But
for all that, help is far from thee. Men will take fright at thy
cries, coming from under the earth, and will fly swiftly as from
a place of sin. I have it in my mind, thou dog, to drop earth
down on thee and stones, and so bury thee. What sayest
thou, ugly one? It would give me joy to defile thy grave!"

Of a sudden the negro made a great leap with hand up-
stretched. His nails grazed Saïd's face, causing him to draw
back in alarm.

"Curse thy father, son of a dog that thou art!" came a
terrible voice from the pit. "May thy life be cut short!
May all thy children rot, and thy woman betray thee to
an enemy!"

"A wise man gives fair words to his master," retorted Saïd, and his voice was like a leopard's paw; so soft yet dangerous. "What art thou to me that I should delay to slay thee? At my elbow there is a nice stone which would break thy head as it were an egg. Speak smoothly to thy master, O Cassim, son of a pig!"

A fresh outbreak of cursing answered from the hole. Then Saïd reflected that he had wasted time enough in play by the wayside. The shadow of the carub-tree, lying like a blot of ink upon the whitening land, tempted him to rest there yet a little while. But two fears urged him onward. The negro might in the end get out of the hole, when Saïd could hope for no mercy if caught napping thereabouts; and the woman he had assailed, alarmed at Cassim's non-appearance, would soon raise the hue-and-cry, if she had not already done so.

Saïd knew that his road lay towards those faint blue distant mountains with the whiteness among their crests, and there his knowledge ended. The plain stretched burning and treeless in that direction, but at a point far away a ripple of foliage broke the level. He could make out the shape of a palm-tree, seeming of no more substance than a blade of grass, so distant it was, and the quiver of hot air between. Palms do not grow solitary like weeds or carub-trees. A village was therefore near it, where he could inquire his road more perfectly. There remained only to take farewell of the prisoner.

He drew near once more to the mouth of the pit. With a look of concentration he leaned over and spat full in the upturned face of the negro. Then he rose lightly and went his way.

IX

IT was towards evening when Saïd left the place where, weary from long walking in the fierce eye of noon, he had sought shelter and refreshment. A crowd of men, women and children—all who dwelt in that place—went out with him from among the hovels as far as a tall palm-tree, which crowned a smooth hillock green with grass. In the midst of the obsequious rabble Saïd strutted a king, distinguished as he was by the missionary's brown dressing-gown, braided conspicuously with red, and girt about the waist with a red and tasselled cord; not to speak of the new scarlet fez bound to his head by a turban of more than human cleanness.

Arrived at the palm-tree, all the villagers pressed forward to kiss his hand or, it might be, only the skirt of his wondrous robe. The glory of his raiment had enthralled them at his coming, and in the first rapture of greatness, in the joy of their cringing and flattery, he had promised to see that all their wrongs and grievances were presently redressed.

So he strode on his way with their blessings, turning ever and anon, with a gracious gesture, to look back at the squalid crowd of fellahìn, who stood grouped about the palm-tree, looking after him with hands shading their eyes. His brain was on fire with arrogance. Every herb on which he trod marked a new act of condescension. The whole earth fell down before him. The sun burned for him alone. Trees and shrubs cast their shadows like garments in his path.

But by-and-by, as the village shrank in distance, the vapours besetting his brain began to disperse. His legs were stiff from his race of the forenoon. He longed for a horse to carry him at ease, and the wish did much to sober him. A great one does not travel on foot, neither does he wander from home in the heat of the day without at least a sunshade in his hand, if not a servant to hold it over him. Sudden shame came upon him like an ague. The villagers would discuss his appearance now that he was gone, and remembering that he had neither horse nor servant, not so much as a parasol, would perceive their own folly and curse him for an impostor. At that he quickened his step so as to be far from a place where he must shortly be held in derision.

The violet mountains, which had seemed so far away in the morning, were now nearer to him than those others from whose base he had set out. The sun, a disc of flame, was sinking down on the uttermost rim of the plain. Shadows were no longer dense and inky under every object, but stretched long and blue to eastward, growing with every minute. Far away across the flat Saïd was aware of a thin bright line, vague and dreamy beneath the setting sun. On that side was the sea. He grew sad as he recalled his little house among the sandhills. The cool breeze of evening was stirring the great leaves of his fig-tree even now.

As he pondered on things past a spirit awoke within him and showed him Abdullah in a new light. He stood still, as if gripped by a sudden twinge of pain. Stretching forth his hands to Heaven he bade Allah witness the trust he had ever placed in his friend and partner, and the consequent enormity of the fraud. In the first frenzy he thought to retrace his steps, to walk day and night without respite, until he had slain the treacherous liar. He even took a dreadful oath before Allah to that effect. But his mind soon changed. There was an evil report of him all along the way by which he had come. He felt ashamed because of Hasneh, and feared to see her face again. And the great city lay before him, where Allah alone knew what joys might be in store for him. Nevertheless, he made a vow : that, when he had achieved the greatness of his hopes, he would return to his native town riding upon a horse, with a company of horsemen, his servants, and would cause Abdullah to be whipped in his sight with a lash set thickly with sharp nails ; and then, when his enemy lay bleeding and faint at his feet, he would recite the story of his crime aloud for all men to hear. And at last, to make vengeance complete, he would spurn his enemy with his foot and gallop off with his servants in a cloud of dust.

Twilight was closing swiftly into night when Saïd reached a place where was a well in the shade among some olive-trees,

and hard by a low, flat-roofed house, from whose open door
and window a faint red light flickered upon the trampled
ground.

"Praise be to Allah—a khan!" he murmured, espying the
forms of two men smoking on stools before the door. Tethered
to the nearest tree, a horse, which appeared black in the half
light, was munching steadfastly in a wooden trough. The
saddle was still on its back, though the girth was unfastened
and dangling.

The two who sat smoking by the door rose courteously at
the approach of a stranger. Saïd returned their salutation as
though it had come from the dirt beneath his feet. He removed a stool to a seemly distance from them and sat down,
calling impatiently for food and drink.

"My horse is fallen by the way," he cried in a loud voice,
for the enlightenment of all who might be in the house. "I
bade my men stay to tend the beast, having yet hopes that he
may recover. A good horse, by Allah, which I bought for
fifty Turkish pounds, but I would not part with it for a
hundred. In a little while they will be here, if they lose not
their way in the darkness, which is very possible, their mind
being little as the mind of a sheep."

At the sound of that high speech the master of the khan
appeared—a tall, black shape on the glow of the doorway.
Behind him other dark forms were discernible—a cluster of
heads, some turbaned, others draped in a shawl bound about
the temples with a rope of camel's hair.

Saïd was not pleased to find the khan so full of people.
In such a crowd there might well be some great one who
might expose him. The fear was vague but sickening. It
was speedily laid to rest. A ray of firelight played on Saïd's
sleeve, showing the fine red braiding, when an awe-stricken
murmur spread among the group at the door. It made him
smile in his beard.

"What is thy will, effendi? All that I have is thine," said
the owner of the house, coming forward with a deep obeisance.
"Deign but to enter the room. It is my shame that I have
no meat to set before your Eminence. But condescend to
wait a little and my woman shall slay a fowl . . ."

"I have little hunger, I thank thee, and I prefer the open
air," broke in Saïd, loftily. "I do but await the men belonging

to me, whom I left to tend my horse, which fell in the way hither. A good horse! Two hundred Turkish pounds would not requite me for his loss. Bring only a little fruit, some bread and some sherbet of roses. And forget not to prepare coffee and a narghileh for when I have done with eating."

At that all was bustle and running to and fro. One ran to the well for water. Another undertook to pound the coffee. A third set a little stool before the fisherman and a lantern to shed light on his repast. A fourth prepared the weed for his narghileh by first plunging it into a jar of water, then wringing it out strongly with both hands. And those who could not be of active use raised their voices officiously in counsel and direction.

Only one held aloof. It was an aged man, one of those who sat smoking before the door. His bearing seemed superior to the rest. He alone remained seated, sucking lazily at his narghileh. Saïd divined a scornful smile on this man's face as he looked on at the slavishness of his neighbours. Night, stealing out from under the olive-trees, had now completely hemmed in the house, so that, as they sat apart, Saïd could not see his countenance. But something told him the contempt was there, and it made him uneasy.

All that he required was presently brought and set upon the stool before him. There followed a hush, as the by-standers, having no more work to do, sat down on their heels at a discreet distance and watched his meal. They conversed together in whispers.

Saïd could hear the horse munching its chaff and barley under the trees hard by. There was now and then the stamp of a hoof, or a faint thud as it pushed against the wooden manger. He found it irksome to eat in state and apart. It came into his mind to call the host to him; but reflecting that true greatness brooks no fellow, he refrained. Instead, he pricked his ears to catch the gist of their whispering.

"Officer"—"Soldiers"—"War" were among the words which reached him. They fired a train of new ideas. Straightening his back, he stroked his moustache and beard with soldierly fierceness.

He was aware of a movement in the group. With the tail of his eye he saw the master of the khan draw near to that aged one who sat aloof and speak to him. Even in the darkness he knew that both their faces were turned in his direction.

"O Faris! Bring the coffee for his Excellency!—and the narghileh also!" cried the host; whereat a man rose and ran quickly into the house. But the innkeeper himself did not budge. He remained whispering with the sheykh, and their eyes were fixed on Saïd.

Presently, when the great man seemed fully and happily occupied with his smoking, the sheykh rose with a show of carelessness, picked up a pair of saddle-bags which lay by the wall, and went silently to where the horse was tethered. Saïd heard him thrust aside the portable manger, and knew, though he could not see, that he was busy strapping the girth. Then came the jingle of a bit.

The fisherman rose with an evil smile. He felt himself the object of all eyes, and in face of that quaking audience which believed in him was bold as a lion to act his part. Without a second's delay he rushed upon the sheykh, and, seizing him by his clothing, swung him round and gripped his throat.

"I have thee, old fox," he hissed, shaking his prisoner gently but with a deft suggestion of worse to come. "This horse is no longer thine. In the name of the Sultàn's majesty— may Allah preserve his life for ever!—I take him from thee. Thou knowest the law. After a little, when the war is over, he will be thine again—if he die not in the meantime, which is very likely, for it is a sorry beast."

With that he left hold of the old man, sending him reeling against the trunk of a tree, and, gathering up his grand robe, climbed into the saddle. All the men of the inn were now gathered to the spot. Their eyes were fierce upon Saïd, but fear sealed their lips. The sheykh, recovered from his stupor, grasped the bridle tightly.

"Yes, it is true, I know the law!" he screamed. "Thou mayst take my horse—good, since there is war. But first thou must write me a paper of acknowledgment. I am no common man, I warn thee, to be robbed and no questions asked. I have friends in power. Give me, I tell thee, a writing of acknowledgment that I may claim my own when the evil time is past!"

Saïd hesitated, aghast. He had never dreamt of any more

D

formality about the levying of a beast of burden for the army
than had been observed in the taking of his own donkey.   In
any case, to give the paper was quite beyond his power, for he
could scarcely write.

"What is this, son of a dog?" he exclaimed at last.   "A
paper, sayest thou?—and the law?   Am I one to take orders
from a dog like thee?   As soon as my men arrive with the
other beasts thou shalt have thy paper, but not now.   Dost
hear—eh, old dotard?   Now stand aside or I ride over thee!
I go to meet my followers."

He urged the horse forward; but the old man still kept
hold of the bridle, and the steed knew his master.   His
hesitation, and the misgiving which showed a little through
his brave mask, had taken something from his prestige with
the onlookers.   They closed in upon him, clamouring for
justice.   It was a lonely place; in all the darkness there was
no friend.   He began to be afraid.

"At least the saddle-bags are mine," cried the sheykh, set-
ing to work to free them.

"Fruit and bread and coffee are worth money, O my uncle!
even without syrup of roses and the narghileh," said the
master of the khan in tones of blandest remonstrance.   As he
spoke his face was very near to Saïd's, and its expression was
terribly at variance with the suavity of his utterance.

All who stood by looked meaningly at one another.   "By
Allah, the right is with him!" they exclaimed.   "All this is
worth money.   It is just that he be paid for it."

Saïd moved uneasily in his seat.

"Take thy saddle-bags, old madman!" he cried.   "What
are they to me?   As for thee, dog, thou mayest count thyself
happy if I send thee not to prison.   I saw thee whisper to the
sheykh here, and knew that thou wast warning him to be gone
quickly with his horse.   Thou art no true subject of the
Sultàn.   If I spare thy life it is payment enough."

At that there was a great outcry from all the group.   They
beset him angrily with intent to drag him from the saddle.
Saïd felt deadly sick.   Only the thought that he was a high
officer of the Sultàn's army upheld him.   Rough hands were
already laid upon him, when he shouted "Praise be to Allah!"
very fervently, with joy in his voice.   They all drew back in
surprise.

"Make haste, Ahmed!—Mustafa!—Muhammed! I, your leader, am assailed by robbers. Hassan and Ali, ride fast! Let Neglb, whose horse is lame, take charge of the captured beasts! I, Saïd Agha, am in peril of my life!"

Turning to the terrified innkeeper and his friends, he said shortly,—

"Dogs, count yourselves dead! Hear ye not the sound of hoof-beats?" And digging the sharp corners of the iron stirrups deep into the flanks of the horse he galloped away into the night. The last he saw of his assailants, they were standing huddled together, like silly sheep, half-dead with fright.

X

IT was evening when Saïd at last came in sight of the great
city. He reined in his horse on the brow of a steep hill,
the last wave of the bare brown highlands through which his
way had lain all day. Hard by was a little shrine, the crescent
fiery above its dome. The sun was just setting among the
dark peaks behind him, and the last gleam of day was warm
upon the shrine and all the hill-top. Horse and man had a
glory at their backs. But beneath, the city and its endless
gardens lay already in the lap of night. White domes and
minarets, mosques and palaces, loomed wanly in the heart of a
vast grove, which stretched, far as the eye could ascertain, to
eastward towards a smooth horizon which was the desert.
Gathering shades spread a thin veil over all the plain, like the
bloom on a purple grape. An amethyst flush suffused the
eastern sky—a spirit flush, soft, yet living, wherein starlight
and daylight seemed mingled. Saïd's heart leapt as he beheld
the mistress of his dreams, set in her gardens, seeming the
fairer and more desirable for the grim, treeless mountains
which were her girdle.

"It is paradise," he murmured in ecstasy.

At the foot of the hill, on the utmost fringe of the gardens,
he could see a little village of flat-roofed houses. A string of
camels was drawing near to it along the base of the steep.
The tinkle of their bells rippled the twilight cheerily. Of a
sudden the noise of chanting arose—a wild, delirious song of
piercing shrillness. It came from the high platform of the
only minaret of the village. Somewhat mellowed by the
distance, it reached Saïd's ears as heavenly music. The
clangour of bells ceased of a sudden. The camels had halted.
Their drivers, obedient to the muezzin's call, were prostrate
in prayer.

Saïd got down from his horse and went through the form

52

of ablution with some dry dust he collected. Taking off his grand garment, a good deal the worse for his five days' wearing of it, he stretched it on the ground for a mat. He turned his face carefully to the south and knelt down as near to the shrine as he conveniently might. He raised his thumbs to his ears and spread his hands over his eyes in the likeness of an open book. He rose, stooped, knelt again, prostrated himself and pressed his forehead to the earth. Then he sat awhile upon his heels with eyes closed, and then glanced to left and right, to exorcise any evil spirits who were thereabout.

At last he rose and resumed his cloak. The orange glow of sunset was fading fast, and the mountains he was leaving were black and grey upon it. He bestrode his horse once more and began to descend. It was night when he entered the city. The streets were almost deserted. The few men he met were wending homeward, some in a hurry, others with the leisure of importance. Light streamed fom an arched doorway, making a yellow pool on the rough pavement. A red glow, sifted through the tracery of an upper lattice, made a delicate filigree upon the wall opposite. But for such chance alms the streets were pitchy dark. The strip of sky above, sprinkled thick with stars, was a brightness in comparison. At the clatter of a horse's hoofs, dogs, seemingly without number, rose grudgingly and slunk snarling from the roadway. Every wayfarer had a lantern to light his steps, either in his own hand or in that of a servant who walked before.

Anon he came to a region where all the streets had roofs which shut out the sky, save a starry shred here and there where there was a rift in the black covering. Here was more life. A few merchants were yet busy stowing away their wares for the night, black shapes in flowing robes and turbans moving hither and thither about their lanterns. At a place where four of these covered ways met, seeming like corridors in a giant's house, a sentry was standing in the door of his little hut talking to two muleteers.

The ride through the dim streets had humbled Saïd. He felt very lonely all at once. In all that wilderness of dwellings there was not one soul who knew him. He would have given much—even his horse, or his brown cloak with the red braiding—to have had Hasneh with him. Fearing he knew

not what rebuff, he had been ashamed to accost any man
hitherto. But now he reined in his horse before the sentry
box and, wishing the little group a happy evening, inquired
after a khan. One of the muleteers knew a good one and
offered to guide him thither. It was plain, by the fervour of
their salutations, that they took him for a superior. He began
to feel more at ease. It was not far to the hostelry. The
muleteer talked glibly all the way, of travelling and of his own
journeys in particular. His name it appeared was Selîm. He
was but lately returned from Haleb the White, and before
that he had been to Baghdad with a hundred camels. Whence
had his honour come? From the South?—from the sea-
coast. Ah, he had been there too, having journeyed with a
caravan to Gaza, and back by El Khalîl and the holy city. It
was·a pleasant land, the lord of all for oranges ; he had the
taste of them yet in his mouth.

Saïd lent a gracious ear to his guide's prattle, which
relieved him of that feeling of loneliness which was weighing
him down. Arrived at the khan, he bestowed a small coin
upon the fellow, who blessed him and went his way.

A bare-legged lad belonging to the inn held his horse
while he dismounted, and led it in through an archway. Saïd
followed closely to be sure that the right measure of fodder
was given and the beast properly cared for. He entered a
huge vaulted chamber, its groined roof upheld by two rows of
pillars.   Couched upon the ground, big, ungainly camels
were pompously chewing the cud, now and then rolling up a
deep gurgling sound like a groan from some nether stomach.
Horses were there, each fastened with a halter to a ring in
the wall. One stallion, a newcomer, was screaming lustily and
tugging at his rope. Patient asses with moving ears and
swishing tails, and sullen mules whose eyes looked wicked in
the lurid glow of the single lantern, were tethered here and
there.   There was a sound of stamping, of scrunching, and a
pungent smell. A little donkey just within the gate lifted up
his voice and brayed as Saïd entered.

Having seen his steed well placed and provided for, Saïd
followed the serving-lad to a door in the wall, whence light
streamed upon a camel's hump. The noise of voices and a
smell of cooking also issued from it, soothing two senses with
the promise of cheer within. He found himself in a long

room with cushions ranged along the wall, lighted by a number of wicks floating in a large saucer full of oil. A numerous company were seated, some smoking and chatting on the divan, others, on isolated cushions, eating ravenously with their hands out of dishes set upon brass trays before them. They all rose in acknowledgment of his salutation and a place of honour was offered to him, which, however, he declined to accept, choosing rather a lowly seat about midway in the room. In an arched alcove or inner room a fire was glowing in a great brazier, whereon were many vessels steaming.

Saïd desired a portion of a savoury mess of pigeons and rice, which the bare-legged lad informed him was almost ready. The meal, though proper enough to his fine robe braided with red and the decent horse he rode, was scarcely in keeping with the sum of ready money in the linen bag upon his chest. But he had no longer any need of a horse. He would sell his steed on the morrow, and the price he hoped to get for it would keep him in comfort for many months.

When hunger was appeased, and a tiny cupful of the bitterest coffee had diffused a pleasant warmth within him, he began to take interest in the conversation around him. A big, sanguine fellow, who by his garb seemed a wealthy fellah —the sheykh of some village, perhaps, or a small landowner —was talking excitedly in a loud voice. His large brown eyes, of ox-like stupidity, were bright, but without a spark of cunning. His close-cut beard was reddish like his moustache.

"My cause is a just one. Also I have set aside much money to secure judgment. My enemy cannot bring forward a single witness in his favour, whereas I have my brother here and my servant who were present at the transaction. It is certain that I shall win."

He took up the hem of his robe—a rich one though somewhat soiled—to wipe the amber mouthpiece of his narghileh.

"Truly thou art an honest man and a trusting," said a bilious-looking person, short and swarthy, with a sneering smile. "It is well seen thou comest from a far village. As for witnesses, I tell thee thy adversary may have ten for thy two. Thou art rash, young man, to quarrel with one so powerful as the tithe-farmer. Thou hast wealth, it may be, but be sure he is richer than thee. Also he has the ear of the rulers, who profit by his exactions. The Mehkemeh is not a house of justice as thou thinkest, but an open market where judgment goes to the heaviest purse. Thou comest from afar; but I am of the city and speak from knowledge. To-morrow, when thou goest to the court, thou wilt be beset at the gate by a crowd of rascals whose trade is to bear witness for money. Twenty piastres will buy thee a plausible fellow who will swear to aught that pleases thee. The cadi will count the witnesses on either side, and will give judgment for the greater number—if he have not sold his verdict beforehand, which is most likely. Bakshîsh is lord of all. A wise man does not fall out with the rich. It is the same all the world over. They tell of countries where justice is for rich and poor alike; but that is all a lie!"

He looked round on the faces to mark the effect of his words. Then he leaned back and began to roll a cigarette.

The young man who had first spoken broke out in fierce invective at such a state of things. Yet he still believed that his own case would prove a big exception. He boasted wildly and a little foolishly of the revenge he would take if judgment were given against him. He even reviled those in authority, so that his listeners murmured, with fear in their eyes. It was ill to speak thus in a public place where none knew his company. The eyes of everyone sought a neighbour's in concern. Saïd above all was singled out for suspicion. His brown cloak of outlandish make, and especially the red braid upon it, had a quasi-official look. It was a relief to all when a fat-faced man with roguish eyes, who sat in the lowest seat and seemed the poorest there, raised his voice in fantastical eulogy of riches. He stood up, and mimicking an advocate or other public speaker, talked nonsense glibly in a high poetic strain. It was rather brilliant nonsense, and it tickled his audience hugely. One and all rolled with laughter, holding their sides. By the time the wag sat down again he was dear as a brother to every man there. As an approved jester he might have taken the seat of honour without offence to the most arrogant.

After that the talk became less general. Men yawned one after another. Those nearest to Saïd made overtures of friendship. They asked questions: whence he came, what his name was, whether he had a son, what might be his business in the city, and so forth—questions Saïd was often puzzled to answer. To escape from their inquisitiveness he declared himself with a yawn to be very weary, and asked to be shown to the place of sleep. One or two of the company had already set the example. He salaamed to the room in general as he went out.

The same bare-legged youth who had served him on his arrival led him now through the dim stable, among the sleeping beasts, to a place where a flight of stone steps was built against the wall. Ascending, he came into a long room like to that he had just left. The lantern his guide carried showed the floor bare save for four mattresses, on which as many men lay stretched, and a heap of dirty bedding in one corner. There was a lattice affording a glimpse of the stars above the uneven blackness of flat-topped roofs. The night air came freely into the chamber—not the sweet breeze of the mountain or the seashore, but a breath of the sleeping city redolent of the day's filth. The lad dragged a mattress and a covering from the heap and spread them close by the window. Then wishing the traveller a happy night, he departed.

Saïd lay awake a great while. Men came in by ones and twos, spread out their beds and lay down, until the floor was strewn with sleeping forms and the sound of loud snoring in every key floated out melodious into the night. He could not be rid of a feeling that he was still on horseback, riding at a foot's pace over hill and dale, breezy mountain and burning plain. A fear was at his heart—a fear that had been with him always of late, that he might fall in with a band of soldiers who would rob him of his horse even as he had robbed the rightful owner. He had indeed learned from a shepherd lad that there was no war but only a general movement of troops changing garrison. But as steeds were needed as much in the one case as in the other, the tidings in no way relieved his mind. By a cautious avoidance of towns and large villages, and choice of a by-path, even though it went a long way round, he had almost doubled the length of his journey, and had approached the city by the way of the hills, whereas the way of the plain was much shorter.

When at length he fell asleep it was to dream that the whole city had become solid, of a single stone, and that

he was immured in a little cavity in the midst of it. The
stone was populous, swarming with human beings who gave
no heed to his cries. There were endless tunnels thronged
with wayfarers, all bearing lanterns — a nation which had
never seen the sun. The weight of the whole stone was
somehow upon him. He called to Allah for relief; but the
thickness of that stone was inconceivable, and Allah very
far away. However, the face of Muhammed the Prophet
(peace be to him!)—a fat sly face like Abdullah's—looked in
upon him and sternly remarked, "It is Paradise." Then
arose a terrible cry for bakshìsh, and Saïd knew that the
stone was no other than a court of law.

XI

SAÏD awoke, as soon as it began to be light, to find the chamber already half empty of sleepers. His forehead was clouded as he went down the flight of stone steps into the stable and threaded his way gingerly among the beasts and merchandise. His mind was busy laying plans for the day. There was much to be done. His horse must first be sold, and then he must look out for a lodging in keeping with his means. He must be on his guard every minute, for the dwellers in towns have ready wits and love to whet them on a stranger.

The ghost of daylight, looking in at the arched doorway, cast a pallor on the stumpy columns, on the humps and heads of camels, on the glossy flanks of horses and mules. He made his way to where his own steed was standing listless, awaiting the morning's dole of chaff and barley. A soft neigh and a pricking of the ears welcomed him. He smoothed the horse's mane lovingly, patted its neck and rubbed its nose, whispering all manner of endearment. It was a good beast, and he was sad to part with it.

In the guest-room he found the young man who had spoken so rashly overnight seated on the floor at a meal of bread, curds and olives. A handsome lad of sixteen or thereabouts, whom a strong likeness proclaimed his brother, sat with him, eating from the same tray. At a becoming distance their servant—a swarthy, fierce-eyed fellow, whose weather-beaten tarbûsh had lost its tassel—squatted on his bare heels awaiting their pleasure. Saïd greeted them politely before shouting for something to eat. While a servant who answered his cry was pouring water over his hands and helping to dry them on a dirty cloth, the voice of the young man rose in flowered eloquence.

He was rehearsing the speech he meant to make before

the cadi.   It must have been written for him by some learned
scribe skilled in all the bewilderment of tangled words; for
no plain man could lay hold of its meaning.   It was all of
one piece from first syllable to last, and as it was recited, or
rather intoned, there was no telling where one thought ended
and the other began.   Saïd's mouth fell agape with admiration.   He listened spell-bound, forgetful even of his breakfast.
Once or twice the orator, finding himself at a loss, drew a
scroll from the bosom of his robe and passed his finger along
and down it till he came to the passage.   Then he replaced
the scroll and went on with renewed fervour.

"Capital!" cried the servant, when a complacent grin of
his master announced the end.   "In all my life I have heard
nothing like it.   It speaks with the mouth of the Coràn, with
the voice of an angel.   It would melt the heart of the Chief
of Mountains, by Allah!   Rejoice, O my master, for our
cause is won!"

"Good—very good!" said the younger brother, his face
eager with impatience.   "Is it not the hour when we should
repair to the Mehkemeh?"

Saïd also lent his voice to swell the chorus of praise.
Such a speech, he protested, would grace the lips of princes.
It was polished as a tray of gold, exquisite as a mosaic of
divers kinds of precious stones, sweet as the voices of girls
singing to the sound of the one-stringed lute.   The ear of
Allah would not disdain it.   This high praise, which was
perfectly sincere of its kind, flattered the orator and his boyish
brother.   Even the surly henchman looked at Saïd with
grudging approval.   The chief of the party informed him
graciously that he had procured the speech of a scribe
renowned in all the city for his learning, and that it had cost
him a pretty sum of money, which he named.   If his enemy
could produce a better he would be surprised, and so forth.
"Moreover," he added, with a smile of such doltish cunning
that Saïd envied his opponent—"moreover, I have laid out
much money already among the servants of authority, and I
have here a great sum to be expended in the court itself.   It
is sure that I shall win."

"There is no doubt!" his companions chimed in, the one
eagerly, the other with a kind of sullen defiance.

"No doubt—not a shred of doubt," echoed Saïd, his bearing very respectful of a sudden as he heard the jingle of coins in the sack which the young man opened his robe to show him.

His fast fairly broken, he called for the reckoning. The lord of the khan appeared—a very fat man wearing a robe of indigo blue, under which dirty white pantaloons showed to his ankles, the reddest of red slippers, and a girdle of many colours which, instead of restraining his bulk at all, bulged out frankly upon the most obvious part of him. His turban was richly embroidered, but old and dingy. His demeanour was important but polite, as became a substantial host requiring payment of a guest of unknown quality. The amount was twelve piastres, he informed the effendi. After a little fruitless haggling, which only served to hurt the feelings of mine host and turn him to a boulder of dignity, Saïd discharged his debt and took leave of the hopeful litigant and his supporters.

Passing out into the stable he found the bare-legged lad of last night zealously brushing his nag's mane and flanks. At a word he left work and fetched the saddle and bridle from a heap of trappings in a nook of the wall.

A group of camels were being laden from a heap of bales which stood piled round one of the pillars. The cursing of their drivers, three in number, was very lusty, as they made them kneel, then rise and kneel again, to get them into position. The foremost of them, already accommodated with a load, stood across the doorway, blocking it. An oath from Saïd, ably seconded by the bare-legged stable-boy, called forth a perfect storm from the camel-drivers, one of whom ran forward and led the unwieldy beast to one side. The horse was taken out on to the causeway. Allah, who was being invoked within the archway to blast and utterly destroy the father, religion and offspring of the half-dozen camels there lading, was humbly asked to increase Saïd's wealth as that worthy rode off leaving a trifle in the brown palm of the hostler.

The long, roofed bazaar, from which others just like it branched to right and left, was already busy with people going to their day's work. A coolness of the empty night still hung in its shadow, but that shadow was no longer grey and thin, but blue and deep, telling of a young sun reddening the roofs above. It was early yet to think of selling his horse; so Saïd rode forward at his ease, bent on viewing the city, taking this turning or that as fancy prompted.

Stalls were opening everywhere in the shady markets. Shutters were opened, bars removed, goods displayed. Merchants were settling themselves in dim nooks like caverns behind their wares. The ways were choked with a humming, gaily-coloured crowd. Cries of "Oäh! Oäh! Look out on your right—on your left!" came in shrill tones or hoarse, as men with asses or mules forced a way through the press. Sweet, languorous odours, wafted from the shop of a vendor of perfumes, a whiff of musk from the shroud of some passing woman, the fragrance of tobacco, a dewy breath of the gardens from a mule's panniers crammed with vegetables—little puffs of sweetness were alternate in Saïd's nostrils with the reek of dirty garments and ever-perspiring humanity, with vile stenches from dark entries, where all that is foulest of death and decay was flung to glut the scavenger dogs that slept, full-gorged, by dozens in every archway and along every wall. Saïd inhaled sweet and foul alike with a relish as part of the city's enchantment.

He looked about him as he rode with wondering delight, shouting always "Oäh! Oäh!" as a warning to the multitude whose din drowned the clatter of hoofs. The greatness and the glory of it surpassed his dreams. Here was a whole bazaar wide, long and lofty, possessed exclusively by the workers in precious metals; another by the sweetmeat sellers; a third by those who inlay wood with mother-of-pearl; a fourth by those who sell rugs—rich carpets of all the hues of the garden, of every make, from Bukhra and Khorassan, from Mecca and Baghdad and El Ajem. In one street he caught glimpses, through mean doorways, of precious stuffs, fine silks embossed and embroidered, the work of a lifetime. In the next there was nothing but the noise of grinding, chiselling and planing as the joiners squatted at their work, with the breath of the crowd in their faces.

He passed out of the shade of the covered bazaars and came at length to a place where the sun shone blinding on the ornate gateway of a mosque. Doves wheeled overhead about a tall and graceful minaret, which tapered dazzling white upon the dazzling blue, pointing to the heart of the great sapphire dome, to the throne of Allah himself. Through the archway he could see a flock of them strutting and pecking on the mosaic pavement of a cloistered court. Their cooing brought the inner stillness to him in spite of the noisy crowd, like a voice in a bubble of silence.

He rode on, rejoicing in the fierce sunlight and the peaceful shadows, in all the busy throng around him.

It began to be very hot, and he had been long riding. The cry of a certain vendor of iced drinks, who was elbowing his way through the crowd, clasping a huge bottle of greenish-yellow fluid and clinking two cups together as cymbals, was like the voice of an angel calling him.

"O snow of the mountain! How pure art thou, and how cold! O juice of the lemon! how refreshing when mingled cunningly with sugar as in my bottle! O drink of paradise, who could refuse thee? May Allah have pity on him who drinks not of this cup!"

Saïd drank of it and smacked his lips afterwards. In truth it was refreshing. He paid the smallest of coins—it was all the ministering angel asked for his elixir—into the dirtiest of hands, and received the parting blessing.

"May Allah have mercy on thy belly!"

Then he bethought him that it was time he took some step towards selling his horse. He had been quite happy till then, drifting with the tide of inclination, having no aim beyond sight-seeing. But the moment he came to harbour a definite purpose he felt crestfallen and ill at ease. The multitude, with which he had but now mingled lovingly as a brother, seemed to fall back from him of a sudden, becoming heartless and indifferent. He felt bewildered as his eyes strayed over numberless eager faces, seeking some person not too busy to answer a question. All at once, even as he drew rein irresolute, his hand was seized and kissed, and a man's voice hailed him with cheerful deference.

"May thy day be happy, O my master!"

"May thy day be happy and blessed!" returned Saïd, graciously.

It was Selim, the muleteer who had been his guide to the khan. The encounter was timely. Saïd straightway questioned him as to the best place for a man to go who was wishful to sell a horse to the best advantage. Selim had the whole day on his hands. On his head, he was at Saïd's service. He would lead him to a place which had not its like in all the world for horse-selling; it was the lord of all such places, by

Allah!   He would not conduct the effendi to a low place, of
which there were many—no, by his beard, but to the best of
all.   He had a great respect for the effendi, and, to be sure,
the horse was a good horse, deserving to be sold in the best
market.

He took Saïd's bridle and led him out of the throng and
the sunlight into a maze of by-ways, narrow, dark and dirty.
There were archways, short tunnels, sleeping dogs and evil
smells.   Saïd saw many women with their faces uncovered.
Most of the men also in this region wore the fez alone, or, if a
turban, it was informal, of black or grey.   He feasted his eyes
on the charms of the maids and matrons with lazy contempt.
They were Christians, unbelievers and accursed.   Yet men
and women walked bravely in the middle of the causeway, and
were in no haste to humble themselves before a true believer
and one that rode upon a horse.

Referring to his guide for enlightenment,—

"This is the Nazarene quarter," replied the muleteer.
"Here, by the mercy of the Sultàn, the infidels are suffered to
live apart under a chief of their own religion.   It is their
ancient privilege, and none grudged it them of old, when the
dogs were meek and obedient to the law.   In those days they
were not abhorred by the faithful, who lived peacefully with
them, claiming only the right of the conqueror.   But now that
they grow fat and insolent, because of the Frankish consuls
who pamper them, they are become loathsome as Jews in our
sight.   The fault is with the consuls, who shield and abet them
in whatever they do.   The worst of them will tell you that they
are French subjects or Muscovite, and will show papers to that
effect given them by the consul.   Your grace marvels—not
so?—to hear a common man discourse of such high matters.
Know, O effendi, that Selìm speaks not of his own knowledge"
—he twitched the hem of his robe lightly to shake off any dust
of responsibility that might cling to it.   "He has kept silence
in the tavern while wise men spoke, and the ears of Selìm
carried something of the matter to his understanding.   Moreover, it would be hard to find a man in all the city at present,
be he notable or beggar, true believer, or Nazarene, or Jew, who
is not possessed with politics as with a devil."

Saïd, whose ears had given heed, though his eyes were
wandering, frowned terribly as his guide ceased speaking.

"It were a righteous deed," he said, "to slay every dog of them and burn their quarter with fire." There was fierce light in his eyes.

"Ah!" said the muleteer, "but the Franks are powerful and their vengeance would be dire. As thou knowest, the French and English gave aid to the Turks in the late Muscovite war, and in return they claim to govern the Sultàn's realm instead of him. True believers are but as dogs in their sight, and they would set up a Nazarene in every high place. Allah! have mercy! Alas for the evil day that has dawned for the faith!"

But the light in Saïd's eyes was no other than the greed of gain. He was a strong man, not without courage. He would gladly slay a man, whether armed or defenceless, a woman, or even a child in the cause of Allah and the Prophet. But he could not forget that these Christians were rich. His mind's eye saw a heap of gold in the darkness of every squalid entry. Also the women were fine and plump. His lips were yet dry from the sight of a pretty girl who had smiled up at him in passing. Truly, it would be a pleasant and a holy thing to harry these unbelievers with fire and sword.

XII

"SPOKE I not truly, O my master, when I said it was a fine place? The greatest of the city come here each day to hear the news and see what horses are for sale. With thy leave, I will stay with thee. It is not seemly that a man of thy condition should be seen without a servant."

A lofty and ruinous gateway gave access to a sort of lawn, worn bare of grass in many places. All round, near to the walls of houses, trees threw great blots of shade over a crowd of richly-dressed persons—Turkish officers in high fezzes and their best uniforms; grave merchants and notables, robed in finest silk, with close-cropped beards and deep-embroidered turbans; one or two men in the official black frock coat and red tarbûsh, and a sprinkling of undoubted Europeans in light suits with queer-shaped hats upon their heads. All these were standing in groups or strolling up and down watching a wild-looking Bedawi and a groom of the town vie with each other in feats of horsemanship.

Selîm drew close to the saddle-bow as they entered the enclosure. "Effendi!" he whispered, "it were well for thee to dismount here and let me go forward with the horse. It is easier for the servant to raise the price than for the master. Selîm cannot decide, it is understood, without first consulting thee. Be haughty, O my master, and show thyself hard to please! Selîm will take care to exalt thee in the ears of all who question him concerning the horse. So men shall know that thou art a great one, and shall be ashamed to offer a small sum."

The advice seeming good to Saïd, he alighted and gave the rope-bridle into the hand of his follower.

"Allah be with thee!" he said. "The saddle and the bridle go into the bargain; I have no more need of them. And forget not to make much of the horse!"

"Have no fear, O my master! Selìm is a subtle man, well skilled in this kind of business. By Allah, though, it is a pity he is not a mare. A stallion may be strong, swift, beautiful, of the best blood of the desert, but he is not productive like a mare. A good mare in foal would fetch a vast price here, effendi. Ah, my beloved, if thou hadst but been a mare!" He laid his cheeks to the horse's pink nostrils lovingly. Then, with a rousing pat between the eyes, he led him away towards where the Bedawi and his rival were galloping madly to and fro in the blinding sun, pulling up short within a hand's-breadth of the wall, so that the steeds were hurled back on their haunches, shouting and yelling all the while as though their lives depended on it.

Saïd, for his part, bent his steps to the nearest tree, where was a group of loungers in the shade, walking slowly with care for his dignity. Never before had he mixed in such high company, and he felt awkward. But ere he had achieved many steps there was the sound of hoofs muffled by the rank grass, and Selìm stood again at his elbow.

"Look, effendi!" he said, pointing with his finger. "Seest thou the old man yonder?—he of the snowy turban and the striped cloak, black and white. It is a Durzi, one of the nation of the Drûz—whether from the Hauran or from the Mountain, Allah knows. A strange race, O my master!—thou hast doubtless heard speak of them. I bethought me that, being a stranger from afar, thou mightest like to see a true Durzi; that is why I come back to thee. They are our brothers in that matter of the Nazarenes of which we were speaking, and they are strong in war. They love not the Mowarni, their neighbours on the Mountain, who call themselves subjects of the French, and are very arrogant. Men say that there are threatenings of war between them. Look well at him, effendi. Mark how proud he stands. By the Coràn he is the finest old man I ever saw. He is lord of all here by a head."

Saïd admitted to have heard much talk of that strange race, of whom the very Government stood in awe, and even to have spoken with some of them on his journey. He agreed with Selìm that he had never met so noble-looking an old man as this sheykh in the black and white cloak, who, though his long beard was almost as white as his turban, yet stood

alert and upright as if still in the prime of youth. He held a
fine stallion, black as charcoal, by the bridle; and some young
men of the city, who were examining the horse's parts, looked
oafish beside him for all their fine apparel. As Saïd took his
stand on the outskirts of the little crowd of grandees his eyes
were still observant of that stately figure. The black charger
was every whit as admirable as his master. The old Durzi
must be mad, Saïd thought, or very short, indeed, of money to
wish to sell a horse like that. He himself would not have
parted with such an animal for all the wealth of Istanbûl.
The small head, the watchful eye, the listening ears, the distended nostrils, the strong, arched neck, the tail falling like a
cascade, not hanging limp between the buttocks; a dainty
trick of pawing the ground and prancing from mere pride of
life—the charm of these things took Saïd's breath away.

He was standing just within the shade of a great tree,
about whose trunk the loungers clustered most thickly. Along
the foot of a sun-baked wall beyond, roses, a little thicket of
them, tangled like brambles over a brash of fallen stones and
other refuse. The pink of blossoms among their dusty leaves
was lustreless, veiled as in haze by the white glare from the
wall. Their perfume reached Saïd faintly on that light breeze
which springs up about the third hour of the day and breathes
its fullest at noon.

The Bedawi had ceased his mad gallop in the sun's eye
and was now busy scraping the foam from his horse's flanks
with a piece of wood. Selîm had taken his place as rival of
the town-bred groom, and the pair were careering about like
madmen. Saïd shouted to him not to tire the horse—a cry
which drew the attention of those who stood near. He caught
a whisper: "He is a soldier—not so?" and knew, with a
beating heart, that the red braiding of his robe was being
canvassed. Then he heard a Turkish officer say, "It is but
a mockery of our uniform paletôt. That is no soldier's
garment, by Allah!" He knew the speaker for an officer by
the clatter of a sword which preceded and followed the words,
and for a Turk by the way he pronounced Arabic. But he
did not turn his head or let it be known he had overheard.
When at length he risked a backward glance it was to find
that most of the company had moved away, leaving only a
young officer and two Franks. They were talking lightly

together, and seemed perfectly heedless of him or his clothes.

Presently, however, a laugh affronted his ears. It was a Frank's laugh or an idiot's, being very loud and quite devoid of understanding. Saïd felt uneasy but did not change his position, nor turn his head the fraction of an inch. Only he strained his ears to listen. Both the Franks were laughing now, and the sound of their mirth was like the braying of twin asses. They were trying to explain something to the Turk in a strange tongue. At last the officer seemed to understand, for he laughed too—not the meaningless laughter of the other two, but a subtle guffaw full of appreciation. Then he stepped forward and touched Saïd's shoulder.

"By thy leave, uncle"—the familiarity of this style of address was gall and wormwood to the fisherman—"I would ask thee a question. The Khawajât, my friends, marvel much at this garment of thine. It is the work of their country, they aver, and one which no Frank wears outside his own house; it being proper only to the harìm and the sleeping-room. They are curious to know for what reason, whether from ignorance or of any set purpose, thou wearest it before all men in a public place."

Then Saïd, with hot shame and confusion at his heart, lifted up his voice and laughed—a laugh even louder and more empty than that of the Franks.

"It was a famous trick," he cried, "Oh, that rascal! He is a very devil for cunning! Listen, O Khawajât, and thou also, O my lord the Bek! I am a man of consequence in my own city, but it is far from here. I set out to come hither in order to get the inheritance of my brother, who is dead. In the way I passed by the door of a Frank—a priest he was, dressed all in black. He called to me to enter and rest awhile, and, as it was the heat of the day, I got down off my horse and sat with him. While we awaited the coffee, he brought this garment to show me, swearing by all his prophets, whom he counts as gods, that it was a robe of price such as kings wear in his country. He wished to sell it, and as he had taken a fancy to me—ah, the devil!—he would let me have it for five hundred piastres. It was equal to giving it, he said, but he loved me like a brother and so would let me have it for that money. So I, desiring the robe greatly (for

I believed his words, that it was a fine rarity), and having much money with me, paid the price at once, and put on the garment, which in truth is pleasant to wear. Ah, the joker! he befooled me perfectly."

The Turk laughed long and merrily. He was at pains to translate the story for the benefit of his Frankish friends. One of these, whose face had somewhat the colour of a pomegranate flower, insisted on grasping Saïd's hand and shaking it, which is a manner of friendly greeting with the Franks. He laughed heartily with his mouth wide open, staring into Saïd's face with stupid blue eyes. His companion, who kept his face—pink and white, like a painted woman's—carefully shaded by a very broad-brimmed hat, held a little aloof, but laughed heartily too. The moustache of this latter was yellow like straw.

Saïd submitted to the indignity of having his hand squeezed to a jelly and his arm all but wrenched from its socket with as good a grace as might be, consoling himself with the thought that the Franks are all possessed with devils. He was quite in the dark as to the meaning of it all till the officer spoke to enlighten him.

"It is because thou art a merry fellow, O my uncle. My friend here loves thee because thou smilest in misfortune and art not angry that a trick has been played with thee."

At that Saïd grinned broadly and pressed the Frank's hand with all his might, working it up and down until he cried laughingly, "Enough! enough!" that being one of the few words of Arabic which he knew.

"Why art thou here, O my uncle?" asked the Turk. "Hast come to buy a horse? Yonder is a fine one, which the old Durzi is holding."

"No, my lord the Bek, I am come to sell a horse," returned Saïd, with dignity. "My servant leads him yonder in the shade of the tree. It is a good horse, not so much for fantasy as for travelling. There is not his equal for a long journey. I myself have ridden him lately for five days; that is why he looks a little thin. It grieves me to have to sell him."

The Turk imparted the substance of what was said to his two friends. There followed a short conversation between the three, of which Saïd understood nothing. Then the officer said,—

"My friend the khawaja has need of a stout horse to carry him on a journey he is about to make into the desert. With thy leave he would like to examine this beast of thine."

It was a wonderful stroke of luck for Saïd, and he saw a special providence in it. He ceased not from praising Allah until the day was far spent and shadows covered all the streets. In a word, the scarlet-faced idiot bought the horse and paid for it, there in the open field, out of a purse that he carried, no less than fourteen English pounds. The bystanders sneered openly at the deed of folly. The Turk strove to reason with his friend, but the Frank was bent on paying the price first asked, which he seemed to think a low one, though Saïd, if beaten down to it, would have taken the half. The old Druze, who had just refused ten pounds Turk for the splendid animal he held, spoke loudly in envy of Saïd's good fortune. Selîm went mad with delight. To crown all, the Frank, having paid the treasure into Saïd's hand, must grasp that hand again, and shake it almost to the time-limit of the fisherman's patience, for the bystanders were laughing in their beards.

Then, with a light heart, Saïd bade Selîm lead the way to some coffee-house of good repute.

XIII

FROM shortly after noon to the eleventh hour Saïd sat with his attendant in a tavern, debating what was next to be done, praising Allah, and dozing between whiles over a narghileh. The place was cool and dark, like a large cellar. What light there was stole upon the gloom through the low doorway from a shadowy alley without. It wakened a bluish sheen on the rim of a great copper vessel, and paled the faces of those who sat nearest to the entry. Behind, in the heart of the gloom, a fire of live charcoal burned redly. Warm steam, charged with the earthy fragrance of coffee stewing, floated among the guests in search of an outlet. About twenty men were there, seated on little stools or lying on the ground. Some few were talking earnestly in low tones, but the greater part were dozing or fast asleep. The fisherman and his humble admirer sat in the darkest corner, away from the fire.

"Let it be as thou askest!" quoth Saïd, at length, after a long silence of consideration. "I hire thee as my servant for one month. If thou art good and faithful in all things, thou shalt be to me as a dear friend, and I will take care of thy prosperity. It is agreed—not so? Sixty piastres shall be thy wage for the month of probation, and after that we will speak again of the matter. Thou eatest and drinkest at my cost. See! I pay thee at this minute, so full is the trust I place in thee."

Selîm bowed low over the hand which enriched him—a hand horny and grimed as his own—and kissed it fervently. "May thy wealth increase!" he said. "Now truly, I am very happy. A muleteer's life is the life of a dog, and in the end he dies the death of a dog by the wayside; often there is no burial for him. Many a time has Selîm said in his mind, 'O mind, it were well to leave this dog's business and cleave to some great one as his servant.' Allah requite thee, O my master, for I am very happy!"

Saïd proposed that they should go out straightway and seek some decent room for a lodging, but Selîm dissuaded him.

"It is best," he said, "that your honour return presently to the khan. Thou art rich, and the khan is a good one, the resort of great ones. While thou art resting I will go to a place I know, where all manner of news is to be had. I will inquire warily what rooms are to let, and what price would be accepted by their owners. Then, in the morning, I will bring thee the fruit of my gleaning. It is ill to buy or hire anything in a hurry. Selîm is a knowing one. Trust him, O my master, and wait a little!"

"I needs must buy a new robe," muttered Saïd. "I have told thee how the Franks yonder, in the garden, did laugh at this garment of mine—a good garment and comfortable; it cost me six Turkish pounds. There are many Franks, thou sayest, in the city, and I have no mind to abide their mockery. Up, O Selîm! Let us go straightway to the shop of a tailor!"

"Rise not, I beseech thee, O my master. It is not fitting that a man of thy consequence should go to a shop and on foot. Moreover, by thy leave, a vendor of garments ready-made is better than a tailor since thy need is pressing. Abide here a short while and I will bring one hither."

Saïd rendered warm praise to Allah who had given him a servant of such a ready wit.

It seemed but a minute ere a shadow darkened the entry —the figure of a tall man clad in a loose robe from neck to ankles, carrying a large bundle. The voice of Selîm cried, "Behold the merchant, O my lord!"

The tall man saluted gravely as Saïd brought his stool to the doorway, where there was more light. Setting down his bundle upon the ground he proceeded at once to undo it. It contained a number of garments, which he held up one by one, shook out, stroked lovingly, and lauded to the skies. One of them chained Saïd's fancy from the first. It was a loose-falling robe similar to that worn by the merchant, tight sleeved, and buttoning close at the neck. It was of silk and cotton mixed, finely striped in blue and yellow. The merchant, observant of the customer's face, swore by the

Corân that it would grace his Excellency rarely. It was just
the thing for a tall, fine, strong, noble-looking man like his
Excellency. Though he searched through the whole city he
would find no robe so perfectly becoming to him as this one.
All the idlers in the tavern, having nothing else to do, were
drawn near to admire the rich stuffs and witness the bargain.
With no idea of purchasing, and, therefore, no reason for
depreciating what they saw, they joined their voices in chorus
to that of the merchant, and praised the garment as a miracle
of workmanship.

"Let Selîm alone to do the chaffering, effendi!" whispered
the sometime muleteer in his master's ear. And again Saïd
had cause to praise Allah for his servant's wit. For Selîm
drew the salesman apart and spoke fiercely with him for the
space of a quarter of an hour, eyes flaming into eyes, like men
on the point of shedding each other's blood. At the end of
that time they returned smiling, the best of friends, to inform
Saïd that the garment was his for fifty piastres, though the
merchant swore loudly by the beard of the Prophet it was worth
twice that amount. He would not have let it go so cheap to
any other than his Excellency, but to oblige his Excellency he
would make any sacrifice. In return, he craved the favour
of his Excellency's further custom, in case at any time he
should stand in need of fine raiment. The greatest of the
city were his patrons : Mahmûd Effendi, his Reverence the
Mufti, His Highness Abdul Cader, the renowned Emîr of
Eljizar, even the illustrious Ahmed Pasha, the Waly himself!
It was true. If his Excellency doubted it he had but to put
the question to any man there present who would certify him
that it was so.   And all they that stood by, being indeed
perfectly ignorant of the matter, testified, with hands on their
breasts, and eyes upturned, to the merchant's honour.

Selîm received the garment neatly folded and nursed it
lovingly, while his master gave an English pound into the
merchant's hand and counted the change for it. Then, when
the merchant had taken wordy leave, they repaired together
to the khan, it being then the cool of the evening, about the
eleventh hour.

In the vaulted chamber cumbered with beasts and
merchandise Saïd stayed to divest himself of the brown
robe braided with red which had so lately been his pride,

and the kirtle of blue which was beneath it, retaining only his vest and pantaloons, which years ago had been white. He gave the discarded clothes to his servant for bakshísh, to the muleteer's unbounded glee. Selîm assumed the dressing-gown forthwith, stroked it feelingly and moaned with delight. The blue shift, which was an old one but serviceable, he stowed in the sack of his trousers. Then he flung himself on the ground and fell to kissing Saïd's feet very fervently, with broken exclamations of thanks and blessing. Saïd chid him for it, commanding him to get up on pain of his displeasure; but at heart he was well pleased. The cup of his grandeur seemed full to the brim at that minute. For the first time in his life he had played the patron.

As he was adjusting his new robe, Selîm helping him, a sound of mighty cursing rose upon his ears. It came from the door of the guest-chamber, where a lamp was burning already. Saïd stood a moment to listen, then entered, Selîm at his heels.

The young man who had declaimed that famous speech so hopefully in the morning was now the centre of a concerned group, roaring, his face distorted, in a towering rage.

"May Allah cut short his life! May the Cadi rot and all his race with him! May Allah destroy that wicked scribe from off the face of the earth! . . . Heard ye ever the like of it? I pay a great price for a writing to lead my tongue when the time should come for me to speak in the Mehkemeh. I give the half of my wealth to that foul pig of a scribe. And when I reach the court, behold the very same words almost in the mouth of my enemy. He has the first word; therefore my speech is valueless—a mere scroll to burn. I go to that scribe of Satan, and he smiles in his beard. Two men came to him in one day. How was he to know them for opponents in one suit? He laughs. . . . By Allah! he may think himself happy if I slay him not for refusing to give back the money."

At this point Saïd withdrew to the far end of the room that he might chuckle unobserved. He was fervid in his whispered admiration of that scribe; and Selîm agreed that it was a quaint and merry trick, though of opinion that the money should be returned.

The young litigant, his frenzy spent, fell to moaning most pitifully and bewailing his wretched fate.

"Add to all this," he blubbered, "that the hearing is not yet over. Judgment is deferred till to-morrow; and I have wasted my money—all that I brought with me—save only a few piastres which I set aside for the expenses of food and lodging. I have nothing left to buy witnesses for to-morrow. . . . My cause is lost! . . . Merciful Allah! I am ruined."

"A zany!" whispered Saïd to his henchman. "But for such blockheads as this, I ask thee, how should wise men prosper?" He called loudly to the servant to bring something good to eat, and after that was silent for a space, his mouth being full for the most part. He made a favour of allowing Selîm to eat with him, though in truth he was most glad of the company. At last, having swallowed a dose of seething, bitter coffee, brought straight from the brazier by the bare-legged one, he gave utterance to his repletion and ordered a narghileh.

Now Saïd, being full and his mind vacant of business, began to indulge a feeling not uncommon with the great and prosperous. His soul inclined to dalliance and the joys of female society. He wished that Hasneh was there; but not for long. The delights of the city must be many, and Hasneh had been his for seven years, so that there was no more sweetness left in her. Moreover, she had failed in her duty of child-bearing. He had long purposed to supplement her with another woman as soon as he should be rich enough. He looked at Selîm, who was still busy gobbling oily rice, with both hands cramming his mouth. Then he whispered a question, slily watchful of his servant's face.

"No, by Allah!" the other sputtered with indignation. "Your honour mistakes. Selîm is not that kind of man. I would do all things to serve thee, O my master; but lead thee to such a place, I cannot."

"Thou mistakest my meaning," whispered Saïd, soothingly. "I never supposed thee other than an honest man—never!— if it were my last word: never! I did but seek thy counsel, being a stranger in the city."

Selîm was soon mollified.

"That is a very different thing, O my master; but in truth I know nothing of such matters. There are houses in the Christian and Jewish quarters—Ah, the wicked unbelievers! It was a good word thou spakest about destroying them.

There are houses, I say, where women sing and dance by night. There be Nazarenes in all the taverns who will guide thee to them for money. But I advise thee not to go; for evil men abound in those places. At the least, if thou art bent on it, leave the bulk of thy money here, with the lord of the khan, who will give thee a writing of acknowledgment and refund it to thee in the morning."

But all the servant could say failed to convince Saïd of the wisdom of placing his money in another man's hands. To exchange gold and silver for a piece of paper seemed to him the last absurdity.

"This is a foolish thing thou purposest, O my lord," whispered Sellm, with a wail in his voice. "Ah, why didst thou omit to bring thy bride along with thee? Strange women bring ruin to the wisest. As for me, I have my house at a village of the mountains, a parcel of ground and two fruit-trees belonging to me. My woman has always remained there, while I gained money in travel as a muleteer. I go thither in two hours from here when I have a mind to visit her. She is a good girl and faithful; and she seems beautiful to one who sees her seldom and in the shadow of the morrow's parting. Ah, effendi, how sweet is his woman with a babe at her breast to a man returning from a far journey! But this that thou wouldest do—forgive me, my master—is a shame for a true believer, and most bitter in the memory. Strange women are ravenous as wild beasts; they will devour all thy substance if thou persist in following after them. Leave but the half of thy wealth here, with the lord of the khan, or, if it please thee, with me who am thy servant!"

But Saïd only eyed the speaker with suspicion, supposing that he had a mind to rob him. He rose shortly, and having paid for the supper, wished the company a happy night. Whereupon Sellm borrowed a lantern from the bare-legged hostler, and hurried after him, past the sleeping beasts in the stable and out on to the deserted causeway, black as night's shadow, where the flap of their slippers resounded as in an empty hall, and dogs shrank from the ruddy glow of the lantern to form in a barking phalanx at their heels. He was determined to light his master's steps, whether Saïd would or no, to mark well what house he entered and what manner of man he was that kept the door.

XIV

"WOE is me! ... Allah have mercy! ... I am ruined!
... all my wealth is gone! ... I have been robbed
by wicked men; may Allah strike them dead for it. ... Oh, that
I knew the thief, that I might kill him! ... Yesterday, in the
evening, I was rich: now I have no resource but to stretch
out my hand. ... But I will have justice—vengeance! I go
straight to the Cadi—to the chief of the soldiers—to the
Sultàn himself! ... Up, Selìm! Let us hasten to inform the
judge."

"Woe is me! ... My heart is very sad for thee, O my
master. Alas! did I not counsel thee to leave were it but the
half of thy wealth behind with the lord of the khan?—but thou
wouldest not! I have done all that it is in a man's power to
do. I have sought out the owner of that house of sin. I
have threatened him with horrid tortures so that he wept.
And now, having achieved nothing, I have come back to
mourn with thee in the place which thou namedst, even in
this garden by the riverside. The Cadi will not help thee,
for thou canst bring nothing in thy hand. Moreover, a part
of the profits of that house of sin is paid to a great one of the
city for his protection. ... Think not that I am careless for
thy loss. For two hours I was with the master of that house,
cursing and threatening. Once I held him by the throat ... "

"Aha! That was well done! And what said the pig?"

"Have I not told thee, O my master? He wept bitterly
and his sons with him. Then he arose, and also his sons.
They took great staves in their hands and ran like madmen
through all the place, belabouring the dancing-girls and the
old woman who mothers them, and the attendants, and him
who keeps the door."

"Merciful Allah! was there not one who confessed?"

"Alas, my master, thy mind is distraught with grief. Have

I not already told thee? not one of them but confessed. The burden of another's guilt seemed a light and easy thing to bear compared with the great pain of being beaten with a stick. They all cried aloud for mercy, saying, 'I and none other am the thief!' It is the same as if none had confessed. Ah, my master, how camest thou to be thus careless of thy money?"

"Woe is me, I am ruined!"

Saïd lifted up his voice and wept, beating his breast and plucking wildly at his new robe as if to tear it. Sellm, seated on his heels, wrapped in the missionary's dressing-gown, looked on at his master's despair with a grin of the deepest concern. He laboured to console the sufferer with divers proverbs and wise sayings from of old—crumbs from the plenteous table of Islam, which the very dogs pick up and pass from mouth to mouth. But the Heaven-taught creed of resignation was hardly Saïd's at that moment—"A man must bear all things, good and bad, with a calm mind." "Allah was above all." It might be He would mete out happiness at the last, as He did of old in the case of Neby Ayûb! "The reward of patience was sure in the end." Saïd rejected all such crumbs of comfort with a furious shrug. He found them very stale.

With a deaf ear to his servant's pleading, he flung himself upon the ground, moaning, howling and blubbering. Writhing in his anguish, he called upon Allah Most High to avenge his cause, to slay the robber and destroy that house of sin with all who dwelt there.

The voice of his rage and grief rent the calm of that peaceful garden as a cry from Hell piercing the heart of Paradise. Sellm, the resigned, rolled a cigarette and looked rueful as he squatted in the pleasant shade. All about them along the ground little thickets and tufts of rose-trees swayed pink flowers and fluttered green leaves to the pleasure of a light breeze which drank their sweetness. The river murmured in its stony bed, sparkling over pebbles in the sunlight of mid-stream, forming deep pools beneath the bank, very willing to dawdle in the shade of the great walnut-trees.

The mourners were quite alone. The voice of the city floated to them out of the distance like the hum of a mighty bee-hive. A little tavern at no great distance from the bank was deserted save for its owner, and he lay asleep in the shade. It was the fourth hour of the day; and not until the flush of evening have men leisure to go forth and drink the sweet air of the gardens. A stone bridge of a single lofty arch, which bestrode the wady lower down, looked at fragments of its likeness in the eddies and seemed nodding to sleep. The vast blue cope of the firmament paled everywhere towards the horizon in pearly haze. Abundance of leafage compassed the place on every side, but at one point, through a gap in the branches, the old wall of the city was visible, the white cube of an upper chamber peeping over it with a bulging lattice, and a single minaret cleaving the soft distance.

"Be comforted, O my master!" said Selîm, at length, when smoking had brought him to a less gloomy point of view. "Look! the very birds are frightened by the voice of thy grieving." He pointed to certain which were flitting uneasily from twig to twig with alarmed chirrup and twittering. "It is a great loss, I grant thee. To a small man like me it would be ruin. But for thee, effendi, it is only a mishap—most grievous without doubt, and I suffer with thee. Thou hast lost what was in thy hands to spend; but the head of thy money remains—those lands and that palace of which thou spakest yesterday, and all the wealth belonging to thee in thy own place."

At these words Saïd writhed as if a serpent had bitten him. The extreme depth into which he was fallen rendered him careless of dishonour in the opinion of this muleteer. There was a ring of peevishness in his bitter cry as he made the avowal,—

"It was a lie—the word that I spake to thee. I have nothing but that thou wottest of, which is lost. True, I was a great one formerly. Men pressed to kiss were it only the hem of my robe when I walked abroad. But there was an end to my greatness. My enemy, who hated me, was appointed Caimmacàm, and used his power as governor to my ruin. I was robbed and my robbers were openly screened from vengeance. One night certain of the Council that were my friends came privily to my house—a palace it was, by Allah!—and told me of a plot to slay me. Then I fled away by stealth, riding upon the horse thou sawest, taking only a woman that was dear to me and money sufficient for the journey. The woman fell ill by the way and I left her in the house of one who befriended me. Alas, it may be she is dead ere now!

"Woe is me, I am ruined! . . . Yesterday I was prosperous, having a servant and money enough : now look!—I am a crushed worm and there is none to pity me. . . . Allah, in mercy take my life also!"

And at that his moaning broke out afresh.

"Now, by my beard, thou speakest folly," said Selîm, gravely. "Thou sayest: 'Yesterday I had a servant,' when to-day thou lackest not a man to do thy bidding. It was not well to hide the truth from me, effendi. It is with a servant the same as with a partner or a woman. Acquaint him fully at the first, for living always with thee he will presently come at the knowledge though thou wouldst conceal it. Am I not bound to thee for one month by token of sixty piastres and this rich garment which thou gavest me? A robe like this is worth much gold, let the Franks laugh if they please. Selîm is not a dog or an infidel that he should forsake his benefactor, whom Allah has smitten.

"Take heart, O my master! Besides the sixty piastres I have other moneys of my own—a little, it is understood—very little. With all that I have I will buy merchandise—small things such as men hawk through the streets in a basket. Deign to share with me, effendi, nor think it shame because I am a muleteer while thou art learned and of a good house. I will find out some shaded place where thou mayest sit at ease behind the basket containing our wares while Selîm praises the goods for sale in a loud voice, luring them that pass by to pause and examine them. Selîm will be thy servant then as now. Only, at the end of the day when there is no more traffic, we shall divide the profits equally as partners. Is it agreed, O my lord? I know well that it is a shame for thee to take part with a man like Selîm in the open street where all may see thee—it is natural. But that is only the beginning. Afterwards, when our wealth increases, we will hire a stall in one of the finest markets ; when thou shalt be a great merchant, I promise thee, and Selîm, being thy servant, and also (secretly) thy partner, shall partake of thy prosperity. What sayest thou?"

It was long ere Saïd would let himself be won over to this

F

or any other compromise with misfortune. For hours he held
out against his servant's entreaties, moaning always and sign-
ing "No" with hands and head. But as the day wore towards
evening and the shadows of the trees and shrubs grew long
and blue to eastward, he became less hot in his denial; and at
last, having consented to smoke a cigarette, rolled by Selìm and
lighted obsequiously for him by that most faithful of followers,
he relented altogether. "It shall be as thou desirest," he
agreed with a wave of his hand; and he entered with some
keenness upon the discussion of their joint plans for the
future.

"And now, O my master," said Selìm, smiling for joy at
the cure he had wrought, "let us repair to the tavern yonder,
for thou hast eaten nothing since the sun's rising. I know
the master of the place well; indeed, he and I are sworn
brothers. He is renowned in all the city as a cook. Ah, by
Allah, his stuffed vegetables have not their like in all the
world! Arise, O my lord! I have money should there be
need of it."

The sun being now near to his setting, a number of idlers
from the city were seated on little stools in the tavern or in
the shadow of a great walnut-tree which confronted it and
partly overhung the stream.

A train of mules passing the bridge close by made music
with their bells. Quite another kind of music came from the
wide porch of the coffee-house—if porch it can be called,
which wanted but one wall to form a room as large again as
the actual dwelling. A man, sitting cross-legged on a stone
bench or couch beside the inner door, was howling most pitifully with closed eyes and a perpetual rhythmic swaying of his
body to and fro; while another, facing him upon a four-legged
stool, thrummed an accompaniment on an instrument of two
strings. Some of the company kept clapping their hands in
time with the melody. Others smiled voluptuously with
closed eyes, sighing out a prolonged "A-a-ah!" or panting,
"O my eyes! O my soul!" in the height of sensual enjoyment. It was a love song of the most rapturous type—one to
which no son of an Arab could listen unmoved.

To Saïd's present mood it appealed very strongly; but
instead of inducing languor, as in the case of the other hearers,
it brought a warmth to his swarthy cheeks and a brightness to

his eyes. The passionate writhing of the singer, his wails, his shrieks, awoke a lively echo in the fisherman's bosom. Old memories were stirred and, like a heap of dead rose leaves, they gave forth a perfume of days gone by. He recalled the hour when he had led a bride to his house, the madness and the thrill of it. The world was full of maidens fairer and sweeter than she had been.

Absorbed in the music, which seemed to his mind, and to the minds of most men there, to harp upon the keynote of all that is sweet in life, he gave no heed to the dialogue of Selîm and the tavern-keeper carried on in an undertone, though aware that its substance was friendly to the cravings of his appetite. The concluding words, however, spoken somewhat louder as the host moved away, reached his brain.

"May thy prosperity increase, O father of a vegetable marrow! Let them be stuffed as thou alone knowest how to stuff them; and ah! as thou lovest me, forget not to soak the whole perfectly in oil!"

At last the song expired on a shrill, quavering note of long duration. The singer opened his eyes and grinned in acknowledgment of the applause. After one deep-drawn sigh of mixed contentment and regret from the whole audience the hum of conversation arose.

Saïd looked westward to where the sun's chin already leaned on the crest of a ridge of mountains, which seemed the dark wall of a monstrous furnace, for all beyond was flame. He could see the shrine whence he had obtained his first view of the city—a minute black boss against the sky. It was but before yesterday that he had reined in his horse up there.

He was lost in reflections to which the thought gave rise, the commotion caused by the love-song in his blood abating gradually to that torpor of resignation which is the frame of mind prescribed to all faithful people, when Selîm plucked his robe and whispered,—

"Look, O my master! Hither comes the man who was befooled by the scribe—thou rememberest last night at the khan? See, there is the boy, his brother, with him, and one of sullen bearing, who seems a servant."

With a start, Saïd glanced in the direction indicated. At the same instant the sun sank totally behind the rugged hills, and the gardens turned blue-grey beneath a burning flush.

The party Selim referred to was close at hand, walking list-lessly with dejected looks. Saïd rose respectful as the litigant drew near with his following. He bowed profoundly and went through the usual show of deference, scooping up imaginary dust with his hand and laying it lightly upon his lips and brow.

"May your evening be in all goodness, effendum!" he cried. "Allah willing you are happy in your suit?"

At that the newcomers raised hands and eyes to Heaven, all three at once, pouring forth a torrent of mingled saluta-tions, curses and complaints. It was plain they were losers by the day's business.

Saïd waited till they were seated, then carried his stool near to them so as to make one of their circle. He expressed his sympathy warmly, inveighing in no measured terms, though in a low tone, against the injustice of things in general and the iniquity of courts of law in particular. He too had suffered grievous things since last he had the pleasure to behold their honours. Robbed in a single night of all he possessed, he could obtain no redress, no justice, not so much as a hearing of his complaint. By Allah, it was mistress of all wickedness, that city!

The defeated plaintiff was warmed by this sympathy of a fellow-sufferer to be communicative. He recounted all his grievances from the very first, which was a dispute with the tithe-farmer for his extortion of three times his due of the crops of a certain village of which he (the speaker) was head-man. It was a long story of insult heaped upon injustice, and aggravation upon injury; but Saïd did not mind its length, so busy was he concocting a tale to beat it of his own misfortunes. No sooner did he espy an opening—a very short pause in the other's narrative sufficed him—than he thrust his fiction into it wedgewise, breaking short the tale of his rival and astounding his three listeners with a brief sketch or outline of such afflictions as never man bore since the days of Ayûb the Bedawi, whom Allah loved and chastened.

"Of a surety thou art more wretched even than I," said the other, gasping. "Indeed, in a measure I may be called fortunate, for I have found one just man in this city of thieves. He befriended me in the darkest hour of my trouble. But for his kindness I had been in prison at this minute instead of speaking freely with thee here in this pleasant garden. Know that there came one to the court to-day—an old man, a friend of the Cadi, who sat by him in the seat of honour, where the Mufti sometimes sits. But it was not his reverence the Mufti, whose face I know well.

"When that wicked judgment was given a fine was laid upon me because forsooth I had annoyed that devil of a tithe-farmer with my suit and hindered him in the discharge of his duties. As I had not with me wherewith to pay, I offered to ride at once to my village and return after three days with the money. But at that my enemy—may his house be destroyed!—cried out that I was seeking to escape the penalty. And the judge, he too declared that if I would not pay the money I must go to prison until it was collected on my behalf. Then up rose that old man of whom I spoke but now—a good old man, and a kindly, may Allah requite him! —none like him in all the world! He begged a favour of the Cadi, though what it was I might not hear, for they conversed in whispers and I was far removed from them in the hall. Presently he came down to me and led me aside from the rest of the people. He said that he would not have me go to prison for so light a matter. He would pay the fine for me but I must promise to pay back the money before a year expired. Allah reward him!

"So it happens that I am free. To-morrow, ere it be light, I shall set out for my home; and within four days from now that just and holy sheykh shall be assured that Habìb ebn Nasr is a good man and no perjurer—"

"Deign to draw near, O my master. The supper is ready," came the voice of Selìm.

"With thy permission I leave thee," whispered Saïd hurriedly, divided between the pangs of hunger and a desire to learn more of this wonder of liberality; "but quick! tell me what is his name! I too am poor—in the deepest distress. My need is even greater than was thine. Doubtless he will help me also, hearing my tale. Say, O sheykh, what is his name?—where his house? I will take no rest till I kiss his feet!"

"His name is Ismaìl Abbás—a Sherìf, of the kindred of the Prophet—that was all he told me. But he is a great one, I assure thee, one whose name and dignities would fill a book.

He must be a learned doctor of the religion, for he bade me seek him always in the gate of the great mosque between the third hour and noon."

"I thank thee," murmured Saïd, with a thoughtful brow. "May Allah keep thee in safety on thy journey!"

He picked up his stool and rejoined his servant.

"I have good news for thee, O Sélim," he whispered. "Glad news—splendid! To-morrow, at the third hour, thou shalt guide me to the great mosque—"

But just then a shrill murmur from the city floated out over the darkening gardens—the chanting from a hundred minarets, the voice of the common conscience bidding all men pray.

Saïd fell on his knees. It grieved him that he had no cloak to spread out for a carpet as he saw others, Sélim among them, do around him. For a space there was silence in and about the tavern, broken only by the fervid muttering of the worshippers and an occasional clatter made with pots and pans by some soulless woman within the dwelling. A single lantern, hanging from a hook in the roof, was already burning though a spirit-blue of daylight still lingered among the trees. It shone on turbaned heads all turned one way, hands blinding eyes for the furtherance of inward searching, lips moving silently; on old and young alike prostrate, with foreheads pressed to the ground; and dimly, in the darkest corner of the hostelry, on the faces of three unbelievers sitting together by the wall, not daring to speak or move. A word at such a time might well have cost a beating.

XV

SELIM had much to say concerning the beneficent and learned doctor whose name and the hopes he had of him Saïd imparted during supper. But where was the subject within the scope of hearsay on which Selîm had little to relate? It is the custom of muleteers and camel-drivers to gather in the khan, or wherever they pass the night, and tire each other to sleep with talk of their experiences, their masters and their native cities. An intelligent man, and one content to listen, may pick up much useful knowledge of the world and its citizens from such converse. And Selîm had sharp ears and a retentive memory.

The name of Ismaïl Abbâs was become a byword for learning and uprightness, and there were many good stories concerning him, all with a certain quaint salt of proverbial wisdom. But though the servant was glad to air a store of anecdotes he said everything to dissuade his master from an appeal for alms.

He was at no pains to hide the motive of this reluctance, but put it forward humbly as a plea, cringing and with anxious eyes. It was a fear lest Saïd, having once more money in his hand, should abandon their little scheme of partnership for some loftier path to fortune. But the fisherman was firm, and Selîm was at last obliged to yield and consent to be his guide on the morrow.

This experience of his master's obstinacy left the muleteer moody for some time. He grumbled to himself, shrugging his shoulders and frowning at his feet. Then, seeming to come on a solution, his face brightened.

"He will not give thee much money, O my master. It would be profitable for thee to lay it out in the manner I proposed. Thus we should be able to buy a better stock of goods than with my money only. What sayest thou?"

"Of course," murmured Saïd, carelessly. "Thou art a good man and a faithful. Be sure I shall not forsake thee."

"Good—very good," said Selîm, gleefully. "With thy leave, effendi, I go to speak with my friend."

With that he rose, and threading his way among the stools went to the door of the inner room, which framed just then a picture of the tavern-keeper stooping over a charcoal fire and his dilated shadow on the wall beyond. He returned almost immediately and directed Saïd's attention to the host, who had come forth with a great mattress of many colours in his arms, and was spreading it out in a shadowy corner remote from the guests. Selîm hoped that his honour would not disdain to spend a night in that lowly place. The bed was soft and clean, his friend, the taverner could vouch for it. The customers would soon be all gone, when his Excellency could sleep undisturbed till morning.

Saïd was beginning to feel drowsy. He rose with a yawn, bidding Allah bless the house and its master, and, with a reverence in passing to the litigant and his supporters, betook himself straightway to rest. For a minute he lay blinking at the crazy lantern, which burned ever dimmer and more blurred upon his sight. Then he knew no more until, shaken by Selîm, he sat up to behold the gardens fresh and glistening to the sun's first rays, and the tavern-keeper, a fat man with a good-tempered face and a soiled turban, in the act of setting down a tray of eatables upon the ground beside him.

Some two hours later master and man re-entered the city in the comfort attending a hearty meal with a narghileh smoked afterwards for digestion's sake. As they shouldered their way through the motley crowd in the streets Selîm was fervent in praise of their entertainer. There was no one like Rashîd in all the world. His honour had seen well what a good man he was, and how generous. How overjoyed, too, he had been to see Selîm, his sworn brother since five years. Rashîd also was formerly a muleteer. They had journeyed in the same company to Mosul and Baghdad, and had loved one another from the first meeting. They had friends and enemies in common. Never had a harsh or angry word passed between them.

The topic was far from exhausted when they emerged from

a narrow alley and found themselves at the splendid gateway of the great mosque. Selîm, however, broke off short in his eulogy to call Saïd's notice to the dazzling white minaret he had beheld in his first morning's ramble through the city. Now, as then, doves innumerable were wheeling and cooing around it.

"Dost thou know its name, O my master, and the story concerning it?" He put the question more for form's sake than as requiring an answer, and went on at once: "This minaret, effendi, is called by the name of Isa ebn Miriam, that great prophet whom the Christians in their blindness worship instead of Allah. Wouldst like to learn why it is so called? It is Selîm who can certify thee. I heard the whole truth, effendi, from a learned dervîsh, in whose company I once journeyed from Urfa as far as Haleb the White."

Selîm drew his master into the bay of the great gate to avoid a long string of camels, laden with stone, which were approaching with a deafening clangour of bells. There he stood still in the shadow, withdrawn but an arm's-length from the throng and the sunlight, one hand on Saïd's arm to beg attention, the other pointing to the minaret of Jesus the Prophet, whom the faithful call Ruh' Allah: the Spirit of God. The eyes of the passers-by dwelt with curiosity upon the pair, but especially upon Selîm, the importance of whose pose combined with the eccentric fashion of his raiment to make him a notable figure.

"Know, O my Master, it is foretold that, in the latter days, when the end of all things draws nigh, Dejîl shall appear in a cloud of black smoke, black as pitch, covering the whole world. He is the Messiah whom the Jews expect, and great multitudes of that race will follow him. Then the Beast of the Earth shall appear, bearing in one hand the rod of Musa, in the other, the seal of Suleyman. With the rod he will trace a word upon the brow of every true believer; and the foreheads of the infidels he will stamp with the seal. The sun will rise in the west; and the Yehejuj—Mehejuj, that nation of dwarfs, sprung from the loins of Yafez ebn Nuh, will be seen plainly of all men. Arabistan will be shaken with an earthquake.

"Dejîl, that false prophet, will have power for a space to deceive even the faithful. But a fire will break out in Yemen

—a mighty conflagration, driving all flesh before it to the place of Judgment. Isa ebn Miriam will come to this very. . ."

Saïd's impatience at being detained in the gate when a man renowned for almsgiving awaited him within here got the better of his politeness. He broke away with an oath and shuffled off his shoes by the threshold. Selîm, with a sigh, held his peace and did likewise.

On the right hand as they entered, in a shaded place like a cloister, a group of little boys was sitting cross-legged on a carpet, forming a half-circle before a venerable man, richly clad, who was instructing them in a droning voice. Each had an inkhorn at his girdle and a reed pen in his hand, with which to write upon the page of a book which rested in his lap. Saïd smiled as he looked at them; for he loved children, and it was a whimsical thing for him to see half a dozen boys of the most turbulent age sitting grave and demure, like little scribes, at the sage's feet. He followed Selîm to the place of washing, whence, having fulfilled their ablutions, they went into the mosque itself to pray awhile. Upon issuing forth again into the sunlight of the outer court, Selîm raised a hand to screen his eyes, and sent a keen glance round the cloister-like outbuildings in search of a green turban. Suddenly he pulled Saïd's sleeve, whispering,—

"Thou seest three men of grave seeming seated in the yonder corner where the shadow is the darkest? He on the right is the Sherîf Ismaîl Abbâs whom thou seekest. Next to him, if I judge rightly at this distance, sits his worship, the Mufti. The third I know not, but he seems a great one. Be advised, effendi: do not disturb them at present. They speak doubtless of weighty matters, and the tale of thy wrongs will but anger them, being busy."

But Saïd did not hear this advice. Even before it was uttered he was speeding across the mosaic pavement. By the time Selîm grew fully aware that he was standing alone he beheld his master prostrate in the shadow at the feet of the three reverend ones who sat there.

Saïd's outcry of praise and compliment as he lay on his face was cut short by a voice that bade him rise. The tones were mild but commanding; not to be gainsaid. He raised himself to a kneeling posture and sat back on his heels, the tide of flattery still flowing from his lips with a sound akin to a dog's whine. The Mufti—a fat man very richly dressed—was frowning consequentially at the intruder. His unknown neighbour was languid in surprise. Only the Sherîf appeared quite unmoved. With eyes fixed on Saïd's face and hand laid thoughtfully to his trim grey beard, he spoke a second time.

"To which of us three wouldst thou speak?" he asked; and with a gesture of the deepest self-abasement Saïd answered, "To thy Grace, O Emîr."

"Thou hast my leave; speak on! Only take care that thy tale be not long, for I am busy."

Saïd needed no further encouragement. Wringing his hands he burst forth: "Alas for me, I am ruined! Know, O Emîr and your Excellencies, that I was once a great one—none greater than me in all the city, by my father's grave!" Thus he began; and he went on to relate something of what had in truth befallen him and much of what had not, the whole freely sprinkled with "Woe is me!" and "Alas!" and strengthened by solemn asseverations of truth.

"But why, O man," broke in the Mufti, severely, at an early stage of the narrative, "why, I ask thee, dost thou now lay the blame of the theft upon thy friend, when at first thou doubtedst not but that a jinni had robbed thee? It is well-known that the jân are numerous and often malignant. Ever since their revolt against Allah, after the fall of Man, it has been their delight to molest the sons of Adam. The mission of Muhammed, the Apostle of Allah (peace be to him!) was, it is written, not to men only, but also to the jân. Nevertheless, there be many unbelievers among them, as among men, and it is likely that one of them had a grudge against thee. I like not to hear of such doubt. It has an evil savour of infidelity."

"Pardon me, brother," put in the Sherîf, mildly, "if I share the doubt of this young man—in the present instance, be it understood. Who can doubt that the jân exist, when we have the highest assurance of their existence? For all that, a treacherous friend is, alas! no marvel. Proceed with thy tale!"

Saïd went on to paint a picture of his more recent misfortunes, with much glozing and many omissions, being desirous that the whole should redound to his credit. Having heard him out, Ismaïl Abbâs turned to his friends.

"What think you of this story?" he asked with a slight smile.

"Lies!" said the Mufti, with a majestic wave of his fat hand, thereby exhibiting the many rings of price with which its fingers were laden—"all lies! This fellow must be some unbeliever—a Christian in disguise."

"Nay, now, my friend, thou speakest injustice," said the third great one, speaking for the first time. "Have I not fought for Islâm, and that with honour? Have I not been a prisoner in the hands of the infidels? It is well-known that I, of all men, have least cause to love the Christians. Yet I tell thee that even among my personal enemies I have known good men and just."

"I assure your Highness I did but speak of the Christians of my own race," said the Mufti, with reverence. "Some of the Franks, I grant thee, have good qualities." Then, turning sternly to Saïd: "But to what purpose this tale of thine, fellow?"

In a paroxysm of humility Saïd replied that he was destitute, friendless, having no resource but to beg. He addressed himself always to the Sherîf, who smiled as he listened—reflectively, as at some inward suggestion. He had heard, as who had not, the fame of his Excellency which was noised abroad through the whole city; how that he was a pious man—none like him—and a kindly. So, being in grievous trouble, ·he had made all haste to kiss the ground between his Grace's feet, to crave were it but a small sum to save him from dying of hunger. He suited the action to the words, falling again prostrate upon the pavement.

"Die of hunger, saidst thou?—Pshaw!" ejaculated the Mufti, stroking his belly, which seemed very full. "What man ever did die of hunger in Damashc-esh-Shâm since Ibrahîm El Khalîl was king over it? Such things occur, they say, in the cities of the Franks, where a poor man is used worse than a dog. But show me the true believer who would refuse thee bread to eat and water to drink! Thou speakest folly, young man."

Saïd seemed not to hear the remarks of the worthy judge, but lay still prone at the feet of the Sherîf.

"Rise!" said Ismaïl Abbâs, presently, in that gentle voice

of his which allowed of no evasion. "Who am I that thou shouldst fall down before me? And who, pray, is this person in the extraordinary garment?"

Saïd, upon his heels once more, glanced over his shoulder and beheld Selîm standing shyly at a little distance behind him.

"This is my servant, may it please your honour!"

"Ma sh'Allah!" cried the Mufti, fairly startled out of the calm appropriate to him as a fat man and a prosperous. "Is there then found a creature to call the dog master? Has the flea then an attendant? Come hither, thou fellow, and answer: Art thou in truth this man's servant?"

Selîm came forward, shamefaced, with the lowest of salaams.

"It is true, O my lord. He is my master and the father of kindness. It is he who gave me this grand robe which I now wear. That was in the day of his prosperity; and now that he is poor it were a sin for me to forsake him!"

"A miracle!" gasped the Mufti, and held his peace, fearing, perhaps, apoplexy.

"Since when hast thou been his servant?" asked Ismaîl Abbâs with a smile more kindly than that he had bestowed on Saïd's wondrous tale.

"Since before yesterday," was the answer.

At that the Mufti's fat quivered and shook with laughter, and even his dignified neighbour was moved to smile.

"Tell me the tale of thy meeting with him, my son," said the Sherîf, stroking his beard.

Selîm complied with seemly brevity; not forgetting, however, to celebrate the bounty of his sworn brother, the tavern-keeper, and his famous plan of partnership in a petty trade. When he had heard all, Ismaîl Abbâs turned a stern face to the suppliant, who blenched at his look.

"Thou art destitute, thou saidst; yet this good man has agreed to share with thee as a partner. Thou spakest of death by hunger when thy belly is full as my own. I tell thee that this man, who has humbled himself as a servant before thee, is thy lord in all goodness. Thou spakest many words concerning thy former wealth and position, whereas thou speakest with the tongue of the lowest of the people.

"Now listen! Thou wast a fisherman before thou camest hither; I have learnt it from thy mouth. Didst thou not liken thyself to a fish that flaps in the trough of the net when it is lifted out of the sea? A tailor would have found his likeness in a garment; a gardener in a piece of fruit. Thou art clever, doubtless: let thy wit suffice thee. I shall give thee nothing."

"A wise judgment, brother!" grunted the Mufti, with an approving nod. "I myself, who am a judge, could hardly have shown more acuteness. Of a truth, our lot falls in a degenerate age," he continued, with an oratorical flourish of his podgy hand. "In the time of the early Khalifs, the immediate successors of the Prophet, a Muslim had something else to do than to lie and steal and betray his neighbour. Then the minds of all the faithful were set to convert the unbelievers with fire and sword. Where is the Imâm, Omar el Hattab (peace to him!)? And Khalid, the Sword of Allah, where is he? Is their memory clean gone from the earth? Truly the end draws nigh. Dejîl is present with us in the person of the Frankish envoys. The Sultân himself is led astray. The Nazarenes sit with us in the place of honour. They pass the faithful in the streets with never a salutation. Is the soul then gone from Islàm that these things are allowed in our midst?"

"Ah, brother, thou hast well said," sighed the Sherîf. "There is indeed now but the shadow of ancient majesty. Yet, for my part, I do rather regret a later time, when Khalifs of the line of Abbâs ruled in the City of Peace, when learning flourished like a young tree, and the desire of knowledge was with every man as the breath of life."

"I hate the unbelievers as bitterly as any man," muttered Saïd, supposing his orthodoxy was somehow called in question.

"Ha! That is well said!" exclaimed the Mufti—"very well! The hour is perhaps not distant when—"

"Hush, my friend!" interrupted his stately neighbour in a low tone of rebuke. "Thy speech is not of wisdom. The idle words of one in authority are like sparks blown on a wind. They may die harmless on the ground; but they have power to set a whole town in a blaze. It behoves 'thee, therefore, to be careful. Because a Frankish consul caused a decree of thine to be revoked yesterday, thou art bitter against all Nazarenes—it is natural. But let thy wrath consume in silence— Why lingerest thou, fellow? Didst thou not hear the words of my friend, that he would give thee nothing, because thou art a rogue? Go in peace!"

Saïd rose, and with a cringing salute slunk sullenly away.

Selîm, whose face was rueful, was about to follow him, when Ismaïl Abbâs spoke to him.

"If ever thou have need of a friend," he said, "come to me. And, I counsel thee, seek another partner! Now go, and my peace with thee, for I am busy."

Selîm kissed the hand that was held out to him with those gracious words, as also the bursting hand of the Mufti and the thin, nervous fingers of the third great one. Then he went to rejoin Saïd, whom he found in the act of slipping on his shoes at the door-sill of the gate.

Saïd's glance at him was lowering. He thought that the muleteer's purpose in coming after him could only be to taunt and revile. The uproar of the crowded streets sounded in his ears as the voice of his woman sounds to one awakening from an evil dream. The court of the mosque was a burden of stillness at his back—a calm full of reproach, where the very cooing of the doves and murmur of the scholars told of his shame. Selîm was part of the scene from which he would flee. With a vindictive frown he bade him depart from him. But the faithful fellow drew all the closer, grinning friendly and saying,—

"Thou art clever, O Saïd—a perfect devil. That was a capital fraud thou didst put upon me. I, who am accounted no fool, was utterly deceived. With a man of brains like thee for partner Selîm will surely rise to great honour. The money thou gavest me shall buy thy share of the business. Since I may no longer call thee master I name thee friend—brother. And indeed I have cause to love thee, other than thy cleverness ; for the rich cloak thou gavest 'me has this day won me favour in the sight of the great Ismaïl Abbâs. When I was clad as other men are, no great one ever honoured me with his notice. Didst mark how they marvelled that one so well-dressed should be a servant? It was all because of this fine garment, and Selîm is grateful to thee. Now come! I will lead thee to a place where such merchandise as we require is sold cheap."

Saïd stood a moment in doubt, as one bewildered. Then, finding Selîm in earnest, and seeing no spark of mockery in his eyes, he fell a-blubbering all at once and swooped upon his friend's hand, kissing it repeatedly, and calling upon Allah to bless him for a good man—none like him in all the world.

XVI

FOR more than a month the partnership of Saïd with Selîm proved to the profit and contentment of both. But at length Saïd began to tire of it. His mind kept reverting to his roving life as to a period of great happiness.

To sit in the shade of an archway, where two noisy streams of wayfarers elbowed and jostled one another all day long, and cry aloud in praise of paltry wares, seemed a tame, not to say shameful, means of livelihood to one who had sipped of the cup of greatness. The wretched room, too, which he shared with Selîm vexed him with its meanness. It was buried away in the heart of the poorest and most crowded quarter. The approach was through a series of stinking tunnels, where one stirred a sleeping dog with every step, up a worn stairway always slippery with offal. Even at noon the daylight never reached it. The squalor and the evil smells were of no account to Saïd; but to abide in a quarter whose very name was a by-word for wretchedness—that it was which disgusted him.

The delight of his partner each night, as by the light of a floating wick he told the trifling gains of the day, was another ground for discontent. What were a few paras to one who had held fourteen English pounds in the hollow of his hand? Of course it was true, as Selîm said with that cheery smile in which his white teeth themselves seemed light of heart, that a little, and a little, and again a little, becomes a great deal. But the slowness and labour of accumulation were irksome to Saïd. At their present rate of profit it would be three years at least before they could think of hiring that shop in the grand bazaar of which Selîm dreamt every night. Meanwhile, he hankered after the reckless life he had left for this; and each day added zest to his longing.

His mind was in this unsettled state as he walked with Selîm one evening homeward from their place of business.

96

The basket carried between them was almost full, for there had been few purchasers. It was the worst day they had yet experienced, so that Saïd's gloomy silence aroused no wonder in his partner. The ways were still thronged, though the time of dealing was past, and forms loomed grey and shadowy in the waning light. Dogs prowled watchful on the skirts of the crowd, aware that man's intrusion was almost over, looking forward with dripping jaws to an undisturbed feast of refuse.

An aged man sat in the entry of a little mosque, holding out his hand and moaning persistently. The crowd, which now consisted of men hurrying homeward impatient of all hindrance, thrust the partners and their cumbrous burden very near to him. Of a sudden he lifted up his voice with alarming strength. The piercing whine had notes of triumph and of raillery.

"Allah will give to thee, O Emìr! . . . Help me for the love of Allah, or I die! . . . May Allah preserve thy Grace's life for ever! . . . See, I have a hand which is withered! . . . O Lord! . . . I know thee, O Emìr, how great thou art! (Wait a little!) . . . Have not mine eyes beheld thy Majesty of old? (Among the olive-trees hast thou forgotten?) . . . Have mercy, or I die! (Depart from here a little way, watch where I go and follow me!) . . . O Lord! . . . There is no compassion left on the earth since the rich and great turn away their eyes from distress!"

The wail for alms was loud, for all the street to hear. Men looked for a prince, and beholding instead a pedlar of mean appearance, grinned and nudged each other as they hurried by. The words in parenthesis were low, for Saïd's ear alone. Surprised, and a little disconcerted, he drew Selìm into the shadow of a wall, where they stood in no man's way. Then he let go his handle of the skep and turned to observe the old beggar. Selìm, of course, did likewise, the basket compelling him.

"What ails thee, brother?" he asked in concern. "What is there between thee and that old man? What was it he whispered thee?"

"I met him once long ago," rejoined Saïd, flurriedly. "He desires to speak with me apart. Maybe he brings news from my city, or of the woman I left sick by the way—Allah knows! Whatever his tidings, I must hear them."

The beggar had got up and was making his slow way

G

across the street, just where it widened forming a little square or open court before the mosque. His goal seemed to be a passage on the further side, just discernible as black and yawning in the hovering night. Saïd could hear the rascal's whine as he hobbled through the stream of wayfarers which thinned with every minute, moaning and beseeching Allah like one in the last decrepitude. He saw him gain the passage and disappear down it. Then, hastily begging Selîm to wait for him, he followed.

The entry was pitch dark, so that peering in from the twilight he could see nothing at all. For two seconds Saïd was mortally afraid. The fall of night is an eerie time at best, and a dark tunnel with no perceptible outlet was just the place an afrît would choose to lurk in. He recalled something devilish in the appearance of the old beggar, and was on the point of taking to his heels when a hand clutched his wrist and stayed him.

"What fearest thou? I am alone!" The voice in his ear was peevish even to anger. "It is well seen thou hast sojourned in the city, for thou hast the courage of a townsman already. Come in here for I must speak with thee!"

The entry grew less frightful to Saïd's eyes. He suffered himself to be drawn into its gloom. Then in a trice the unseen speaker changed his tone to one of the gladdest welcome. He fell on Saïd's neck and kissed him repeatedly on both cheeks, in spite of a curse-strengthened warning to keep off.

"Thou art the very image of my son," he explained with a rapturous laugh. "In truth I am minded to adopt thee as the child of my soul. Now tell me, beloved, how has it fared with thee since last we met? Thou wast carrying a basket, I observed!—art become a trader? Thou silly one! By the time thou art old like me it may be that thou shalt have wealth enough to purchase a rich garment. Out upon thee! Hast exchanged the merry game of life for drudgery?"

Saïd drew a glowing picture of his altered fortunes, desiring to make his listener recognise the gulf fixed between a thriving and respected merchant and one who lives by alms. The embrace rankled in his mind as an indignity. He felt sullied and was eager to rid himself of the stain, which could be done only by greatly humbling his insulter. The old beggar heard him to an end, then he went on eagerly, as if nothing had been said,—

"Now listen!—leave thy paltry business and join with me! I had once a son on thy pattern but I drove him from me because he would wed with a girl whose father was a leper. I am proud and have ever counted lepers as dirt under my feet; so I cursed him and let him go. If thou wilt thou mayst replace him as my partner. Mark well, I do not require thee to beg. Allah be my witness—no! It is for other business that I need thy strength and youth."

He sank his voice to a whisper, which seemed a snake's hiss in the darkness. A lantern, borne swiftly past the grey mouth of the passage, illumined his face for a moment and showed it distorted with passion.

"I seek revenge—revenge," he repeated, clutching Saïd's arm. "There is in this city a certain dog—an unbeliever, rich and thriving—may his mother's grave be defiled and his religion perish utterly!—who wronged me years ago. I have waited a long time—too long—for the chance to strike back. I grow old, and he also. It may be I shall die soon, or he may die; and in the grave there is no satisfaction. I tell thee, the time narrows. But I am old and alone; I sometimes fear lest I prove not strong enough. My son—may Allah destroy him!—might have helped me had he not been faithless. Thou canst replace him. I promise thee all good things instead of thy trade. Every month is Ramadan in the life of a man like me. We fast all day and stretch out our hands to chance comers, and when the night is come we feast and are merry. I give thee this choice—a prince's life or a mule's; and in the end thou shalt have great riches—the treasure of the Nazarene I told thee of. What sayest thou? Nay, answer not hastily, but go to thy house and ponder this that I have said to thee. To-morrow I shall remain till noon in the cellar of Nûr, the harlot. Go to the coffee-house of Abu Khalîl, which is against the castle—he will direct thee further. Depart with my peace. By my beard, thou art mighty like my son—mighty like Mansûr—may Allah blast him!"

Saïd lingered to question further, bidding Allah witness that to injure a Nazarene would give him the keenest pleasure, but he must have some notion of what would be expected of him. He was curious, too, to know why he, of all the city, had been singled out for confidence; but the old beggar checked him with,—

"To-morrow, when thou hast weighed the matter, I will enlighten thee. Thou calledst thyself Emìr when first I met thee in the olive grove. It may be others shall so call thee after a year or two if thou consent to throw in thy lot with me. Go in safety, O my dear!"

When he emerged again on the rough pavement before the mosque it was to find it deserted save by skulking dogs, and the stars intent upon it. The muezzin had long ago ceased chanting up in the gallery of the minaret. He had turned his face upon the spot where he had left Selìm, when,—

"I am here, O Saïd," came a low voice from close behind him.

Glancing back he beheld his partner dragging their basket out of the gloom of the near wall, where he had been squatting. He must have overheard all. Saïd turned on him fiercely, ready to fly at his throat.

"What dost thou here? Did I not bid thee await me over yonder? Art thou my keeper, and am I a child that thou must needs dog and spy upon me?"

"Nay, O my brother, be not angry with Selìm! I listened not, though a word reached me now and then. How could I suffer my friend to be alone with a stranger in a place of evil seeming?—I know only that he tempted thee to forsake a thriving business and Selìm who is thy brother, and to cast in thy lot with him who is known for a beggar. Also I heard him appoint the house of a certain woman where thou mightest find him. The house of Nûr is infamous for a place of sin, the chosen resort of the most wicked." His tone grew sad and reproachful as Saïd took the spare handle of the basket and they set forward once more.

"In what have I failed, O my brother, that thou shouldst desire to leave me? Have we not all things in common? Have I withheld aught from thee that was mine to give? I have great love for thee, O Saïd, because of the days we have toiled together and the nights we have slept side by side. Also I am bound to thee for the sake of that rich robe thy kindness bestowed, which procures me honour in the sight of all men. Heed not, I entreat thee, the words of this stranger, but continue with me. It is slow—not so?—this laying of a little to a little. But in this business of ours, with care wealth is sure at all events in the end, whereas the fortune which he holds out to thee may come suddenly and without pain, but it is not sure. I once heard a wise man say that wealth gained without labour does not profit a man. He that said it was old and had been rich; I believe that he knew."

They threaded the stinking black tunnels and climbed the foul steps which led to their room. There, having set down the basket in a corner, Selîm busied himself with getting a light and then went out to fetch some supper from a cook-house, leaving his friend sitting thoughtful on a cushion by the wall. After a while Saïd rose and went out also, mounting to the roof of the house by an obscure stairway. Alone under the stars, with the murmur of the city like a floating veil around him, he prayed and gave thanks to Allah, facing southwards to where the dark mountains frowned like a stronghold. When he returned Selîm had ready a mess of lentils such as he loved and smiled to him to fall to.

Saïd fell on his friend's neck and kissed him.

"By Allah, thou art a good man!" he cried. "Kinder than a brother hast thou been to me. May Allah blot me out if ever I forsake thee!"

XVII

AT sunrise Saïd sat with the old beggar in the vault of Nûr the harlot. A beam of young daylight glanced through the open door on the worn flags of steps which led down from the alley without. A dewy mist of dawn flooded also a kind of small court, like a shaft between the houses, which pertained to the cellar and gave air and light to it through two open arches of masonry. By one of these arches a stone stairway was seen mounting up along the wall to a platform or landing, formed of a single slab, which was the doorstep of an upper chamber. There was a sumptuous room, old Mustafa told Saïd in an ecstatic whisper, softly carpeted and furnished with couches such as the maids of Paradise would not disdain. It was there that lovers of distinction met by Nûr's contriving and spent happy hours together.

Abu Khalîl, the taverner of whom, according to the advice of Mustafa, Saïd had inquired his way, had wagged his fat head knowingly when questioned concerning this woman.

"The shameful name sticks," he had said, "being like pitch—very hard to rub off. Yet she is now a recognised matchmaker and has access to every harîm. Young men who would have sight of their betrothed find a friend in her, and ladies who love other than their lords employ her, it may be, as a go-between. I speak not of my own knowledge," he had added, shaking the dust from his robe. "That is what is said of her. . . . Thou askest why does she harbour a beggar? Allah knows! It may be she has a liking for Mustafa, who is a queer old man and says things to make one laugh. It may be that he gathers news which is useful to her in her business. There be many who bless her—this is sure. Perhaps a few curse her—that is not known."

Saïd found her tall and upright, strong and masterful as a man. She was quite old in spite of the enamel mask of pink and white which hid her wrinkles. Darkening matter artfully rubbed under her eyes to give them a languishing look could not altogether conceal the crow's-feet beneath, and the eyes themselves had the hard, unnatural lustre of jewels, very different from the sparkle of youth. Her brown fingers, which she did not whiten until after noon, were loaded with rings, of which the large common stones—sard and coarse amethyst, onyx and amber—stood out like bunions. Bracelets and armlets of tarnished brass and silver rattled and clanked like fetters with every movement of her limbs; strings of glass beads and amulets of all kinds adorned her scraggy neck and her bosom. She was kneeling just then by the brazier, with swelled cheeks fanning a feeble glow that was loth to become a fire. She wore no veil, being at home, but the hood of her blue garment, richly embroidered with gold thread, which she could draw across her face when bashfulness was required of her.

The old beggar sat with Saïd on the threshold of a dark inner room, of whose furniture no more was discernible through the doorway than a cushioned divan running round the walls. He was talking eagerly and fondling Saïd's hand, touching now his leg, now his arm, as if he gloried in the strength of his new ally.

"Now thou knowest why I have chosen thee and no other," he was saying. "I loved thee on that day when first I saw thee because of thy likeness to my son, Mansûr. Since then I have been to thy city, where all men tell of thy flight as a strange thing. It was not known whither thou wast fled nor why, nor to what purpose. But I, being shrewd, asked them: Who profits by his departure? and they told me, 'Abdullah abu Azîz, for the house and the fig-tree and the nets of Saïd are fallen to him.' (Ah, he is a clever one—that Abdullah!—one who will surely rise to honour. I sat once in a tavern where he spoke of thee as a dear brother he had lost.) I perceived clearly that this Saïd the Fisherman of whom they talked was no other than the Emîr Saïd with whom I conversed by the way. I thought much of thee for the sake of my son, Mansûr, who forsook me, and also because I knew thee destitute. When a man has nothing he is not particular what work he undertake if only there be profit in it, and I stood greatly in need of such an one to help

me in the business which thou wottest of.   By my head, when
I saw thee last evening in the street my heart leapt with joy
as if thou hadst been in truth my son.   Allah is merciful!

"Now, hear the story why I hate Yuhanna the Nazarene.
Attend now and judge whether I have not cause enough to
execrate him.   Many years ago I slew my sister with this right
hand."   He sank his voice to a whisper with a meaning glance
at the old woman.   "She would have become even as Nûr
there, I tell thee, had I suffered her to live.   He lured her to
the city, and then, after he was sated, he cast her out and
placed her in a house of shame of which he was owner.   But
I found her.   We were but poor fellahîn of no honour or
account, yet not one of all my family but would have done
as I did.   I slew her and she bared her own breast to the
knife.

"It was in the days of Ibrahîm Basha the Egyptian—a
good time, by Allah, though one must not say so now that the
Turks are again our masters.   But there was strict justice for
all men then, a Christian being the equal of a Muslim in the
eyes of the Government.   I went to the house of the Cadi and
I kissed the earth between his feet, and I told him all my
story as if it had been a figment of my own brain.   I asked
him : 'What would your honour do if it had been his sister?"
and he replied, 'By Allah, I would slay her and destroy that
infidel with all his father's house.'

"I answered : 'Good, O my Lord : the first I have accomplished; the second I will perfect ere I die.'   At first he was
angry at the fraud, for he had supposed me a professed tale-
teller; but afterwards he laughed, and called me a rogue, and
bade me mind to do nothing which the law forbids.

"The dog Yuhanna and the old jackal, his father, were
rich after the manner of unbelievers, that is to say secretly and
by foul means.   Acting as the agents of a notable of this city
they lent money to us villagers wherewith to buy seed and
took the greater part of the harvest in payment.   Between
them and the tithe-farmer there was little left for us on our
threshing-floors.   They lent money also to the great ones of
the Government and claimed no payment at all, thus gaining
protection and influence beyond all others of their accursed
race.   After the abduction of Lulu, my sister, they conceived
a hatred for my father's house.   They persecuted us—may

Allah quench the fire on their hearth! Ah, they were clever!"

He raised eyes and hands to the vaulted roof and remained thus a minute lost in admiration of their subtlety.

"There came a bad harvest. They clamoured for immediate payment of the seed they had advanced to us, pretending to act merely as bailiffs for Muhammed Effendi, but the mind of the unbeliever was well seen in what followed. Our houses became the property of the notable, so they said, the property of Muhammed Effendi, but in practice theirs. My father and my brethren lived on in the village; they were like trees which have struck deep root in the ground, which to transplant is to kill. But I, being young and full of pride, chose rather to roam the land as a beggar than to feed as a slave from the hand of my enemy. I have had much joy of life since then, yet have I never forgotten the shame of my house nor the oath which I swore solemnly before the Cadi himself. And now that the allotted hour grows nigh, behold, Allah sends thee to me in the nick of time. By my beard, I blame thee not for forsaking thy woman; it seems to me that thou didst well to get rid of her. What use, I ask, in keeping her since thou sayest she was barren? And thou art more serviceable to me as a lone man. Allah is just!" He thought fit to embrace his new adherent and slobber over him in a very fatherly way, much to Saïd's annoyance.

"Enough! enough!" muttered the fisherman, pushing him off. "Of a surety I will aid thee in this business. But tell me, I pray thee, O my uncle, how came thy hand to be withered."

The old beggar threw back his head and laughed so that the whole roof of his mouth was displayed and its horse-shoe of broken yellow teeth. The subject considered, such merriment was frightful to Saïd; it made him shudder. The woman started up in alarm to her full height, and, with an oath, pronounced him mad.

"Ah, ha, ha! I have a withered hand. It is curious—not so? Know then that it befell me in this wise: While I was yet new to the work I met a beggar who had his arm withered to the shoulder like the dead branch of a tree. He told me

that it brought him great wealth and marvelled much how I
could move pity, being whole and in the best of health.
Inquiring if he had been born like that, he laughed at me for
a simpleton. He said it is easy—nothing easier in all the
world; and he promised to teach me the way of it. I had
thought to take service as a muleteer or otherwise, but the
talk of his riches and his merry life changed my mind. We
were together two days and became friends. On the third
day we reached the town and he sought out a certain dervish
and brought me to him. I went in whole and sound even as
thou art; I came forth with this hand in the state thou seest.
It is a trick—no more. At first one has to be careful lest the
blood should flow back to it; but that is all. It has been my
stock-in-trade, the head of my wealth."

Of a sudden he bent down and pinched Saïd's leg rapturously. "Aha, what a leg! Behold, O Nûr, how stout and
strong it is! I know one in the city who would treat it for
thee—up to the knee! By Allah, that is all I ask—only to
the knee! Ah, it would look sweet—beautiful! It would
bring tears to any man's eyes when he compared it with its
brother, and on one so young. Only up to the knee; what
sayest thou? I tell thee, my dear, there is wealth
in it — money — much money! But no, alas! it cannot
be; for all thy strength may be needed in the work of
vengeance."

There was something foul and inhuman about this
rhapsody which made Saïd kick and edge away with loathing
as from the touch of a ghoul. The old beggar eyed him re-
proachfully.

"Ah, now thou art very like Mansûr—very like my son!"
he murmured, with a remembering shake of his head.
"Mansûr would never consent to have so much as a finger
treated, though I besought him with tears for hours together.
The young are ever so boastful of strength and blind to their
own advantage. And now, O my soul, if thou art ready I
will show thee the house of Yuhanna the Nazarene that
thou mayest know it among others for the house of an
enemy."

He rose and went to where Nûr was munching bread and
olives, with jaws cramped by the stiff coat of paint on her
cheeks. He whispered a few words to her, while Saïd stretched

himself and yawned, glad to breathe free of a place which the queer behaviour of his new friend had rendered distasteful. Then together they mounted the broken stairs and issued forth into the dewy shadow in which the newly-risen sun steeped the narrow roadway.

XVIII

MUSTAFA led on by unfrequented tunnels and passages, avoiding as far as might be the main streets, where professional pride obliged him to put on an appearance of extreme feebleness and whine despairingly as one in the clutch of a devil. At last, in a narrow lane between high walls, with never a lattice, he stopped before a low door which was open.

"This is the house of the pig—the house of Yuhanna!" he whispered. "I will enter—it is the beggar's privilege. Do thou follow as far as thou canst without being seen!"

A narrow passage turned at right angles after a few yards, so that the interior of the house could not be looked into from the street. This notion of an entrance the wealthier Christians and Jews had borrowed from their Muslim neighbours. With the latter it secured the harīm from wanton intrusion when taking air in the courtyard, as common politeness prompts every visitor to cry aloud on crossing a threshold. In the case of the former it served chiefly to screen the inner luxury of the house from envious eyes, and so preserve its owner from extortion or robbery. In each instance plenty of rubbish and offal was strewn at the outer gate and the passage maintained in as foul a state as possible, as a blind to the tax-gatherer going his round of observation, that the house might be assessed at a low rate.

On turning the corner Saïd was quite unprepared for the scene of splendour which burst upon his sight. There was a small quadrangle of two storeys high, its walls inlaid with arabesque figures as a frieze under the roof and as medallions between the windows. The pavement, worn uneven in places, was arranged in a chequer of black and white stone. A few lemon-trees in the centre formed a bower over a tank of clear water fed by a freshet that flowed through the midst of the court in a toy channel. But what charmed him and held his eyes, to the exclusion of all other beauties, was a girl twelve or thirteen years of age, with black hair plaited in two long tresses, and a skin like cream. She was playing with a baby boy in the rich shadow beyond the space of sunlight. A creeping plant upon the wall behind her had large green leaves and trumpet-flowers of gorgeous purple. A pair of white butterflies flirted above her head just where the sunlight veiled the shadow in golden dust.

Her laughter, ringing clear and silvery in Saïd's ears, seemed part of the spell which held him motionless there, at the angle of the passage, with a new hunger in his eyes. He licked his lips, which were parched of a sudden, and tingled from head to foot.

The old beggar tottered across the open space of sunshine, making a great clatter with his staff upon the pavement.

"Allah will give to thee, O my lady! I am a poor man and very old. . . . Have pity! . . . O Lord! . . . See, I have a hand that is withered! Allah will give to thee! . . . For the love of Allah, help me or I die. O mistress of beauty, O daughter of kindness, turn not thy face from my misery! . . . O Lord! . . . Allah will give to thee!"

Saïd watched every movement of the girl ravenously, feeling uplifted by a great yearning. He saw her start in terror at the first sound of the old rascal's plaint; but fear changed swiftly to compassion, and, with a gesture bidding him wait, she disappeared in the gloom of a doorway. His eyes remained steadfast on the place where she had last been.

The old beggar stooped down as if to fondle the little child, but in reality to pinch him spitefully. A howl of pain uprose, which the honeyed words of Mustafa, spoken soothingly in a loud and whining voice, were powerless to abate.

Presently the girl returned, followed closely by an old woman, who seemed a servant. With a smile which caught at Saïd's breath she put some money in the old man's palm and bade him go in peace. Mustafa kissed her lily hand repeatedly, while the old serving-woman took the baby in her arms and strove to quiet it. Then he hobbled away, ceasing not to praise Allah in a loud voice, calling down all blessings on the illustrious lady's head, till he was in the gloom of the passage close to Saïd, when he muttered, with virulence,—

"May the girl be ravished! May her father be slain before her eyes, and her little brother butchered in her arms! Allah witness, I have waited long enough. The hour of the ruin of this house draws nigh."

"She is a darling—a pearl!" breathed Saïd in his ear. "I am sick for love of her. As one athirst in the desert craves a cup of water, so is my desire for her. O my soul! O my eyes! O my beloved!"

They were out in the street by this time. The narrow way was very quiet, the sun beating down fiercely upon it. There was no one in sight.

The old beggar stopped short and confronted Saïd, striking his stick on the paving-stones.

"Thou sayest well," he hissed, surprise and glee together in his eyes, "very well! By Allah's leave thou shalt enjoy her—if it were my last word, thou shalt possess her; so the dishonour of my father's house shall be fitly avenged. Allah reward thee, O Saïd! child of my soul. A young man's passion sees further at times than an old man's forethought. Wait a little while in patience. The faithful grow mad against these pagans, who sit in high places by favour of the Franks they serve. I see the wrath of Islâm gather like a storm-cloud black and low over the dwellings of the infidels. I hear the voice of the thunder afar off. The heavens quiver because of the white lightning. A little while and the storm will burst to overwhelm the whole race of them."

Leaning on his staff, the old man lifted pious eyes to the strip of living blue stretched like an awning above the high white walls. There was something noble in his bearing as a prophet denouncing the wicked. For the first time Saïd felt in awe of him.

"If Allah will thou shalt have her, I say! Of a truth thou lackest not understanding. I who am wise had never thought of it in all the years that I ponder the matter. Now thou art dearer to me than Mansûr—dearer than my own son! Have a little patience and I warrant thee thou shalt have her. Only forget not, when thy desire is spent, to put her away into a house of shame. Forget not that, I say, for it is the crowning point! So shall my vengeance be perfect. Praise be to Allah!"

"May Allah increase thy wealth," said the fisherman,

moistening his lips. "By the Coràn, I care nothing for the treasure of the Christian pig so that I may have his daughter."

"Thou shalt have her and half of the treasure as well," said Mustafa, rapturously, as they moved forward; "and when I die the whole of the treasure will fall to thee. Let Mansûr cleave to his leprous wife; I wash my hands of the dirt of him, for he is no more my son. In truth, I am very happy. I must not stretch out my hand to-day, for glad laughter would come in the midst of my plaint, and who would give to a joyful beggar? Come with me to the house of Abu Khalll, where the coffee is worth a Turkish pound each cupful . . ."

He broke off and collapsed in a second from a hale and upright old man to a starving wretch with one foot in the grave. His withered hand thrust out before him, he tottered along, leaning heavily upon the staff; and his piteous moans wrung their meed of compassion from the heart of every passer-by. Saïd followed a few paces in his rear. Thus they traversed the junction of three busy markets—a place thronged to overflowing with a hustling, multi-coloured crowd, through which a train of camels laden with pelts were pushing a slow way, not without frantic shouting on the part of their drivers.

Striking into a dark and deserted byway, Mustafa resumed his natural shape. Saïd was inclined to be loud in his admiration of these rapid changes; but the old beggar dismissed all such flattery by a majestic wave of his hand.

"It is habit, O my son! After well-nigh forty years of practice thou couldst do it as well as I—perhaps better—Allah knows!"

XIX

ABU KHALÌL, the fat taverner, sat in the doorway of his
shop, blinking at the sunlight on the rough stones of
the castle wall. Piercing cries of importunate salesmen,
warning shouts of donkey-boys and muleteers—all the hubbub
of the neighbouring market reached him as a hum of insects.
He nodded with it after the manner of the very fat, to whom
the world's bustle is a perpetual lullaby.

A few dogs lay stretched in the sun's eye as if they had
a mind to be well roasted throughout. Beneath a dirty
awning, spread to shelter a stall of candies and sherbet, a
white-turbaned negro, its owner, was dozing in the yellow
shade beside his wares, his cheek reposing on a certain dainty
of white sugar, fine-spun and silky, which hung tangled tresses
over the end of a wooden case. A tod of hyssop, springing
from a rift in the old stonework, had dusty leaves and
looked sickly in contrast with its pendant of deep shadow.
A green lizard slumbered on a jutting stone. Abu Khalìl
blinked at all these things until they mixed in rosy haze before
his eyes. The lizard seemed to fall upon the awning, the
negro and his sweetmeats were lifted up to meet it, the hyssop
.swelled to a great tree, and Abu Khalìl's head dropped
forward with a grunt of surrender.

When Saïd and the old beggar came upon him he was
fast asleep and snoring. His fat chin formed three several
folds upon his breast, his hands were clasped loosely upon his
well-filled girdle. He looked up with a start as their shadows
fell short and black on the cobbles before him ; but it was
more likely the clap of their slippers which awakened him.
With a noise between a camel's groan and the puff of a
swimmer he half rose to welcome them. The huge mass
moved grudgingly, forming strange creases at the joints.

"May thy day be happy, O Mustafa ! How is business ? "

he muttered sleepily, and fell back at once to the restful posture which suited his bulk. His glance of recognition at Saïd was keener, being mixed with curiosity.

"So thou didst find thy way, effendi? I am happy." His eyes expressed an indolent wish to know what could have drawn a young man whose beard was nicely trimmed, who was clad in a decent robe of striped silk not very greasy, to consort with that aged scapegrace.

"What is there to eat?" asked Mustafa, choosing a seat within the tavern. "This day is a festival with me, for I have recovered my son who was lost. So I said to my soul: O Soul, we must rejoice and be lazy until the evening, because it has pleased Allah to restore my son to me who have been long desolate. Furthermore I said: O Soul, we will repair to the house of Abu Khalîl, the illustrious—may Allah preserve him to us!—where the coffee is worth a Turkish pound the cupful, and the smell of the fried beans would make a prince hungry. Ah, beans are excellent, O my uncle, and it is near noon. What hast thou in the house?"

The fat host returned thanks for the flattering terms in which this demand was couched by half-rising as before, saluting, and wagging his head humbly. He called upon Allah to shower all blessings on the head of his friend Mustafa, to make him happy in his son; and then in the same breath—a long one for him—shouted crossly to someone within, by the name of Camr-ud-dîn, to pound coffee with all speed and prepare a mess of beans to fry. Then the spark of excitement died down and he became torpid once more.

Saïd and his adopted father were earnest in their discussion of the beans when they appeared. The bowl might have been licked out by dogs, so clean they left it. Each drank two cupfuls of the famous coffee and accepted the offer of a narghileh. And then their words became ever less frequent, until they went the way of Abu Khalîl, falling fast asleep one after the other.

For hours they dozed on by fits and starts. The place was very quiet except for a distant murmur from without, soothing as the sough of reeds in the wind, and an occasional din of pots and pans from the inner closet, where Camr-ud-dîn and his mother were always at work.

H

When at last Saïd became wide awake it was towards
evening and the tavern was crowded. With strained knuckles
he rubbed the cobwebs of a dream from his eyes and let off
the remains of sleep in a mighty yawn. Mustafa had removed his stool to a little distance, so as to be within earshot
of a group whose talk appeared to interest him greatly.

A young man, who seemed of consequence, was holding
forth to a half-circle of humble admirers hanging upon his
words with mouths agape. His turban, finely embroidered,
bound a fez which, if not new, was certainly newly-blocked.
His overcoat of emerald green, falling loose to his heels when
he stood upright, was edged all over with fur. It was now
flung carelessly open, displaying a robe of striped silk, own
brother to that which Saïd wore, though the relationship was
somewhat obscured in the latter's case by dirt. The gravity
with which he stroked his beard, at the same time letting his
keen brown eyes range over the faces of his hearers, was very
impressive. The confidence of his speech, and the rhetorical
flourishes with which he emphasised each point, spoke him a
lawyer, and might have spared him the frequent statement of
his calling. Following the example of his companion, Saïd
hitched forward his stool to listen. "I that am a lawyer and
know what right is—I tell you," the orator was saying, "that
this state of things cannot endure. It is not to be borne. In
the olden time, when the infidels were duly held in subjection
under us, was there any strife?—I ask you, was there any such
bitter hatred as there is nowadays? The fault lies with the
Franks, who play the rulers in this land and presume to guide
the hand of the Government Is the Sultàn the servant of
any man that they should thus lord it in his dominions? But
two months since occurred a flagrant instance of their
meddling, when a judgment of his Eminence, the Mufti,
against a certain Nazarene was set aside as a thing of nought
by the Waly's order. And for what reason?"

The lawyer spread out his hands and smiled fiercely.

"And why? Think you that his Excellency, the Waly,
would incline to act thus of his own volition? Never! It
was because certain of the Frankish consuls went to him and
said in his ear that Fulàn was under foreign protection. Is
the pride of Islâm dead that such things are borne with
meekness? Is the tiger become a lamb? . . . I ask all of

you here—Who is the governor of Damashc-ush-Shâm?—and
you tell me, His Excellency, Ahmed Basha, his honour,
the Waly. I say no! and again no! Ahmed Basha—may
Allah preserve him!—and all who bear rightful authority over
us are but the servants of the Franks. . . . Behold they
gather upon us like vultures, they contend which shall have
the greatest share of the spoil—that is, of the wealth of Islâm.
Woe is me, for the end of all things draws nigh! The cross
is set above the crescent, the feet above the head. If any
oppose them they cry aloud to their masters, the powers of
Europe, and great ships are sent across the sea to lay waste
our coasts; as was done, you may remember, not two years
since at Jedda, where the townsfolk had risen as one man to
exterminate the Christians. O Allah, Most High, how long
must these things be? How long wilt Thou suffer the
heathen to triumph over Thy faithful?"

He paused with hands and eyes upraised. A fierce
murmur of applause spread to the uttermost corners of the
room. All the idlers had left their talk to listen. One or two
that were unbelievers slunk out at the door, thankful for the
excitement which allowed them to escape unheeded.

"The Turks themselves are not much better than the
Franks," said a short man, hardily. "They say that the Sultàn
is a pagan secretly. It is sure that his likeness—a thing
forbidden and accursed—hangs over his head where he sleeps.
Ah, if we sons of the Arab had but a Khalífa of our own race
we would shake off the Franks as a waking man brushes fleas
from his raiment!"

An awe-stricken hush followed this bold utterance. All
looked to the lawyer, whose eyes were wrathful on the rash
man who dared to speak treason in his presence in a public
place. Himself had no great cause to love the Turks, but
spies were everywhere, and it was always wise to speak good
of the authorities. Besides, he hoped one day to obtain the
post of Cadi, and to that end was anxious to stand well with
the Government. Very sternly, therefore, he bade that madman hold his peace. The rebuke he thought fit to administer
was thickly interspersed with praise of all the Sultàn's
delegates, from Ahmed Pasha, the nervous old general set to
rule over a turbulent province, to himself who hoped some
day to be Cadi. Then, when the seditious one had no more

treason left in him, but was become limp all over and hung his head, he took up the burden of his previous speech.

"These Christians wax rich. They multiply beyond measure while our numbers dwindle by reason of the thousands of our young men who are slain in war. The Christians furnish no men to the army; they swoon at sight of a sword or a gun. Yet they murmur because a tax is required of them in place of soldiers. They go weeping to their consuls because each of them is obliged to pay—it may be twelve piastres a year! Of old, as is well-known, all the world that is under the hand of the Sultàn was divided into two houses—the House of Islâm and the House of War. Now the Nazarenes, being dwellers in the House of War, had to pay, each man, a small sum yearly for his life. It was just, for are they not the vanquished and their lives duly forfeit to Islâm. Now, by favour of the Government, that tax is remitted, and the bedelleh askerleh laid on them instead. Yet they grumble, saying that the tax —a very light one—is too heavy for them to bear. Are they not rich? Do they not thrive and grow fat among us by trade and usury? The Frankish consuls, I tell you, are the root of their discontent. They stir them up to anger us, that there may be an excuse to destroy us. The Franks move us all as pieces in a game. They pit us one against another and stand by, ready to fall upon the conqueror and overcome him while he is weary. O day of misfortune! O day of ruin for the Faith!

"You have heard how a Nazarene did lately pollute the harîm of a respected Muslim in this city. The culprit— Jurji by name—is now in prison awaiting his doom. Of right he should die, for a man's house is a sacred place and a breach of hospitality is the blackest of all crimes in the sight of Allah. Yet it is known that a Frankish consul—one who has the ear of the Waly—is active on his behalf. He may be released without punishment. What say you to that? Is so great a wrong to be borne tamely? Since these things are so, were it not seemly that the faithful should rise as one man against the heathen and slay every living soul of them, and burn their houses with fire? Allah is just!"

The sun had set behind the mountains and twilight was stealing on the street without. The shadow in the tavern from being blue and limpid was become black and opaque. The coo of the doves floated on a tired murmur. Through the open door the negro merchant was seen to take down his awning, bestow his wares carefully in a battered packing-case, and finally to invert the trestle which served him for a stall, and laying the case and the folded awning between the legs, drag it away with him. The wall which closed the outlook was pale and dead-looking, the bush of hyssop making a dark blot upon it. Abu Khalîl was awake at last. He stood by the threshold of the inner room, trimming a lantern with ponderous leisure.

The old beggar leaned forward with flaming eyes. He laid his sound hand on the delicate woof of the lawyer's sleeve.

"I am with thee, effendi!" he cried. "Whenever the cry of the Faith is raised, Mustafa will be ready! I will spare none of them!" he yelled with sudden frenzy—"not one! Old men and young, women and little ones, shall die, and in their death I will spit upon them and spurn them with my foot. But the girls, effendi"— he sank his voice to an eager whisper—"the girls should not be slain. There are sweet ones among them—not so, Saïd, my son? They whose fathers hate and revile the Faith shall give birth to true believers. Each one of them shall suckle a Muslim at her white breasts. I am with thee, I say! But wait, thou hast not heard what was done to my sister, nor yet the oath which I swore before the Cadi in the time of Ibrahîm Basha the Egyptian. Aha, that is a good story—capital! . . . "

With a gesture of contempt and impatience, in which there was a leaven of terror, the lawyer shook himself free of the old man's grasp.

"Thou art mad!" he exclaimed. "What have I in common with thee?" Then a little ashamed of the fear he had shown, he continued, in a very firm voice,—

"Am I he that gives orders to the faithful? I do but utter that which every believer knows to be true. You have heard how it has been foretold that when the first of the sevens shall fall the ruin of Islâm will begin; when time shall invert the second it shall be completed. Are we now in the year 1277 of the Hejra? The first of the sevens is about to fall, and with the third year hence the second will fall in its turn. In the insolence of the Nazarenes and the growing power of their protectors we see the seed of destruction. If the sun of the Faith must set—which Allah forbid!—I say let its setting be like unto its rising long ago! Let flames of burning houses lick the sky, and the blood of the idolaters flow like a great river. I foresee war. It breaks out in the Mountain, where the Mowarni openly declare themselves to be subject to the French alone. They grow boastful and overrate their strength. Soon they will provoke the Drûz, who, though less numerous than they, are braver by a great deal and better skilled in warfare. Who but Allah can foresee the end of it? But I, being a lawyer and learned, tell you that as a spark falling amid a heap of touchwood, so is a little war in a land of discontent. Though but ten men rise boldly against the heathen, in a few days there will be slaughter from Haleb to Oman! Allah be with you! May your evening be happy, O my friends!"

With a slight reverence to the company, which called forth a storm of compliment and blessing, he rose, and gathering his furred garment about him sauntered forth into the twilight.

Abu Khalîl had lighted the lantern by this time, and it hung from a hook beside the inner door. Its ruddy beams shone on swarthy faces of excitement, turned one to another in the flow of talk which comes, like a sigh of relief, after the strain of a thrilling story. To most men there it was nothing but a tale they had just heard; a little more stirring, perhaps, than other tales, because it told of a future they might all see instead of a past which they had never known. They speedily dispersed once more into groups, chatting eagerly of more homely topics.

It was night—the time when devils lurk in every dark entry and keep festival in every ruined dwelling. One man told a gruesome story of how his brother once slew a jinni by accident. It had happened in that very city, in a street not a hundred paces from where they were sitting. Even at that early hour the flesh of every listener crept deliciously, and close-shorn heads put forth bristles under turbans.

His brother—the narrator laid proud stress on the relationship—was belated one night on his return home. His name was Kheyr-ud-dîn, a good pious man and a true

believer. Walking down a certain street he came suddenly
to an unseen barrier. He could pass his hand along it as
along the surface of a wall; the feel of it was smooth like
glass or tight skin. Yet there was nothing to be seen in the
way; only the narrow lane in moonlight and shadow, and the
dogs prowling in search of offal. Then he espied what seemed
a sewn goat-skin for holding water, lying collapsed and empty
in the midst of the causeway. And as he looked, behold it
filled out and tightened, and began to roll. Kheyr-ud-dìn,
who was a pious man, praised Allah, and marvelled much to
see it rolling thus of itself, with none to push it nor any slope
of the ground to cause displacement. And as it rolled, lo !
it grew and grew until it was huge like an elephant. Then he
began to be afraid, and desired to go quickly to his own
house. But the unseen wall prevented him, and all his
strength availed not to break through it. Then he cursed the
father of that wall, and its religion, and its aunt, and its first
cousins, and its offspring down to the third generation, kicking
it all the while and beating it with his hands. At last, being
very angry, he took the knife from his girdle—a sharp knife
with a fine handle inlaid of brass and silver—an heirloom in
the family. With that he struck at the barrier and it ripped
down like flesh.

There was a hideous shriek; he was snatched suddenly
out of the moonlight and the streets and whisked away to a
place of darkness, where the king-jinni sat on a throne of
fire. All the people of the jân were there, lurid in the red
glow of their monarch's seat. The king's eyes were set slantwise in his head; his ears were long and leaf-shaped like the
ears of a pig. He wore no turban nor any covering to his
head, which was bald and dome-shaped, of the same colour
as his face—that is to say mouse-colour. Flames shot from
his eyes as he leaned forward to frown on the prisoner. All
the people of the jân grinned horribly upon Kheyr-ud-dìn,
and gave forth a hissing sound. He stood accused of slaying
one of them, by the name of Yusuf. In vain he disclaimed
all knowledge of the crime.

"Thou liar !" said the king, turning a glance of fire upon
him, which burnt right through clothes and flesh, and shrivelled
the marrow of his bones. "Didst thou not rip open his belly
with thy knife there in the open street ? Is not his death-

shriek yet present in our ears? By my head, thou shalt die for it!"

And all the people of the jân yelled frightfully, "He shall die! He shall die!"

Then in his great distress he called aloud upon the name of Allah; when lo! in a trice he was back once more in the quiet street, and there was no barrier nor any waterskin, but only a few dogs skulking in the moonlight.

Another spoke of serpents.

"There is a kind of snake," he said, "which has his dwelling on the skirts of the desert. He has neither head nor tail, but is round like to a pigeon. When one approaches him he does not hiss like other snakes, but barks like a jackal, and picks himself up and hurls himself at the man. You may laugh at what I tell you, but, by Allah, it is extremely true. My grandfather shot one of that kind with a gun which is now mine. I will show it you if you will favour me with a visit at my house. It is a good gun, and I wish to sell it. It is worth much money."

Quoth another,—

"By the Corán, but thy pigeon-snake is a light thing as compared with the mighty serpent of which I have heard old men speak. He traversed the land of old, devouring all things, even men and women, until at last he slid down from the crest of the mountain, glided under the sea as under the lid of a box, and was no more seen. He was clothed all over with long hair, part black, part white, like a goat's; and his length was a day's journey from head to tail. Allah have mercy—a strange thing!"

Saïd would gladly have drawn near to listen. It was a kind of talk that pleased him, as befitting the hour. The tavern reeked of good cheer, the company was numerous enough to preclude real terror, while a glimpse of the gruesome, populous night from the open door gave a shuddering zest to each new story. The cellar of Nûr, too, where he was to sleep, was not far distant, and he was sure of Mustafa's company in the walk thither. He burned to tell a marvellous story of what had befallen his uncle on a journey into Masr. The yarn had become popular, almost proverbial, in his native town, where it was known as Saïd the Fisherman's story of the Blue Afrît. Of all the dwellers in Damashc-ush-Shâm,

Selîm alone had heard it. The adventures of other men's
kindred dwindled to everynight blunders wherever it was
told.

But the beggar's skinny hand clutched his arm, enforcing
attention. He yawned as he hearkened to the old man's raving
of blood and vengeance. The wild looks and wilder talk of
his companion made him fear that he had cast in his lot with
a madman. But when Mustafa gripped his arm tighter and
looked into his eyes, and laughed, saying, "Aha! that was
a good thought of thine. By the Coràn, I hold thee
dearer than Mansûr—dearer than my own son! Shalt have
her, dost understand? In sh'Allah, thou shalt possess her!"
Saïd was reassured on the score of his sanity.

Abu Khalîl, the fat taverner, looking round benignly upon
the faces of his guests, marvelled much in his sleepy way to
observe those two speak so earnestly together. Mustafa was
hatching some beggar's plot, he supposed; but the dutiful and
submissive bearing of the young man towards his sire made a
deep impression on his flabby brain. Camr-ud-dîn had that
day cursed his father's religion, which was his own, and Abu
Khalîl had been properly indignant. In return he had cursed
his son's creed, as also his father and his mother. He felt that
he was not blessed in his offspring, and in a dim, fat way he
envied Mustafa.

XX

BETWEEN the cellar of Nûr and the tavern of Abu Khalîl the summer days passed lazily for Saïd. The year's last rain had fallen. Each departing night left a burnished blue canopy over the city, on which the sun crept slowly like a snail of fire. The cry of the water-carriers grew sweet and ever sweeter in the ears of all men; and the street dogs panted with lolling tongues as they slept.

Every evening drew forth a great multitude to the pleasure-houses studding the gardens by the river bank. Men sat on stools, or cross-legged on the ground, sipping sherbet of almond or tamarind or rose, and chattered with the birds in the respite from a sultry day; while the sky glowed amethyst, then emerald, then beryl, and the earth's bloom among the trees became a paleness of lilies.

Once at sunset time Saïd went to the coffee-house of Rashîd, where he had slept that night with Selîm, to make inquiries concerning his former partner. But the landlord was gruff and slow to answer, so that Saïd abstained from further questions and returned thither no more.

Every morning, about daybreak, the old beggar arose. Having broken his fast upon the soured milk and bread prepared for him by Nûr, he took up his staff and set out for some mosque or archway where was both shade and concourse—the two main requisites for a beggar's seat. Saïd, rising perhaps an hour later, had the livelong day idle upon his hands, after he had brought water for his hostess and helped her to order her dwelling. He stood high in the good graces of the grim old woman: partly, no doubt, because of the little services he was ever willing to render, but chiefly owing to the lover-like attitude he adopted towards her.

He used her reverently yet fondly, as the desire of his soul. It seemed a humorous thing for a free man to serve an old woman of evil repute; and Saïd, having once grasped the fantastic side of their relation, played his part thoroughly and with all the fervour of a devotee. From constantly cajoling her with flattery and impassioned words he himself came near to forget that a hag's face underlay her mask of paint; and she, for her part, though alive to the cozenage, grew to dote on him as the apple of her eye.

Sometimes, when the fragrant smoke of a narghileh made a philosopher of him for half-an-hour, he contrasted the lot of this old woman with that of Hasneh and other wives of poor men. Here was one whose name had been a byword for infamy living as a queen in her old age, extending bounty and protection to whom she would, exacting service as her due. The greatest of the city came under cover of the night to beseech her aid in secret business of the heart. Grand ladies of some notable's harîm, veiled from all peril of recognition, sought her in their way from the bath or the perfumer's on a like errand. Clandestine lovers made their heaven in her upper room. Each and all, fearing, blessed her and left gold in her hand. "Allah grant me as prosperous an old age!" thought Saïd. And yet Hasneh, the rough-handed and meanly clad, would have deemed herself the better of such an one. It was a strange thing!

Another person who had conceived a warm liking for the fisherman was the fat taverner. As the bright pattern of filial devotion, Saïd was always welcome to meat and drink and a narghileh afterwards in return for occasional help in the service of the coffee-house. Abu Khalîl loved to ply him with parables and hard sayings, beginning always, "There was once a son," and ending mostly in an attempt to cuff poor Camr-ud-dîn, the "son" in question. This unfortunate youth inherited his father's tendency to fall asleep at odd moments. He would have become fat, too, like his father, had he been allowed to remain long enough in one spot. It was his constant chagrin that he could enjoy no rest, between waiting on customers and obeying his sire's behests; for Abu Khalîl, though always dormant himself, would not let his son indulge in a moment's lethargy. Camr-ud-dîn carried his grievance plainly written on his dirty brown face. He did everything under protest; and he loathed the sight of Saïd, who was for ever being held up to him for an example.

Once or twice Saïd caught a glimpse of Selîm among the crowd in the streets, but on each occasion was able to dodge aside and avoid him.   He would have rejoiced to know him happy and doing well, but was ashamed to meet him face to face.   For this reason he shunned the great bazaars and more crowded ways in his walks abroad.

At least once in every day he was drawn to the house of Yuhanna the Christian.   Sometimes he went thither at evening, when a deep earth shadow wrapped the city, and the western hill was black against an orange glow; more often in the early morning, while the ways were yet shady.   Hid in the angle of the porch he could observe all that passed in the court within. The very stones of the pavement had charm for him.   His beloved came and went, appeared and disappeared, now crooning a love-song with her baby brother in her arms, now mocking the coo of the pigeons, now romping with a maid-servant.   Whether she stood on tiptoe with head thrown back and arms uplifted, her long tresses reaching almost to her heels, to pull down the branch of a lemon-tree and see if a certain fruit were yellowing; whether she stamped her foot in sudden anger at the clumsiness of a servant, or slapped the child, who loved to bury his tiny hands in her hair and some-times caused her pain—whatever she did was full of grace in Saïd's eyes.   He would con over her moods and postures afterwards as he lay awake at night, tossing feverishly with a fire at his heart.   Crouching in the shadow of the entrance he feasted his eyes on her beauty of form and motion, until someone came to disturb him, when he stole back in the blue shadow of narrow alleys, shunning instinctively the sunlight and open places, with a singing in his ears.

At such times he went not to the tavern of Abu Khalîl, but straight to the cellar of Nûr.   The old woman listened kindly to his ravings, and soothed him with hints of hope, bidding him have but a little patience and he should be satisfied.   The girl's father, she said, was a wealthy merchant, a Nazarene, and under protection.   It would be unsafe to carry her off in a time of quiet, for the Frankish consuls would be sure to clamour for vengeance.   Alas, in these days none but a true believer could be wronged with impunity.   But a change was at hand. Wherever she went—in the palaces of the great as in the cellars of the poor—she heard murmurs of discontent.   Men's forbearance was taxed to the utmost. A little more—a feather, it must give way, and then Allah knew what would happen! There would be riot—that at least was certain—and amid the confusion of a whole city's rising one girl could be abducted and no man know it. Saïd must therefore wait and trust in Allah.

He drew some momentary comfort from this assurance, but his desire grew with every day, threatening to consume him. Old Mustafa rejoiced secretly at the haggard looks of his young ally. He strove by all means to foster a longing which promised to fall in timely with his scheme of revenge. He spoke rapturously of the charms of Yuhanna's daughter when they sat together among the gardens in the pale evening; and he would hug himself with glee when the fisherman leapt up and cursed the day he was born, beseeching Allah to strike him dead, for what was life to him without his darling!

One morning, as Saïd lounged in the tavern of Abu Khalil, a dehlibash entered, followed by an obsequious private. His uniform was that of the irregular troops distributed for a safeguard among the country towns and villages. He cast a keen glance round the coffee-house, passing over Camr-ud-dîn and his father and two Christian lads drinking arak together in a corner, until his eye rested on Saïd.

"Yonder is the man for us—what sayest thou, 'brahîm?"

"A strong man!—a fine man!" agreed the soldier, bending his right arm and feeling the muscle thereof to confirm his meaning.

"Look here, O what is thy name?" said the officer, addressing Saïd; "if thou hast a mind to earn ten piastres, rise up and follow me!"

If he wished to earn ten piastres! O day of blessing! O day of good luck! Upon his head he would serve his Excellency. To hear was to obey. Might Allah preserve his Honour's life for ever! What might be his Grace's further orders?

The officer strode out of the tavern again, motioning him to walk with the private soldier. In this order they traversed the city. Passing out at an eastern gate they came to a wide-open space where grass grew in ragged patches. Under some big trees which bordered the parade ground was a motley gathering of men and horses. The arrival of the dehlibash was hailed with loud blessings and cringing salaams. A steed was apportioned to Saïd, while the officer counted his men.

"Praise to Allah, the tale is complete!" he said with a sigh of relief; and then, looking at his watch, "It is lucky that it is so, for it wants but a half of the appointed hour. Here, 'brahìm, let this man wear thy paletot and give him a gun! At present he has nothing of the soldier about him. At an ordinary time it does not matter; but a friend whispered me this morning that the Waly himself purposes to review us; and it is likely Abdul Cader will be with him. He is a great general, by Allah, is Abdul Cader—his eyes are as the eyes of an eagle. Well"—he shrugged his shoulders and spread out his hands in deprecation—"if the Government can only afford to pay seventy soldiers and I am obliged to maintain a hundred, is it my fault that they be not clothed like the Sultàn's body-guard?"

Saïd donned the soldier's overcoat. The hood hanging between his shoulders irked him like a burden, so that he twisted his neck to see what was there, provoking shouts of laughter. Then he swung the carbine across his back, just as the order to mount was given.

The dehlibash marshalled his troop, two deep, in the middle of the parade ground. Even thus, in the full glare of the sun, with glint of gun-barrels and prancing of steeds, the show was not a brave one. A few half-naked urchins, smitten with awe at the sight, stood to watch, and idlers from the city gathered to the spot. Presently there was a noise of shouting and a pair of outriders cantered out at the gate, followed at an interval of about a hundred yards by a group of horsemen in civil dress surrounding the person of the Waly.

Ahmed Pasha wore the official frock coat and dark trousers, his sober Frankish garb contrasting strangely with the gorgeous trappings of his charger. His pale, intellectual face appeared the whiter for the scarlet fez pressed low on the forehead. Beside him, on the left hand, rode that great one whom Saïd had seen in the court of the mosque, sitting with the Mufti and Ismaïl Abbâs. Two Franks, whose top-boots were very prominent, rode on the Waly's right, and a servile official or two completed the party.

"Who is he?" Saïd inquired of a neighbour in the ranks.

"Who? O stupid! Ahmed Basha, of course!"

"No, I speak not of the Waly; but say, who is that great one who rides at his left hand?"

"Whence comest thou? Who art thou who dwellest in Es-Shâm and dost not know Abdul Cader, the mighty chief of Eljizar whom the French took and imprisoned and at length banished hither! Hist!"

The troop saluted after a fashion, and the Waly began his ride along the ranks, chiefly to ascertain that the right number of men were there. He seemed mortified by the wretched appearance of the troop. The two Franks smiled openly, pointing out individual scarecrows one to the other. As luck would have it, something in Saïd's bearing pleased Ahmed Pasha. He reined in his horse before him and made a remark over his shoulder to the Franks, who drew near with expectant faces.

"Now, my man, thou that art a servant of justice in this province, I put a case to thee: Suppose thou foundest a Muslim and a Christian fighting together, what wouldst thou do?"

Saïd reflected a moment.

"May it please your Excellency, I should take the Kâfir to prison."

The Waly bit his lip and rode on. The Franks tried in vain to stifle their laughter. Even Abdul Cader smiled and his eyes twinkled.

His round of inspection over, Ahmed Pasha addressed some sharp words of admonition to the troops; and refusing to listen to the officer's excuses, rode back again into the city. The crowd which had followed the governor dispersed after him. The soldiers retired to the shade of the plane-trees and there dismounted. Saïd and some fifty other faggots were paid off; and, being deprived of their guns and such soldierly garments as they had assumed for the nonce, sauntered away as civilians.

In his road to the tavern of Abu Khalll, the fisherman saw signs of unwonted excitement. The faces of the men he met had a fierce and eager look. Once or twice a Nazarene passed him, slinking along by the wall with the furtive side-glance of a dog that one stones. Drivers of camels and mules who seemed to come from the way of the mountains were beset by an eager crowd begging for news; while others coming off the

desert passed unheeded save for the curses of those whom the
advance of their laden beasts threatened to crush against the
wall.   Khans and coffee-houses were full to overflowing, and
the sound of many voices in agitation came from their shadowy
doorways.   It was near noon—an hour when men are wont to
move lazily, and the very camels seem to slumber as they rock
heavily onward with jangling bells.   But to-day all was animation.   Even the street-dogs opened an eye, drew in their
tongues at intervals and stirred uneasily in their sleep.

Saïd accosted two men who were arguing and gesticulating
in the shade of a merchant's awning.

"What is the news?" he asked.

"Great news, O my uncle—news of moment!   There is
war in the Mountain and it is sure that the Mowarni have
arisen and have destroyed twenty villages belonging to the
Drûz.   One that has but now arrived from Beyrut assured me
of it.   He saw the flames like stars on all the seaward slopes
as he passed the ridge at sundown.   It is sin, by Allah! for
the Drûz are our brothers in this matter.".

"Nay, by Allah! it is a lying report thou hast heard!"
cried the other man, vehemently.   "It is the Drûz who have
risen up suddenly and have destroyed thirty villages of the
Mowarni.   It is true, however, what thou sayest, that the
Drûz are our brothers.   May their power increase!"

The merchant before whose shop they were squabbling
removed the ivory mouthpiece of a narghileh from his lips
and crossed his legs more comfortably.

"It is likely both of you are wrong," he said.   "The event
occurred only yesterday, so the tidings are not yet confirmed.
This is but the first rumour which we hear.   It is surely
greater than the truth."

Saïd hurried on his way with a full heart.   Wild fancies,
that were half hope and half project, throbbed in his mind.
The time foretold of the lawyer was come; the day to which
Mustafa looked for vengeance was at hand.   A fire was kindled
on Lebanon, and a strong wind blew from the sea.   The
smoke was driven over the great city, and there were sparks in
the smoke.   Es-Shâm was as a heap of tinder carefully prepared.   Through vague pictures of riot and bloodshed he saw
the daughter of Yuhanna as he had first seen her, fondling her
baby brother in a blue shadow which the intervening sunlight

dusted with gold.   The vision was perfect even to the purple flowers on the wall at her back and a pair of white butterflies sporting above her head.   The vividness of it pained Saïd, causing heart and brain to ache.

The tavern of Abu Khalîl was crowded and uproarious when he reached it.   Just within the threshold, forced outward by the press, stood the host himself with back to the sunlight. By his manner of standing he seemed anxious and ill at ease. The expression of his face when he turned was the same which Saïd had seen it wear when knives were drawn in the house or a customer flew at another's throat.   With a touch of the hand and a whispered salutation the fisherman slipped past him and edged his shoulder into the throng.   Stools overturned were being kicked about among the feet of the disputants.   Clenched hands were shaken fiercely in angry faces.   Every man believed himself to be possessed of the truth of the matter and resented his neighbour's statement.

"Thirty villages!"—"Twenty!"—"No, a hundred, I tell thee!"—"The Drûz, by the Corân!"—"The Christians for certain!"

In the thickest of the crush Saïd descried an emerald mantle edged with fur.   It shone out brightly amid the ruck of soiled robes of every conceivable colour, blue predominating.   An embroidered turban binding a newish fez was conspicuous in like manner.   The young lawyer, who came thither to converse with clients, was struggling to obtain a hearing.

"I who am a lawyer tell you that it behoves all men to keep peace at this crisis!" Saïd heard him cry.   "Let the unbelievers extirpate each other—Durzi and Marûni.   The Franks are powerful and wish ill to Islâm.   They will cause all who take part against the Christians to be put to death. What profit has a man though he destroy his enemies if he die for it?   The Waly has summoned the Council of Notables. They will take strong measures to prevent a disturbance.   Calm your minds, I entreat you, all of you!"

Derisive shouts drowned his prayers.   The old beggar sprang forward and gripped his shoulder.   He swung the lawyer round so that he could grin in his face.

"What is this, effendi?" he said with a mad laugh.   "Does a man change his mind with each moon?   A little while since, when the chance of war seemed remote, thou wast a lion, ex-

I

horting us to battle with brave words. But now, on the eve
of the tumult thy heart grows faint. In the beginning, when
there is but a spark, it is easy to fan it or blow it out, which-
ever one please ; but afterward, when it is become a great fire
all the breath of a man avails not to extinguish it. Courage,
O Excellency ! It is a creditable thing to be chief among
men. Be sure I will give thee all honour, and praise thee as
my leader in this business ! "

With an oath the lawyer tore himself away. His face was
livid as he pushed through the noisy crowd to the door. He
passed quite close to Saïd, so that the latter could hear him
mutter under his breath,—

"A madman—dangerous to the peace of the city—I go
straight to denounce him. With Allah's leave he shall be in
gaol ere sunset ! "

Saïd watched him shuffle away in the direction of the
Waly's house, keeping close to the castle wall, as though its
strength were a protection, the skirts of his emerald coat
bellying behind him. Then he elbowed his way to where
Mustafa was leaping and dancing like a maniac in the midst
of the press, screaming curses on the Christians to the joy of
all.

Saïd plucked his robe and whispered, but the old man
shook him off at first and raved more frantically than ever.
But by dint of repeating his warning in a louder tone, and
dragging him by main force towards the door, he at length
won him to hear reason. They went out together into the
blinding sunshine, Mustafa cursing all lawyers and their
kinsfolk.

On reaching the cellar where they lodged, "Allah is
gracious ! The time is come, O Nûr ! " cried Mustafa, capering
and waving his skinny arms in a frenzy of glee.

XXI

IN those days the taverns of the city were never empty except at dead of night. Each sun brought fresh tidings of a rousing nature; and the excitement of the vulgar is a gossip who must chatter or die. It was soon known for certain that the Maronites had been the aggressors in the first place; but now the Drûz were slaying them like sheep all along the mountain.

"Of a surety, the Drûz are our brothers!" was the judgment of every true believer. "It is not true, what is commonly told of them, that they worship a calf in secret places. By the Coràn they are no idolaters. They fall not prostrate before pictures of women and sheep, as do the Nazarenes; but worship Allah even as we do. May they utterly destroy their enemies, who are ours also!"

Men went about their work distractedly with brains on fire. Unrest was everywhere. The sunlight itself, which baked the roofs, quivered of anticipation. The crescent gleaming on dome and minaret had a message for all the faithful.

Only in the Christian quarter fear reigned amid a death-like hush. The few inhabitants who ventured beyond its limits were hustled and spit upon. True believers cursed and reviled them so that they grovelled in terror of their lives. There was menace in the very air, so that they breathed it with deprecation.

In the dewy shade of an early morning Saïd bent his steps towards the house of Yuhanna. Wrapt in thought of his beloved he walked as in a dream. The ways were cool, he was conscious of a strip of radiance overhead, he saw men move as shadows. At a joyful shout of his own name he started as though one had struck him.

131

"Is it indeed thou, O Selìm?" he cried. "O day of joy! How goes thy business?"

The memory of his former scurvy treatment of the muleteer made him a little backward in cordiality. But upon Selìm embracing him tenderly as a brother, with no more than a playful reproach on the score of his desertion, he was truly delighted to see him once again; and they walked on, hand in hand, so far as their roads lay together. Saïd had little to relate. His life since their parting had been lazy and uneventful. Of the all-absorbing topic of Yuhanna's daughter he cared not to speak, being far from secure of his friend's approval. But Selìm, on the other hand, had much to tell. Alone, he had carried on the old business for a few days, in the hope of Saïd's return; but things had not thriven with him. The voice of the master was gone, and he might shout till he was hoarse in praise of the wares, yet few paused to examine them. So he sold the remnant of his stock to a dealer for what it would fetch, and journeyed to the mountain-village where was his home, to dandle his baby and take counsel with his woman. On his return to the city he applied for help to Ismaìl Abbâs, the Sherìf—Saïd remembered?—who received him very kindly and gave him a letter—guess to whom! to Ahmed Pasha, to his Highness, the Waly himself! In short, he was now a member of the Governor's household, receiving bakshìsh from all desirous to curry favour in his master's neighbourhood.

He was in the way of honour, and (under Allah) he thanked Saïd for it. Had it not been for that rich garment Saïd gave him he would never have caught the eye of the great Ismaìl Abbâs in the first instance. Moreover, he praised his friend's generosity and self-denial in that he had not taken his share of the slender profits of their partnership away with him. It was a magnanimous action, but then Saïd was ever the father of kindness. He had grieved much for the loss of his brother, and had even been to the cellar of Nûr seeking news of him. But the mistress of the house—a tall old woman with painted eyes—had been short with him and he could learn nothing from her.

Saïd's heart smote him as he listened. Allah had blessed him with the truest friend ever man had, and he had slighted the gift. He squeezed Selìm's hand and swung it lightly to and fro as they walked. Might Allah destroy him utterly and quench the fire on his hearth if ever again he gave this good man cause to reproach him.

"I rejoice in thy happiness," he said when the time came for them to part. "And what is the mind of his Excellency the Basha with respect to the war of the Mountain? Wait a little and there shall be war in Es-Shâm on the pattern of it."

"Alas, O Saïd, they say in the palace of my lord that should the men of Es-Shâm follow the example of the Drûz, then the downfall of Islâm is sure, for the Franks will avenge the Nazarenes, that is known. The Waly himself is very anxious: it is said that he weeps at night in his chamber. He is a great general of renown, but he loves study better than government. One of the soldiers of the guard, who has served under him in the wars of Europe, tells me that he was ever a great general—none greater—upon paper: victory waited on his science; but he loved not the turmoil of a battle and its perils.

"His mind is now torn asunder by the demands of the Franks wishing one thing, and the advice of the elders of Islâm, who desire the opposite. In truth, it seems to me who am a small man and no politician, that he hearkens too willingly to the speeches of the Franks, the sworn enemies of the Faith. It was no wise thing that he did yesterday in ordering the dog Jurji, who did outrage on the harîm of Asad Effendi, to be released without punishment. The Franks speak as lawyers on behalf of their clients, and they strengthen their pleading by threats. This pardon of an evil-doer, simply because he is a Nazarene, will madden the faithful. As I came just now through the long bazaar, a band of youths armed with sticks passed me, running towards the Christian quarter, vowing they would do justice on Jurji with their own hands. I fear the Waly has been ill-advised in this matter. He is a great man and a politic, but he is weak, and the Franks overbear him. I fear there will be trouble. Thanks be to Allah that Selîm is not the great Waly of Damashc-ush-Shâm, but only a small servant whose duty is plain. May Allah guard thee in safety till we meet again!"

They parted. Selîm was quickly lost in the shifting crowd of a roofed bazaar, while Saïd, striking into a quiet alley, pursued his way to the house of Yuhanna. The news of the release of Jurji rankled in his mind, making him venomous towards the Christians.

As he passed the threshold of the outer door, seeking that corner of the entrance passage whence he was used to spy on his delight, he stumbled on a pitcher someone had left there. The earthen vessel crashed upon the stones and was shattered to bits. The noise was enough to bring the whole household running to the spot. Bitterly cursing the accident, Saïd took to his heels. A little way up the lane he hid himself in the angle of two walls.

Presently, as he stood there waiting till the alarm of the broken pot should have had time to subside, he heard loud voices approaching. A rabble of Muslim lads burst into the narrow way, cursing all the Nazarenes, and yelling that they were come to do justice on Jurji the evil-doer and destroy his father's house with fire. Most of them carried sticks; some had long knives in their hands. Seeing a man look out from the door of Yuhanna's house they chalked the sign of the cross ostentatiously on the pavement, spat upon it, and trampled it underfoot. The head was quickly withdrawn and the door shut and bolted from within.

This seemed rare sport to Saïd. Lifting up his voice against the Christians, he joined himself to the mob.

They paraded the entire quarter, reviling all they met. Here and there a man cried shame upon them, but the most part slunk past them along the wall with a cringing salutation. At length, growing weary of their unchallenged progress, they were about to disperse, when a happy thought occurred to Saïd. He imparted it to his comrades, who were loud in acclamation. Such as had knives set to work to cut short lengths of stick, which they bound two and two together so as to form rough crosses. Then they took hold of the street-dogs, which lay around them by dozens, tied a cross under the tail of each, and with a kick sent them howling in all directions.

The fun was at its height when a man dressed in the Frankish fashion, but swarthy and wearing a fez, emerged from a doorway close by in earnest conversation with a Muslim in a fur-edged mantle of emerald green. He of the foreign garb cast one searching glance at the crowd, and then, seeing its occupation, walked off hurriedly, dragging the lawyer along with him.

"Dîn Muhammed!" Saïd yelled after them in derision.
"Behold we follow thy advice, effendi!"

"Dîn Muhammed — Allah! Allah! Perish the unbelievers!" shouted a few of his companions; but the greater
part were silent, seeming afraid.

"It is the dragoman of the Muscovite consul," one murmured with consternation. "He knows me well, whose son I
am. He will surely lodge information against us and we shall
be imprisoned for this day's work."

"Let us after and slay him!" cried another, valorous from
a whole morning spent in insulting men with impunity.

"Let us go quietly each to his own place!" pleaded a third,
who had cause for alarm, being well-known to the dragoman.

His advice seemed best to all, and they disbanded forthwith. Saïd went to the coffee-house of Abu Khalîl, where he
smoked a narghileh. The tale of his morning's pastime made
the fat taverner quake with inward laughter. Camr-ud-dîn and
his mother stopped work to listen; the customers applauded it
as a merry jest. He was obliged to repeat it from the beginning
for every newcomer. At midday he made a hearty meal of
lentils and bread, drank a cup of coffee, and disposed himself
for a nap.

About the second hour after noon he was roused by a
strong hand on his shoulder shaking him. To the first blurred
glance of his sleepy eyes the whole tavern seemed full of
soldiers; but when he sat up he found there were but four of
them.

"A scar on his forehead," one was saying, as if he read
over a description in writing, "the beard black, tall and robust,
the son of perhaps twenty-three years, his raiment striped of
blue and yellow, soiled. This is the man, by Allah! . . .
Arise, O my uncle, and come along with us!"

"What means this? What evil have I done?" Saïd
rubbed his eyes and stared aghast.

"Who said thou hadst done any wrong? Not I, by Allah!
To my mind thou didst well to spit upon the infidels; would
to Allah thou hadst slain a few of them! But it is the Waly's
order that thou go to prison. Make haste, O lazy one!"

Saïd was dimly aware of Abu Khalîl quaking and wringing
his hands somewhere between him and the sunlight, of the
voices of Camr-ud-dîn and his mother mingled in curses upon

the soldiers and their ancestry.   Then he was led out into the white glare of the street, where a small crowd of idlers and ne'er-do-weels gaped upon him, and ran along with his captors as an additional escort.

It was clear that the guards had orders to avoid all crowded thoroughfares, for they hurried him through dark tunnels and passages and along mean alleys of an evil savour.   But with all these precautions they were obliged to cross the open space before a large khan at an hour when traffic was at its height; and such a group was sure to attract notice, even without the little crowd which followed it implicitly as the tail the dog. The person of the prisoner was much scrutinised, and questions were put to the soldiers, who answered with an "Allah knows!" and a surly shrug.   All at once a well-known plaint struck Saïd's ear.

"Allah will give to you! . . .   For the love of Allah, take pity or I die! . . .   O Lord! . . .   Allah will give to you! . . ."

He started, and then howled "Mustafa!" with all the strength of his lungs.

"Hold thy peace, O fool, lest I strike thee on the mouth!" hissed the chief of his escort fiercely.

But the old beggar had heard his cry.   The crowd parted suddenly, giving way to a wild, lean figure a-flutter with rags. Mustafa raised hands and eyes to Heaven for horror of what he saw.

"What is this?" he shrieked.   "Allah cut short their lives! They have taken my son—the staff of my days!—the light of my eyes! . . .   These sons of iniquity have robbed me of my son! . . .   O Allah! . . .   O Lord! . . .   O men of Es-Shâm—O fathers of kindness, will you suffer this great wrong to be done in your sight?   By the Prophet, there is no sin in him! . . .   O Lord! . . .   He has ever been a good son and a pious.   Say, O Saïd, for what cause have they taken thee and bound thy hands?   Let all men judge of thy innocence!"

"For the cause that I cursed the heathen!" shouted Saïd, at the cost of a smart blow on the mouth, which made his gums bleed.

"O Lord!" screamed the old beggar, dancing and rending his clothes as one gone mad with grief.   "See, they strike him!   There is blood on his lips! . . .   They side with unbelievers! . . . They buffet the champion of Islâm and lead him to prison! . . . O men of Es-Shâm, O faithful people, you have heard his crime from his own mouth! . . . O Lord! . . . Rescue him!—rescue my son!—my only son!—the staff of my life!"

The soldiers and their charge were at a standstill, a crowd pressing upon them from every side. There was a sound of muttered curses on all hands, and the shrieks of the old maniac seemed ominous to the guardians of law and order.

"Bah! it is nothing," shouted the chief of the party so as to be heard afar. "He will be rebuked and lie idle in gaol for a few hours. . . . By Allah, we are no infidels but true men. That old rogue there lies when he says that we side with the Nazarenes. Allah be my witness, it is a lie! But the Waly's order is upon us, which to hear is to obey, and those who dare to resist us do so at the risk of heavy punishment. . . . Oäh! Oäh! In the name of the Sultàn, make way, I say!"

By soft speaking, mingled deftly with threats, he managed to force a path through the press. In the quiet alley into which they plunged directly he cursed Saïd for a madman and threatened him with every kind of torment as the guerdon of his misbehaviour. There was peace again, and the soldiers were able to breathe freely. They waxed courageous and blustered as Saïd became sullen and crestfallen. But the old beggar had joined the faithful few who clung to them through all vicissitudes of the road; and he ceased not to revile and execrate them, imploring Allah to strike them all dead and so release his son, until he had watched Saïd disappear within the gate of the prison. Then he sped fleet-foot to the vault of Nûr, to take counsel what was next to be done.

XXII

SAÏD'S first impression of the gaol would have been a pleasant one but for the dejected looks of its inmates and the foul stench pervading its atmosphere. His captors left him unshackled in an open quadrangle. An arcade supporting a flat roof made a sort of verandah on two sides of it, affording shelter to the prisoners from the glare of noon. The remainder was shut in by a high wall, in which was the entrance gate, strongly barred and further secured by a small guard of soldiers hardly less wretched in appearance than the criminals themselves. On one hand the rays of the sinking sun were warm upon wall and pavement; on the other, a deep blue shadow stretched out from the arcade before mentioned almost to the middle of the court.

Saïd stood for some time where his escort had left him, just within the gate. His eyes strayed over the various groups lying or squatting in the shade or striding wearily up and down in the red glow that dyed the eastern wall. Most of them were ragged; all were dirty, with the exception of three young men, who sat aloof together, cross-legged, on the edge of the sunlight. The gaiety of this little party, talking and laughing bravely in the face of misfortune, attracted Saïd even before he knew them for his associates in transgression. His approach was hailed with shouts of welcome, and he was made to sit down with them.

They affected to treat their imprisonment as a jest. It was not likely, Saïd agreed, that men would be greatly punished for so slight a misdemeanour. The Waly was a Muslim, and all believers must surely feel with them. Their arrest was only a sop to the Franks. That dragoman—curse his religion!— had complained to the Muscovite consul, his master; and the consul had gone in a rage to Ahmed Pasha, who was ever ready to humour a Frank in small matters. The consul's word

138

was law : the ringleaders were put in prison. On the morrow they would be brought before a council of true believers, gently reprimanded and set at liberty.

Thanks to these assurances, and a good supper which a soldier gladly brought in for them from a neighbouring tavern, Saïd slept well enough that night, though on the bare stones. He had no money to procure bedding such as his friends obtained from the gaolers for a trifle of bakshìsh. But having supped well at their expense, and being used to rough couches, he scarcely envied them the luxury. He awoke in gladness to the prospect of a speedy release. But the day wore on, and the little company sat ever in the shadow of the arcade, gazing at the gate until their eyes ached. They murmured and grew despondent ; darkness returned and they were still in durance. Saïd slept ill that night ; his companions moaned and stirred uneasily in their sleep. They were forgotten, or the Franks had poisoned the Waly's mind against them. In either case they had small cause to rejoice.

About sunrise, Saïd was awakened by the clank of an iron chain. A peevish voice bade him arise and that quickly. He scrambled to his feet and looked for his companions. They were standing a little way off, under a strong guard of soldiers. Their limbs were fettered, and they were linked together by a heavy chain. He read blank dismay in their faces.

"What is this? What have we done to deserve such usage ? " he asked indignantly, as two men, detached for that purpose, fitted irons to his wrists and ankles. There was no answer ; the men seemed morose yet handled him gently. Upon his repeating the question in a louder tone the officer in command, who appeared in a towering rage, turned on him fiercely.

"Thou mayst well ask what is this ! I myself know not the meaning of it ! Perhaps the Waly is possessed with a devil—Allah knows ! To hear is to obey ; but to carry out such an order is a shame for one who is a Muslim. May all the Franks perish utterly ! . . . Know that the dragoman of the Muscovite consul—a Christian and the son of an Arab, may his house be destroyed !—was closeted with his Excellency yesterday afternoon. And a little later I received the order for your punishment ; that you are to sweep the streets of the Christian quarter in chains. Allah witness, I count it a sin and dishonour to the faith. Notwithstanding, to hear is to obey!"

He turned aside with a shrug to give a word of command to one of his men. Four common brooms were brought and distributed one to each of the convicts. Saïd was coupled on to the chain with the others, and thus bound together they were marched out at the gate, while every prisoner that was a Muslim ground his teeth and howled with rage at the indignity. The ragged privates who kept the door murmured together with lowering brows.

"Jurji, the Nazarene, that was a malefactor, was set free without punishment," Saïd heard one of them growl; "while these believers, who have done nothing to be called a crime, are condemned to dishonour the faith. In truth, the end of all things is at hand!".

Their road lay past the gateway of the great mosque. The sight of the white minaret with its crescent glittering upon the blue brought scalding tears to men's eyes for the honour of Islâm which was dead. The cooing of the doves had a new and mournful note in it. The prisoners walked listless with downcast faces; the soldiers closed in to screen them, as far as might be, from the stare of the populace. But the guard themselves were sullen and dejected; the work in hand being a heavy burden on their minds. Suddenly a piercing cry broke upon the hush in which they moved.

"O Lord! . . . I behold my son—my only son—the staff of my age—whom the children of sin took from me! The slaves of iniquity have loaded him with chains—Allah, cut short their lives! . . . By the Coràn, he is no evildoer, but a pious man and a faithful—who did but curse some Nazarenes and spit in their faces. It is for that they have fettered and bound him! . . . O Lord! . . . Shall these things be done under the sun and in the sight of all men? Merciful Allah!"

The soldiers quickened step, but the voice went along with them, as it were a knife stabbing their hearts, which were sore enough already. Why did not the sun veil his face and spread a darkness over all the city that the shame of Islâm might be hid? Oh, that Allah would cause the earth to yawn and swallow up the infidels, as he did for Neby Musa of old; that all the world might know that God was still watching over his faithful as in the time of Nûh and Ibrahîm and Ismaïl,

as in the days of Daûd and of Isa, and of Muhammed (peace
to him!), his apostle. O day of woe! O cursed day of
infamy!

That was a proud morning for the Christians. They
swarmed in the streets of their quarter with exultant faces.
The day of their deliverance was come at last. The con-
querors were become the slaves of the conquered, to sweep
their streets for them. They gloated on the sight with the
coward's triumph, who, seeing his foe laid low by a stronger
than himself, spits valiantly in his face and cries, "Mine is
the victory!" Secure of protection, they took pleasure in
taunting the prisoners, cursing them for sons of dogs and
mocking them with proffers of water when they seemed weary.
The pent-up venom of centuries was on their tongues. The
poor earthworm hissed like a snake.

A number of the faithful had flocked into the quarter,
drawn chiefly by the frantic outcry of the old beggar. They
failed at first to grasp the position. The valorous attitude of
the Christians only shocked and bewildered them. But no
sooner did they learn what work was doing than their eyes
grew fierce with the old pride of Islâm—the battle-pride of
their forbears, who had carried the white crescent on the green
flag victorious from India to the Atlantic. There were scuffles,
and Christians were hurled to the ground. The press grew
menacing about the sweepers and their guard. The soldiers
looked anxious. The prisoners were ordered to cease work,
and the officer, foreseeing a riot, was minded to take them
back to prison on his own responsibility. The courage of the
Nazarenes began to waver. The older and wiser of them
slipped quietly into the nearest houses. But the younger and
more turbulent, loth to forego one tittle of the unwonted
pleasure of retaliation, remained in the street, hurling insults
at the religion of Muhammed, and all professing it. Even
thus they outnumbered the believers, who, however, were
constantly on the increase as the rumour of a tumult spread
through the city. In vain did the captain attempt to draw
off his men, for they were locked in the heart of a seething,
yelling crowd. It was all they could do to hold their ground.
All at once the voice of the old beggar was raised in triumph,—

"To the rescue!—Dîn! Dîn! Dîn Muhammed!"

There was a rush of turbaned men, a sharp struggle; the

soldiers were torn away like trees by a winter torrent, and a
hundred hands were eager to free the prisoners from their
fetters.   Files, knives, iron bars—every kind of tool and
weapon was thrust forward to serve in the work of release.
Rescuers and rescued were rocked too and fro in the battle
raging around them.   For once the Christians fought like
wild beasts.   Here a turbaned head was seen to fall, there a
fez.   Death shrieks mingled with the howls and shouts of the
fighters.   The uproar was frightful.   For a while the issue of
the fray seemed doubtful; but soon the Christians began to
give way.   The war-cry of Islâm gathered volume, until it
seemed to roll along the sky in waves of sound.

"To the house of Yuhanna!" cried the old beggar,
dragging Saïd's arm.   "Dìn Muhammed! to the house of
'hanna, the pig who protects Jurji, the evildoer! . . . Y'Allah!
. . . Death to the heathen!"

Saïd, freed of his chains, forced his way earnestly through
the crowd.   Mustafa dogged him, screaming, laughing, and
yelling like one possessed, keeping tight hold of his raiment so
as not to lose him.   A number of the faithful, fired by the
hated name of Jurji, followed frantic as they.

XXIII

THE house of Yuhanna was at some distance from the
scene of riot. Its outer door stood open as on other
days, and at the moment when Saïd burst into its pretty court,
the girl Ferideh was seated on a cushion in the shade of the
lemon trees, her little brother in her lap. Suddenly, as if the
stillness had been some brittle thing, it shivered to a great
roar. There was a whirr and a flutter as the pigeons rose in
a cloud from their researches on the pavement.

Snatching up the child, she sprang to her feet. The
menace of the wild inhuman faces appalled her. She fled
towards the door of the house in terror at that inroad of madmen as she deemed them. But the old beggar, outrunning
Saïd, caught her by the arm and shook her brutally.

"Say, girl, is the pig, thy father, in the house?"

Ferideh winced for the tightness of his grasp. Outraged
pride and a certain fearful wonder were blended in her
answer.

"Be not so rough, I pray! . . . Know that my father
receives no man to-day, for he lies upon his bed, having fever.
To-morrow he will perhaps be well, and, when well, he is
accessible to all who seek him."

Mustafa laughed aloud and pushed her so that she
staggered backward a few paces.

"He receives no man, sayest thou? By the tomb of the
Prophet, he will receive us! Aha, O 'hanna, thou old rat,
thou devourer of women, the avenger of blood overtakes thee
at last!" He drew a long knife from his girdle and flashed
it in the face of the girl.

"Dìn Muhammed!" he cried. "Death to the infidels!
Y'Allah!" and rushed into the house, hurling to the ground
an old woman, almost blind, who had come to the door

143

seeking querulously to know the meaning of the uproar. The crowd raised a loud shout and pressed after him.

"O holy Miriam! O Yesûa, Redeemer of the world, save him, save my father!" shrieked the maiden, falling on her knees, appealing to the sky above, whose bright peace mocked her anguish. The mob, bent on plunder, only laughed at her and praised her looks in passing. She grew white and red by turns, and her lips moved with difficulty as she prayed.

The scared pigeons circled overhead, whirling great flakes of shadow over wall and pavement. Their cooing and the tinkle of the rill from the basin, heard despite the tumult, were heartrending as memories. The still foliage of the lemon trees cast a dark pool of shadow on the flags. The leaves of a creeper on the wall trembled a little.

Saïd made no attempt to enter the house. He had no thirst for blood, no desire for gain. The screams and yells that arose within only confused his brain. He drew near to the kneeling girl, and she did not see him; but the child saw him and clung closer, burying its face in her bosom. He felt bashful—at a loss how to proceed. The court was deserted now; he thought he would have felt bolder in the presence of a crowd. The shouting and the noise, though friendly, numbed his wits. Forgetful for a moment of what was going on within the house, he began to make playful overtures to her baby brother.

Through an open lattice a frightful shriek rent the air, deadening all other sounds. Another, and then another . . . The girl leapt to her feet and listened, hugging the little one so tight that it cried fretfully.

"O just Allah! they are killing my father!" she cried, and was rushing blindly towards the open door when Saïd caught her in his arms.

"Unhand me, loose me, wild beast! Let me go to my father. Dost hear his cry? They kill him—an old man and sick, lying on his bed with none to help him."

She fought him frantically for a moment with teeth and feet, always holding the child fast to her breast. Then, as if all her strength were spent, she gave one bitter cry and was still.

Holding her thus in his arms, Saïd felt uplifted beyond all care of life or death. What matter though a hundred old men were butchered if only he could manage to convey her away from that place to the upper chamber of Nûr, the harlot.

"I suffer with thee, O my beloved!" he murmured soothingly. "But thy father was old; the days that remained to him were few in number. Also the people are mad this day against every Nazarene. . . . Listen, pretty one! If they find thee here they will surely slay thee, and this child also. Now I have so great love for thee that I would not let a hair of thy head be harmed. By Allah, I would slay the man who dared to touch thee with a finger! Come with me, O my soul, and I will lead thee to a place of safety."

She gave no answer nor any sign that she heard, but weighed heavily upon him. Looking down, he realised that she had swooned.

The little boy, escaped from her embrace, was trotting eagerly towards the door of the house, through which rich carpets and other furniture of price were being flung out pell-mell. Saïd, who was fond of children, called to him that there were devils in there, and bade him fly to some neighbour's house. Whereupon the little fellow toddled for the street in terror of his life.

He had raised the fainting girl in his arms and was bearing her swiftly towards the outer gate, when Mustafa overtook him.

"Aha, thou performest thy part? It is good—very good! Now listen!—I slew him. See, his blood is still warm on my left hand. . . . I was the first to plunge a knife into him; but, before I smote, I made him teach me the place where his treasure lies hid. At my bidding the multitude held their hands and stood back, knowing that I had private cause to hate him. He told me readily, in a whisper, thinking to save his life. But I slew him—with this knife I slew him. It is a good knife—a sharp knife. By Allah, I love this knife as my brother from this day forth. Ha, ha!"

He sank his voice.

"I go now to secure the money. There is a fountain— thou knowest it?—out yonder among the gardens, built on the pattern of a little mosque. In the pavement of its recess is a loose stone covering a hole where I am used to bury trifles. There I will conceal the wealth, and afterwards I will seek thee at the house of Nûr. Make haste, O my son! . . .

K

Look, there is smoke: they set fire to the house! . . .
The girl is pretty, and some of them might quarrel with thee
for her sake. My peace go with thee! "

Saïd strode out into the street with his burden and
plunged into the network of dark passages and byways he had
threaded so often for desire of her. He had not gone far
before she began to give signs of a return to consciousness.
He paused awhile in a secluded place to give her time to
recover. Presently, to his great relief, she was able to stand
on her feet, though still dazed and needing support for
every step. She asked not whither they went, nor seemed to
care. Indeed, she evinced no mind or will of her own, but
moved wherever he led her, without reluctance as without
eagerness. Her beauty, and the strange sight of a Muslim
shepherding a Christian maid, caused the men they met to
stare at them; so that Saïd, having no wish to court notice,
bade her draw the fall of her white hood across her face,
as the Drûz women used to do. She obeyed by a vague
movement which told that her mind wandered.

Nûr was cooking her noon-day meal on the brazier when
they entered. She welcomed Saïd with delight and cast a
searching glance at his charge. Then, as he began to explain,
she checked him with an impatient gesture and a nod of
intelligence. She understood perfectly. He had been sent
to sweep the streets of the infidels. Oh, the sin of it! She
had heard the news from the son of Abu Khalîl when he
brought some figs she had asked of his father. The whole
city was ashamed. There had been a riot — not so?—
and he had been rescued. And then Mustafa — the old
madman!—had led the mob to the house of 'hanna, his
enemy. And this then was Saïd's beloved?

She thrust her painted face close to that pale one and
scanned the features narrowly. Then she passed her hands
down the loose robe, feeling the limbs beneath.

"She is sweet — a pearl!—a darling!" she exclaimed.
"By Allah, thou art in luck's way, O my soul! Art happy
at last? . . . She neither sees nor hears us. Poor love! she
is distraught with grief. It happens timely that the upper
chamber is ready. I prepared it for the pleasure of a certain
effendi, but his girl is a Nazarene and, in these troublous
times, will not dare come hither. I will tend her there, the

priceless gem! And thou must not come nigh her until the evening. Dost hear, O Saïd? She must sleep and take refreshment, and Nûr will tend her. Wait until the evening, I say; and then, when she is a little rested, I will present thee as her deliverer."

With that she put an arm round Ferideh's waist and supported her very tenderly up the flight of steps to the guest-chamber. And Saïd sat on his heels, rolling cigarette after cigarette, drinking glass after glass of rose sherbet, too perturbed to eat though Nûr pressed him to share her repast. And Nûr, for her part, took a malicious joy in his distress, looking forth from time to time from the door of the upper room to wag her head at him and whisper, trumpeting with her hand,—

"She is sweet, I tell thee!—white as milk!—a darling! I that am a woman cannot choose but kiss her!"

XXIV

THE first lilac gloom of night had fallen on the city ere the old beggar regained the vault of Nûr. A feeble glow from the brazier showed his wrinkled face ghastly pale and distorted with nervous twitchings. Madness burned in his eyes. His fingers clenched and unclenched spasmodically; his staff fell from them with a thud upon the earthen floor.

"O Nûr, hear me! Where art thou?" he cried, peering about in the darkness. "I have slain him, I tell thee—I have slain the pig 'hanna—the enemy of my house . . ."

"Hist!—Hold thy peace!" The door of the upper chamber was opened and shut. There was the rustle of a dress and clank of trinkets as the old woman came down the steps. "She is up there—his daughter, dost understand? Saïd has been with her, but against my advice he was violent and frightened her. She fought like a tigress and screamed so that I had to interfere. By my head, it is lucky that my house is a place apart, walled off and secluded, else all the quarter must have come together, seeking the cause of her out-cry. For long I have been trying to soothe her; now at length she is silent and I am glad of it. As for Saïd, she has scratched and bitten him finely. A little while since he went out to gather tidings; he will return presently. Now sit down, O my uncle, and I will warm up thy supper, which was ready long ago."

But Mustafa gave no heed to what she said. Except that he lowered his voice somewhat it seemed that he heard nothing of it. Clutching her arm, he launched into a sort of chant of praise and thanksgiving.

"Allah is bountiful! . . . I slew him, I tell thee! He lay on his bed shamming sickness; and I held the rage of the

148

faithful in check till he had whispered me the secret of his treasure. He thought to preserve his life thereby, deeming we were come to rob him. But I spoke the word, I called on the name of Allah! I shouted in his ear the name of the girl, my sister, whom he ruined. A hundred knives struck down at him as he lay; but mine was foremost and it cut his life. . . . Praise to Allah!

"Ha, ha! He was fat and lay on a soft bed, whereas I am lean and used to sleep on the earth. Yet I slew him! . . . See the stains on my left hand—O hand of honour, O blessed hand! . . . The fat who dwell in palaces must reckon with the lean beggar at their gates. I would, O Nûr, thou hadst seen him in the death-throe. He looked so funny that all men laughed. Ha, ha, ha! . . . Thanks be to Allah! The reproach is taken away from my father's house. Allah is gracious!"

"Thou art overwrought, O father of Mansûr," she said soothingly. "Sit down and rest. See, thy supper is ready! . . . By Allah, thou art very old for this work, and I fear lest it prove harmful to thy health. Sit down, dost hear me? After a little while Saïd will return and we shall learn what news there is. In the meantime I will make some coffee for thee."

The old beggar allowed himself to be persuaded. He sank down cross-legged by the threshold of the inner room, while she, having made fast the door, shook an earthen lamp to be sure it had oil enough, lit and set it in a hollow nook of the wall opposite to him. By its light she observed him furtively as she busied herself about the brazier, and she shook her head bodingly from time to time. A torn strip of his filthy turban dangled over one ear. His scanty robe, all ragged, displayed the thick growth of grizzled hair upon his chest. His bare limbs were shrivelled and sinewy, of the colour of a sun-dried apricot, the legs dusty almost to the knee. His withered hand was extended as when he sat by the wayside for alms.

It was as if mere change of posture had been a charm to quench his excitement. The life was gone from his limbs, the fire from his eyes. He was become bowed and very feeble—an old, old man whose hours are numbered. His mouth hung open slavering. The underlip moved perpetually as he gurgled certain phrases, always the same, seeming catch-words to something he would fain recall.

"Allah is bountiful . . . I slew him . . . Dìn Muhammed . . . O blessed left hand . . . Allah is bounti-ful ! . . ."

Nûr shook him with rough kindness as she set a smoking bowl of chopped meat and rice at his knees with the charge to wake up and eat. She held the dish under his nostrils that the savoury steam might beget a craving. She grew poetical in praise of its contents ; but all in vain.

Mechanically he thrust a trembling hand into the mess and raised a portion to his mouth ; but he let the rice slip through his fingers without so much as licking them.

Nûr was greatly concerned. He must be on the brink of death, she told herself, thus to neglect good victuals, he who was always wont to come in ravenous from a day's begging. She made shift to feed him with her own hands and rejoiced to find that he swallowed the morsels placed in his mouth.

While she was thus occupied the door was tried from without. A knocking ensued, and the voice of Saïd calling to her to open. She left her charge and flew to shoot back the bolt.

"Where is Mustafa? . . . Bid him come away with all speed ! It is said that search is made for us for our part in the destruction of Yuhanna's house. Ah, there he is ! Rise, O my father, and come with me. The carnage of this day is nothing compared with what to-morrow's sun will see. Know that a great multitude of Christians, fugitives from the Mountain, have entered the city seeking refuge. And many Drûz, both from the Mountain and the Hauran, have pursued them hither. I met a party of them in this minute as I came through the street. They are strong men of war and armed like soldiers. They are eager as ourselves against the pagans. . . . Arise, O Mustafa, and come away ! It is known that we frequent this place, and it were a shame to be taken a prisoner on the eve of so great a festival. . . . Arise, I say ! What ails thee? Art ill? Speak ! What is this, O Nûr?"

The woman clung to his arm.

"Merciful Allah ! I fear he is at the point to die. At his first coming he was as one possessed, shouting and screaming and waving his hands. It was very hard for me to quiet him.

Now he is like one in a swoon; he sees me not nor hears me, and is weaker than a baby."

"I warrant he is only tired. If Allah will I shall find means to rouse him. He is as my father, and this place is dangerous for him."

He strode to the place where Mustafa sat cross-legged, mumbling fragments of sentences, and staring at the basin of rice and meat. He grasped the old man's shoulder and bent over him, raising his voice as if to overtake the wandering mind and call it back.

"Fie upon thee, O my father!" he cried, "thou who hast this day slain the enemy with thy own hand, and hast done battle so bravely for the Faith, to sicken and faint like a vaporous girl. Allah witness I am ashamed for thee! Awake, O Mustafa! This place is not safe for us. The soldiers—Allah blast them!—may be seeking us even now. If we stay here we shall be taken and put in prison, and must forego all the glory of to-morrow's slaughter. The wrath of Islâm burns like a great fire to consume the infidels. From the hour of sunrise the slaying will begin. Men will look for thee, O my father, in the front of the battle. They will marvel greatly and say one to another, 'Where now is that old lion which devoured Yuhanna, the pig?' They will look for thee to lead them on; it were a sin to disappoint them. Up, O Mustafa! The danger grows with every minute. Awake!—y'Allah!—for the faith of Muhammed!"

The last words were of magic virtue. The dying embers of the old man's wit leapt up at them in lurid flame. With a cry he sprang to his feet, staring wild-eyed at Saïd.

"Dìn Muhammed!—I slew him! O glorious left hand! Allah is bountiful! Yes, I hear thee, my son, and I understand. I was asleep, not so? I was weary and so I fell asleep, and methought the angel of death was with me. But it was a dream surely. I will go with thee, O my eyes, whither thou wilt, so that there be men like him, who lie on beds of down.—Ha, ha!—while I who slew him am used to lie on the hard-trodden ground. I must be strong, sayest thou? Now, by my beard, that is a foolish word; for who is stronger than Mustafa? 'Hanna was weaker for I slew him easily, witness Allah and the blood-stains on my left hand. O glorious hand! But it is true what thou sayest, that a man's

strength must be nourished with meat.   Of course, I will eat;
and to-morrow I will do great slaughter—thou and I together,
O my soul.   O blessed left hand !   Allah is bountiful !"

He swallowed the food hastily by great mouthfuls, with no
signs of relish.   When the bowl was empty Nûr brought him
a cup of hot coffee, which he gulped down in like manner.
He grew reasonable, taking counsel with Saïd as to the best
place for them to lie till morning.   The old woman, seeing
him fairly in the way of health, wished them both a happy
night, and returned to the upper chamber to look after the
girl Ferideh, whose moans and lamentations, though unheeded
in the greater anxiety attending the beggar's plight, had long
been audible.

"Take care that she do herself no mischief: she is a very
tigress !" Saïd called after her as he and his adopted father
stepped out into the night.   They went stealthily, by
narrow ways the moonbeams seldom fathomed, to a small
tavern kept by a Muslim, which was towards the Christian
quarter.   Others of the insurgents had likewise chosen that
place for their night's shelter.   There were blithe greetings.
A discussion was going on, in which Mustafa, having no care
to rest, joined eagerly.   But Saïd, being very drowsy, yawned
cavernously at all that was said.   He soon stretched his length
on the floor and fell fast asleep.

XXV

"DÌN! Dìn! Dìn Muhammed!" . . . "Allah! Allah!"
. . . "Death to the unbelievers!" . . . "Perish the
Nazarenes!" . . .

Saïd awoke to the consciousness of a frightful uproar
streaming in with a sunbeam through the open door. The
whole city was filled with it—wrapt in it as in a mist.
Frenzied shouts for Allah and the Prophet, devilish yells and
cries of exultation mingled with the run of a great multitude
in the street without, the distant beat of a drum and a sound
of desultory firing.

The tavern, in deep shadow, was empty save for the old
beggar, who stood over him brandishing a curved knife like a
sickle in his sound hand, while with the withered he pointed
to the piece of an iron bar which lay on the ground close to
Saïd. A fierce devil looked out at his eyes.

"Arise, O sluggard!" he cried with a mad laugh. "Is this
a time to sleep and be lazy? Come, let us out! There will
be blood!—blood!—blood of unbelievers to flush the streets
like water! Aha, the dogs of the city shall drink rare wine
to-night!"

Saïd's eyes caught fire from the speaker's. Grasping the
iron, he sprang to his feet. "Ready!" he cried; and with a
bound like a wild beast's they cleared the threshold together.

A live stream filled the alley—a torrent of men and boys;
all with the murder-light in their eyes, all flourishing weapons,
all racing in one direction. The current caught them and
swept them along.

"In case we be sundered in the tumult," breathed Mustafa,
"meet me in the place thou knowest—in the secret place of
our treasure among the gardens—at the hour of sunset. Forget
not!"

153

Saïd turned his head to answer; but the old man was torn away from him in a sudden eddy of the human tide to avoid the frantic kicking of a donkey which held the middle of the causeway. He found himself roughly shouldered between two Drûz of giant build, clad in the black-and-white cloak and white linen turban of their tribe. Each had a long-barrelled gun slung across his back and a knife in his hand. They ran steadily, with teeth clenched and eyes full of a grim purpose, hustling Saïd along with them unawares.

"Dîn! Dîn! Dîn Muhammed!"... The mountaineers, though unbelievers, joined lustily in the cry of El Islâm. They had come fifty miles in pursuit of their quarry and now they had run him to earth. "Dîn 'hammed!" a child's voice piped manfully; and Saïd beheld a little boy in a man's arms, brandishing a toy knife as he was borne along, crowing for joy of the merry race and the shouting. There was a stoppage in front; but those behind still continued to push on, regardless of the protests of such as were tall enough to see the nature of the obstacle.

The giant on Saïd's right proclaimed that certain persons of authority were sorting the crowd, sending some this way, others that, to join bands already at work. He licked his lips as he added that he himself had slain fifty Maronites between the first hour and the fourth, at the taking of Zahleh. By Allah, it was the business to whet a man's appetite. He remembered to have eaten a whole sheep that day—to have rent it limb from limb and devoured it yet warm and uncooked, he was so hungry. But his remarks were lost for the most part in the general uproar.

"Dîn! Dîn! Dîn Muhammed!..." Saïd was past the obstacle, speeding over the rough pavement of a lane in shadow. The sky, a narrow streamer of living blue, seemed to flutter and wave overhead as he ran with throbbing brow and panting chest. With the two Drûz and a hundred others he was told off to join a part of the mob who were gone to raze the house of the Muscovite Consul, whose ill-timed meddling had fired the people. The two Drûz lost their eagerness.

"What have we to do with this Frank?" Saïd heard one say to the other. "Let us turn—what sayest thou? Our enemies are yonder!"

"True," breathed the other; and they slackened so as to drop behind.

The house of the Consul was already in flames when Saïd's reinforcement came up. Little pillars and wreaths of brown smoke curled upward from it, to condense in a low cloud like a frown upon the tranquil sky. A seething, roaring throng, close-packed from wall to wall, choked every approach. By mounting on a high stone beside a doorway Saïd contrived to see what was doing.

Furniture and other goods, which the greed of the insurgents had dragged from the burning house, were being tossed back into the blaze by order of an aged man invested with some sort of authority. This person seemed some prophet or dervish—a holy man in any case, for he was naked save for a loose shirt of sackcloth, and his legs and arms were almost black through long exposure. He capered about in a solemn measure, screaming, praising Allah, and exhorting the faithful to fresh exertions.

There was a movement on the outskirts of the crowd. Where was the good in standing idle, looking on at the prowess of others, when there was work enough for every man that day?

"Dîn! Dîn! Dîn Muhammed!" . . . Even to Saïd's maddened brain it occurred that there was some rough order in the mob. A band of butchers were there in their slaughter-house garb, with long knives dripping blood not of beasts. Men forced their way into homes, he among them, upsetting costly furniture, trampling rich carpets in their zeal to seize on the inmates. These they spat upon, spurned, insulted and dragged out into the street, where the aforesaid butchers waited to despatch them.

Girls were embraced brutally and borne shrieking away in the arms of men whose clothing was bespattered with the blood of a father or mother. Crones strained and knotted their wizened throats in supplication for the spark of life that yet warmed them. Dwellings were looted, then set on fire. Saïd, in his search of the house of a rich merchant, saw a foot peeping out from a heap of bedding. He laid hold of it and, pulling with a will, elicited an old, white-bearded man whose face was grey with terror. He shrieked to Miriam, Mother of God, to help him; but Saïd had him fast by the throat, thin and gristly as a hen's, and soon pitched him headlong down a short flight of stone steps. He toppled senseless at the feet of one of the butchers, who, being idle for the moment, knifed him at once.

The thought of Ferideh, awaiting his further pleasure in the safe-keeping of old Nûr, filled the fisherman with a kind of drunken joy. She had bitten his arm last night and the wound pained him yet. What matter! There would be plenty of leisure to punish and tame her by-and-by. She would learn to worship him in the beautiful house he would build for her out of her father's hoard. His brain whirled. He had the strength of two men. He saw all things in the redness of eyelids closed against the sun; felt and cared for nothing save the lust of blood and the joy of killing. . . .
"Dîn! Dîn! Dîn Muhammed!"

A sound of firing came out of the distance—a single volley followed by faint cries. One or two strained ears to listen; but the hoarse shouts of the slayers and piercing shrieks of their victims made it hard to ascertain noises more remote. Zeal continued unabated. Men, women and children were dragged out of the shadowy doorways to be hacked to death on the causeway beneath the ribbon of peaceful blue sky which the smoke of burning houses began to veil in part. The mob jeered and reviled their last agonies. Some were found to spit in the faces of the newly slain. And the name of Allah was in every man's mouth.

Of a sudden a tremor ran through the multitude. The uproar dwindled to a murmur, above which terrified cries were heard, growing louder and nearer.

"The soldiers!"—"The soldiers have scattered us!"—"Allah destroy them!"—"They have killed Ahmed, my brother!"—"I am wounded even to death!"

The broken remnant of some other band poured headlong from the arched entry of a by-street and made haste to mingle and lose themselves in the stagnant crowd which choked their way. They came running, beards on shoulders, faces blanched with fright, and slipped in among the throng as a lizard slips under a stone for safety.

The butchers stayed their hands and wiped their knives on the skirts of their clothing. The feeders poured out of doorways to hear the news. Saïd struck a squealing Nazarene on

the head with his iron bar and looked out from the lattice of
the upper storey where he found himself. He glanced down
upon the press of dark fezzes and light turbans in fierce sunlight
and plum-coloured shadow. The sea of heads rolled purposeless like beads unstrung from a chaplet. All at once a yell of
rage uprose.

"The soldiers!—Allah cut their lives!—The soldiers!—
let us slay them!—Let us fly!—Let us stone them to death
who favour the infidels!" At the street end, where there was
a great pool of sunlight, Saïd caught the glint of gun-barrels
and recognised the uniform of the irregular troops. He saw a
sword flash as an officer of high rank flourished it; and
through all the cursing of the mob he heard a word of command, short and gruff like the grunt of a pig. A howl of exe-
cration rent the air. The front rank of the troops were taking
deliberate aim at the rioters.

Saïd beheld the surging sea of heads with the unconcerned
pity of an angel or a sage. Packed close as they were down
there, every shot must tell. He gave warm praise to Allah
Most High, who had placed his servant in that upper chamber,
whence he could observe all that passed without peril.

Then he saw a strange sight. The rabble had shrunk back
before the muzzles of the rifles covering them. Across the
space of pavement thus deserted rushed the wild figure he had
observed before the consul's house. The holy one ran up to
the officer and confronted him with gestures of command and
entreaty.

"Shall Muslim war with Muslim?" A shrill voice rang
clear on the hush which ensued. "Will you then separate
yourselves from the cause of Allah and His Apostle to side
with pagans and idolaters? Will you shoot down the servants
of the Highest like dogs? I heard a voice in the night saying, Go to the city, Es-Shâm, and tell the dwellers there: The
word of Allah to such as are faithful. Slay me the unbelievers
which aspire to sit in high places! Slay the whole race of them,
the child with the strong man, the woman giving suck with the
aged one whose eyes are dim! Let not a soul of them remain
alive, for the welfare of Islâm is in it!—Will you then anger
the Praiseworthy? Will you then . . ."

"Dîn! Dîn! Dîn Muhammed!"

The words of the saint were drowned in a shout which

thrilled Saïd to the marrow and made tears start in his eyes. The officer took a written paper embodying his orders and tore it to little pieces. The soldiers flung down their rifles with a great noise. With frantic exclamations the crowd surged towards them, enveloped them, embraced them and made them one with it. The Colonel waved his sword on high, shouting for Allah and the Prophet. It was who should kiss his hand, his scabbard, his clothing—anything that was his.

"Dîn! Dîn! Dîn Muhammed! . . ." The mob, thus reinforced, set to work once more. "To the French convent!" someone shouted. "Let the nuns be ravished and then slain!" The cry was taken up on all hands with laughter and coarse jibes. "The nuns! The nuns!" "Aha, the nuns are sweet!" "They have kept their flower for us, the darlings!" "Let us see how the nuns are fashioned!"

There was a breathless rush, of sheep following blindly the track of an unseen leader. Saïd was more than once crushed against a wall of the narrow ways they traversed; but he was stalwart and held his own. Then there was a standstill. Those in front hammered at a strong door, while those behind stood on tiptoe and craned their necks to see what was doing.

All at once there was a backward movement. Another panic got hold of the crowd. A cry, "The soldiers!" was again raised; but was received with jeers by such of the mob as were of that calling. A small troop of armed men rode up to the door of the nunnery. They were seen plainly of all, towering as they did on horseback above the seething mass on foot. Most of them rode their chargers at the foremost, who drew back in alarm; while a few, among whom was the leader, dismounted and entered the convent, the door of which was promptly opened to them.

A mighty roar went up from the multitude.

"It is Abdul Cader!"—"May Allah preserve his Grace!"—"He goes to take vengeance upon his enemies!"—"It was the French who wronged and imprisoned him, though he fought them brave as a lion!"—"He is come to claim the French nuns for his harîm!"—"Allah is just!"—"May all the Franks perish, and their women be dishonoured!"—"Long live the might of Islâm!"—"May Allah preserve Abdul Cader, the glory of the Faith!"

But applause was turned to oaths and howls of rage when the hero and his officers reappeared, escorting with respect a train of black-robed nuns, each with the obnoxious cross shining on her bosom. The horsemen closed around them as a bodyguard ; the leaders sprang to their saddles. Then the fury of the crowd broke all bounds. The coolness of the rescuers as they rode away had a point of contempt which stung the rout to madness.

"Dîn! Dîn! Dîn Muhammed!" . . . "Death to the enemies of Allah!" . . . "Who dares protect those whose lives are forfeit to Islâm!" . . . "Perish Abdul Cader!" . . . "Death to the traitors of Eljizar." Raging like a winter-torrent, the crowd surged forward in pursuit. The horsemen were constrained to a foot's pace, having regard to the women in their midst. The mob was close upon them. Stones and other missiles began to whizz through the air. Of a sudden the whole mass swayed back, every man jostling his neighbour.

Abdul Cader had turned his horse about and was sitting motionless, his eyes ranging sternly over the sea of turbaned heads and swarthy, malignant faces. A last stone, flung at random from the heart of the throng, struck his arm and made him wince. He raised a hand to his tarbûsh, commanding silence. An awe-stricken hush spread like a breath over the crowd. This man was the established idol of the populace. He was the greatest living hero of Islâm, and at heart they gloried in his intrepidity.

"What is this, O my friends?" His voice rang out clear and measured. "Will you provoke the wrath of Allah against this city? Will you anger him so that he turn away his face from us for ever? It has been told you how I have fought for Islâm—ay, and borne imprisonment and exile for our holy Faith. But I tell you I would rather be the meanest Christian slain this day in the sight of Allah than one of you whose hands are red with his blood. Shame on you, Muslimûn!—Shame on you, I say! Would to Allah I had gone to my grave ere ever this day dawned for the Faith!"

He gazed for a moment, silent on the silent crowd; then, turning, set spurs to his horse and cantered away. But the foremost, among whom was Saïd, saw that his eyes glistened.

"Dîn! Dîn! Dîn Muhammed!" It was the holy man

who raised the shout once more, waving his gnarled brown arms above the crowd. "Who dares withstand the justice of Allah? Slay him also, who rescues the condemned of God! Onward! Dîn! Dîn!"

But the words of Abdul Cader had wrought a change in the temper of the multitude. Some there were who lagged behind. Saïd's thirst for blood was somewhat slaked by this. There was time, he bethought him, to visit Ferideh and snatch a kiss from her before keeping his appointment with Mustafa. He slipped aside into an archway which gave access to a shady passage barely wide enough for two to walk abreast, and made his way by forsaken paths to the prison of his desire. And ever as he went the roar of the tumult was in his ears, now loud and near, now soft and melting in the distance, like the thunder of surf upon a rock-bound coast:

"Dîn! Dîn! Dîn Muhammed!"

XXVI

FOR once Nûr was cross with Saïd. No sooner did she understand the reason of his coming than she lifted up her voice and chid him roundly. Upon his persisting, she threw herself in his way and forbade him to advance another step. The girl was ill enough already without the aggravation of his presence. If he so much as set foot in that upper room, she (Nûr) would cease to befriend him and would let the girl go free.

Cowed by her vehemence, Saïd grumbled that he had no instant wish to harm the maid, but was come just to see how she did; with much more, scarcely audible, about his own property, and kissing, and no sin. Whereupon the old woman became herself again, called him the light of her eyes, and detecting some tell-tale stains upon his raiment soaked a rag in a vessel of water and made haste to sponge it. The strong perfume of her unguents kept him quiet and submissive while she purified him. His eyes languished and his lips parted as he inhaled it.

Bending close to him over the task,—

"It is a kindness I do thee, O my soul!" she said. "Suppose soldiers or other slaves of authority met thee with the marks of blood on thy robe, by thy beard, I think it would fare ill with thee. As for that girl thou lovest, she has been all day like a madwoman. She is deaf to all my comfortable words, and cries ever to Allah that he should take her life. She boasts that she will beat herself to death against a stone of the wall sooner than endure thy embrace; that is why I stayed thee. To-day is but the morrow of her disaster. Leave me alone to deal with her, and, after a few days, I warrant thou shalt find her tractable. When she is tame enough I shall send thee word. With thy share of the treasure of which

Mustafa speaks, thou mayest well afford to hire a fine house for her. With a fine house and a gift in thy hand what girl could gainsay thee? For thou art handsome, my dear, straight as a palm-tree, strong as a lion. Does the work of slaughter flag that thou comest hither thus early?"

Saïd told her something of the day's doings, while she, vowing that he must be famished, brought some bread and dried raisins from the inner room. He was in truth pretty hungry, though the fact had escaped his mind. His jaws worked as a busy mill to which grist came unfailingly by great handfuls. Nûr wished him two healths, and, squatting on her heels, kept her painted eyes fixed on him in a kind of dotage.

"I am sorry thou didst lose sight of Mustafa," she said at length, speaking chiefly to herself. "He was ill yesterday in the evening—very ill, so that I deemed him at the gate of death. Allah restore him to us in safety and good health!"

Saïd's utterance was somewhat choked, his mouth being crammed with leathery bread.

"Hadst thou been with us in the tumult, O my eyes, thou wouldst not marvel that we were forced asunder," he mumbled. "No man thought of his neighbour, but each ran alone for himself, taking care not to stumble lest the multitude behind should tread out his life. Praise be to Allah that he has granted me to see this day! Not a street of that quarter but has dark pools of blood on its pavement—blood of the heathen, of the unbelievers, which to shed is a pious deed. At the hour of sunset I am bound to meet Mustafa in a place appointed among the gardens. O happy day!"

"In sh'Allah, thou wilt find him in the extremity of good health!" exclaimed Nûr, rising to prepare herself a narghileh. "As for the maiden, the daughter of Yuhanna, I have said that I will tame her for thee. Seek not to approach her until I send thee word. Prepare a fine house for her and bring a gift in thy hand. Force is one way to succeed, but there is a better, I do assure thee."

The sun's rays were red upon the upper roofs when Saïd left the cellar. He saw no man in the streets save such as were very old and feeble. Veiled women and girls, some with babies in their arms, stood chattering together in doorways or at the cross-roads. They called to him for news.

In passing the tavern of Abu Khalîl, he beheld the fat host seated on a stool in the doorway, wide awake, his face expressive of the deepest disgust. He appeared to be afflicted with an itch in the calf of his leg, for he was scratching the place slowly and woefully with a shard.

"Peace on thee, O Abu Khalîl!" cried the fisherman as he sped by.

"Upon thee be the peace, and the mercy of Allah and his blessings!" retorted the taverner, with a dismal groan. "But say, why dost thou hasten? Stay a little and tell me, hast thou heard aught of my son?—of Camr-ud-dîn? The villain escaped about the second hour. Doubtless, he is with the slayers—curse his religion! and behold there is none left to serve in the house, his mother being sick this day. Wait a minute, I say—may thy house be destroyed!"

But Saïd only cried "Allah comfort thee!" over his shoulder as he hurried on. The thought of Mustafa and the treasure lent wings to his feet. Besides, it seemed a small matter that Abu Khalîl should lack his son's help that day, seeing it was a dull time of business, all likely customers keeping festival elsewhere. A surge-like roar was ever in his ears, loud or distant according to the trend of the streets he traversed.

Turning a sharp corner, he collided with a man in as great a hurry as himself. The shock was very great. Saïd rubbed himself ruefully, and so did the stranger. They were about to curse each other and pursue their several ways when recognition turned their gall to honey. The fisherman blessed Selîm, and Selîm blessed the fisherman. They embraced, and Saïd, having a view to his own profit, inquired with what eye his Excellency, the Waly, deigned to regard the disturbance.

"Alas!" cried the other, lifting hands and eyes towards as much of the purpled heaven as was visible between the roof-lines, "my lord is distraught with grief. The Franks ply him ever with angry demands that he take instant measures to put down the tumult. Allah knows that he has done all that was in his power to do. The garrison was divided in two companies, and sent forth with orders to fire on the rebels without mercy. One division with its officers deserted to the people; the other, after firing one volley and wreaking great havoc, was withdrawn lest they too should make common cause with the insurgents. The Council was summoned, and Ahmed Basha signed with his own hand a paper declaring that the Government can do nothing. He sent an express for Abdul Cader, but was refused because Abdul Cader and all his followers were busy rescuing great numbers of the Nazarenes and conveying them by families to the castle. He invited the Basha to bring but fifty armed men and ride with him, saying that with so small a reinforcement as that he would undertake to quell the riot in a few hours.

"It was Selìm who was charged with the message, and I would to Allah it had been some other. For my lord began to weep and wring his hands, being, as I guess, afraid for his life to ride forth, yet ashamed to play the coward in the sight of an old lion like Abdul Cader. Before I left his presence he took a leaf of paper and began to draw upon it what seemed a plan of the city, crying, 'Thus and thus it should have been. So and so I should have acted.' It was as though the squeak of the reed on the leaf brought comfort to him. Poor great man! I tell thee, my heart was sick for pity of him. All in the palace agree that the Franks will have him slain for this hesitation which is his infirmity.

"I go now to buy a little food for those who have taken refuge in the palace-yard. There is a great crowd, and who can tell how long the slaughter will last? Many must die of hunger, and that is not pleasant to see in the court of the house where one dwells. To slay a foe in anger, and his woman, and his sons and daughters, is natural for all the Franks say. It is natural that a man should seek to destroy his enemy once for all, and wash the land clean of his name. Vengeance of blood, from what they say, is a thing unknown among the Franks. The price of blood has no claim among their customs. Were it otherwise, they would better understand our manner of warfare. But what do I, loitering by the way? In thy grace, O my brother! Allah guard thee till we meet again!"

When Saïd at length passed out at the town-gate, twilight was rising from the ground. Shadows, which were half a light, floated among the tree-trunks. He had yet a good way to go, and the sun was set; he hurried on, therefore, along a fair road almost roofed with leafage and bordered by hedges which smelt sweet. In a place where black trees of mournful seeming grew sparsely amid a wilderness of white stones, he beheld veiled figures flitting darkly among the tombs and knew them for women caring for their dead.

The zeal of the faithful must have waned with the sun, for he overtook and passed several groups of men, dusty and disordered; and, as he crossed a bridge, the twang of an aûd and wailing chant of a singer reached him from some tavern down the stream. Nevertheless, he still heard the roar of the tumult through a tremulous veil, as it were, of nearer sounds—the droning plaint of the singer, the bark of a dog, chirping of birds, croaking of frogs, the murmur of the stream and the rustle of leaves. It was the same roar that he had heard on awaking, only fainter and with a note of satiety. He wondered what the drum was that had been beating all day, and was beating yet somewhere in the city. And even as he listened and wondered, the cry of the muezzin rose shrill above the din, followed by another—by a host of others, until all the plain was filled with their message. The turmoil sank and died away. The drum was no more heard. The unbelievers enjoyed a respite while the faithful said their prayers.

Selecting a little patch of grass by the wayside, beneath a great mulberry-tree, Saïd fell on his face and gave praise and thanks to Allah. It pleased him to think on how few days of his life he had omitted to pray at each appointed hour. He asked Allah to forgive him the omissions, not to let them weigh against his virtues to destroy him. Then, shrugging his shoulders resignedly, he rose, inhaled a perfumed breath of the night, and murmured, "Allah is just!"

At the point where a garden-track branched from the main road, and blunting the angle, stood a building one would have taken for a large wely or saint's tomb, flanked and dwarfed by twin cypress-trees. A pious foundation from of old, it served the double purpose of a fountain and a place of rest for wayfarers. It consisted of a centre arch, admitting to the spout and trough, and of a recess on either hand; and was surmounted by three domes in proportion to these divisions, that in the middle being much higher than the other two, which peeped over the square roof as a skull-cap shows above a turban.

The fountain whitened in the half light amid the gloom of the surrounding foliage. The two cypress-trees stood up blackly, their tufts cutting the green sky. Saïd's eagerness grew apace. He walked faster and faster, and was on the point of girding up his loins to run when a loud voice turned him to stone. It was the voice of Mustafa, but it had a new intonation which made his flesh creep. It came from within the building, very harsh upon the evening murmur and the twilight, which, between them, were soft as velvet.

"Allah will give to you!" There was something fierce and exultant in the cry, which assorted gruesomely with that prayer for alms. "Allah will give to you! . . . I slew him, I tell you. . . . See, I have a withered hand. O hand of my honour—O blessed hand! . . . O Lord! . . . Take pity, O my masters, or I die. . . . Allah witness, I slew him. Aha, he was fat and lay on a bed of down, whereas I. . . . O Lord! . . . Allah will give to you! . . . I am poor and lean while you are fat and dwell in palaces. See the stains on my hand. . . . O hand of my love—O happy left hand! Take pity, hear you?—or I will slay all the race of you, fat men that lie on soft cushions. . . . Aha, you look very funny, all you fat ones with your mouths open, lying on green couches and your eyes turned over in your heads. It is a merry sight. . . . O Lord! . . . Have compassion or I die. Merciful Allah, is there none to pity me? . . . Behold my father's house is washed clean of the reproach. . . . Blood! . . . I see blood!—blood everywhere—blood of pigs—blood of unbelievers. Lo! the stream of it rises up to heaven, and it is counted to me for righteousness. Allah rejoices! The Prophet smiles at God's right hand! . . . O Lord! . . . Death to the unbelievers! Perish the Christians! Dîn! Dîn! . . ."

Daunted by the hideous outcry and the gathering night, Saïd stood still, shuddering, until the voice died away upon a frightful shriek. Then he ran forward.

"May his house be destroyed," he breathed ruefully between his clenched teeth. "It is sure he is possessed with a devil. Why else should he cry aloud to summon all men to the secret place of our wealth!" The recess on either side of the fountain was very dark. Saïd stood by the trough of stone and whispered his friend's name. He spoke it aloud, then shouted it, then made the vault ring with it on a despairing yell of terror. Dead silence and a darkness which the tinkle of a slender thread of water made hollow as a bell; more than all, the echo of his own voice almost killed him with fright. He was haunted, the sport of malicious fiends. They were mocking him somewhere in the gloom, pointing at him and laughing noiselessly. He was minded to run, but his feet were become of one piece with the uneven pavement. It was that hopeless, blind terror which knows no beyond—the despair of a child alone in the dark. He shut his eyes; but fear lined their lids with eyes and wheels of flame, which rolled and dilated, scathing his very soul. Sure that dreadful shapes were drawing near him, he opened them from excess of fear; and, seeing nothing, was ten times more frightened than before. He breathed hard.

However, as long seconds passed and nothing happened, little by little the panic left him, and his wits, faint and trembling, returned to him. The arch by which he had entered was full of dark forms of trees quivering upon a starry sky. He heard the howl and yelp of a jackal; no doubt there were vineyards near with green clusters of half-formed grapes such as foxes love. The well-known sound and the everyday thoughts it engendered calmed him somewhat. A jangle of bells approaching along the road wholly reassured him. For all that, it was with heart in mouth that he stepped into the recess whence the cry of Mustafa had seemed to proceed.

Straining his ears to retain the friendly sound of the camel-bells, he passed a hand along the wall. All at once he stumbled on something. He stooped down to feel what it might be.

"O Mustafa!" he whispered fiercely, "what is this? . . . Arise! Awake! Say, where is our treasure? Let us take each his share and return with speed to the city. Come, awake, I say! Make haste!"

No answer. The mass was inert as he shook it; an arm flopped and that was all. He had nothing wherewith to get a light, and it was very dark. Yet he felt brave and master of himself, for the clangour of bells was drawing near and he could hear the voice of a camel-driver chanting in praise of love.

He found the old man's head and placed his hand over his mouth.   There was no warmth of a breath; the lips were cold and sticky.   Then Saïd knew for certain that he was handling a dead body.

XXVII

SAÏD shuddered, not so much for the knowledge of his own uncleanness, nor for the fear of death, as for the loneness of this end by the roadside and for horror of the wild cry he had heard. Since last the sun rose he had been present at the killing of many men and women. But they all had perished in the open street in the sunlight, amid the shouting of a great multitude, with prayers and curses on their lips; whereas Mustafa had met death in the dark, in a lonely place with none to witness.

He thought of the treasure, that it was now all his own; and sorrow, like a spring of sweet water, welled up in his heart for the loss of his more than father. But the next minute he wished Mustafa no good for dying ere he had made him privy to the hiding-place. By Allah, a loose stone in the pavement was not so easy to find in the darkness, without lamp or direction, and with a corpse for company.

The clash of bells grew very near indeed. The chant ceased, and the singer shouted to a comrade at some distance. Then the bells lost their rhythmic chime and jangled confusedly. The train of camels had halted.

Soon an unwieldy, groaning bulk was led in to drink at the fountain. Saïd stood very still against the wall of his recess, watching the black shapes fearfully, quaking for his treasure, lest the drivers should strike a light or any movement of his should rouse suspicion. There were sounds of sucking, gurgling and groaning, the swinging tramp of great beasts, and a hairy smell. He heard the voices of the men debating whether to enter the city in its present disturbed state or to sleep at a khan they named without the gate. He grew fretful, burning to begin his search for the treasure. It must be taken away at once, lest the discovery of Mustafa's body should lead to a thorough search of the place.

At length the last camel was watered and he could hear the men swear as they marshalled the train. The rhythmic clangour broke out afresh. With an oath of relief he began to crawl upon his hands and knees, feeling the pavement stone by stone as he went. He felt everywhere to within a hair's-breadth of the corpse; but not a slab was loose, though he fancied one or two rang hollow as he rapped them. The camel bells were but a tinkle in the distance. He was alone and fear breathed hot upon him.

In a kind of fury he gripped the dead man's arm and dragged him into a corner. With the shiver of that contact upon him he knelt down to examine the place where the body had lain. There was a stone cast up—a wide hole. Oh, for a little light!

He let his forearm down into it; and his hand felt gold, both coinage and jewellery, which seemed to be contained in a strong coffer of iron or brass, of which the lid was open. Lying flat on his belly, with both arms in the hole, he long strove to lift that chest—by the lid, by the side—but it would not budge. Then he thought if he could only get his fingers under it he would have better purchase. He needed something thin yet strong to thrust beneath it as a prise.

"May Allah cut short his life!" he panted. "Who but a madman would have left our wealth thus exposed? By the Prophet, it is lucky that I alone was at hand to hear his last cry. . . . May his house be destroyed."

"Peace to him," he added as an afterthought, setting to work once more. He took a knife from his girdle, and managed so to force its stout blade under the treasure-box that his fingers could take hold. He tugged and strained, tendons cracking, sweat streaming from every pore. At last, after many failures, he raised it clear out of the hole and set it on the pavement. Praise to Allah!

Sitting back on his heels to recover breath he mopped his face with the lap of his robe. Mustafa was indeed a marvel of strength to have carried that burden with anything like secrecy from the house of Yuhanna hither. He turned the miracle over in his mind, seeking its human side. Of a sudden he recalled how the old man had spoken of the fountain as a place where he was used to hide trifles of price. The riddle was solved; there was no great wonder after all. The strong chest was the beggar's own. He had brought the wealth of Yuhanna hither in a sack, or some vessel unlikely to raise suspicion. He had then uncovered the hole, opened the chest, and poured the treasure pell-mell upon its contents. This evening he had naturally wished to gaze upon his riches. And even as his eyes were glutted the angel of death had passed over him.

Saïd's heart grew faint with rapture as he thought that here was more than all the treasure of the Christian. Allah alone knew what hoards Mustafa might have amassed during long years of begging and pilfering.

"Thanks be to Allah!" he murmured. "May Allah increase thy goods, O abu Mansûr!"

But the question was urgent—How to dispose of all this wealth for the time being? He dared not replace it, lest, when men came to remove the body of Mustafa, they should chance upon the loose slab and haply discover it. To bury it somewhere in the darkness and return with a sack in the early morning seemed a bright thought; but he could not regard it with perfect favour, knowing what mischievous devils lurk at night in lonesome places. A jinni might see him bury the chest and play some vile prank such as turning the gold to dross, or ashes, or salt, or freezing the ground above it to solid rock.

At last he resolved to take his fortune along with him in the pendant sack of his voluminous trousers. A weight down there would attract no notice, for it is the custom of all men to carry their marketings thus—their implements or whatever is cumbrous in the hand. He stood and pulled up his over-robe. Holding up the placket of his pantaloons, he took money and jewels by handfuls and dropped them in. Passing his hand along the bottom of the coffer to be sure it was quite empty, he found a small coin which he left for an alms or gleaning. He took a step to and fro to see how it felt. The treasure swung as a solid whole, bumping his ankles, his shins, and the calves of his legs. There was no clink or jingle to betray its nature. It was clumsy, very uncomfortable, but (praise to Allah!) quite safe.

He squatted to replace the chest and close the hole. The posture was restful, for while it lasted the pavement bore his burden. Then he rose, and, with a faint glance towards the carcase of Mustafa, moved gingerly away. But no sooner had he turned his back upon the dead than a panic got hold of him. He stumbled through the archway out into the whispering night as fast as the weight of his treasure would allow.

Weary and bruised all over, he sank within the threshold of Nûr's dwelling, bumping against a small donkey, saddled and hung about with gaudy tassels, which stood there patiently with swishing tail. A lamp was burning on the floor of the inner room, and Saïd could see the vast bulk of Abu Khalîl seated beside the mistress in a languorous attitude. Nûr rose full of reproach on beholding the fisherman.

"Thou art returned, O my soul? What is this? Did I not counsel thee not to come nigh her for a while? Moreover, it is not safe for thee to be here. Search may perhaps be made; all wise men concerned in the riot sleep beyond the walls to-night. Our friend, Abu Khalîl, is come seeking news of his son, Camr-ud-dîn . . ."

Peering into his face she broke off and cried,—

"How is Mustafa? Where is he? Speak!"

"O Nûr, Mustafa is dead!" murmured Saïd with a woeful shake of the head. And in truth his heart was near to breaking, for the treasure had barked the shins of both his legs, not to speak of ankles and the great weight to carry.

She screamed,—

"Just Allah! Hearest thou that, O Abu Khalîl? . . . O day of disaster! O evil day! . . . Where is he? Lead me to him! None but Nûr shall lay him out for burial! . . . Hearken, O Saïd—O son of his soul and heir of all his wealth! I will hire a goodly company of women to bewail him with beating of breasts and tearing of hair. Thou wilt not grudge the money, for thou art a rich man through his death. . . . Where is he? Lead me to him!"

Very mournfully Saïd told her that the body lay a long way off, in the chamber of a certain fountain among the gardens. He recounted the cry he had heard, the sudden silence, and his finding Mustafa dead in the black recess.

"Allah is just!" he said. "It were well if some men set out at once to fetch him hither, for I heard the voice of a jackal near to that place, and I would not have my father's corpse a prey to unclean beasts. For myself, I am weary and broken with grief, I may not return thither. I am now a rich man, as thou sayest, the wealth of Mustafa being greater than any man supposed. Let the burial be according to thy desire."

During the narrative Abu Khalîl had risen slowly from the couch and dragged his vast bulk to the door to listen. Hearing talk of the wealth of Mustafa, he appeared dazed, and exclaimed, "Ma sh'Allah!" under his breath. He strove to treat Saïd as the heir, with a deference which old habits of patronage made to sit awkwardly upon him. Nûr was suddenly inspired. She laid her hands wheedlingly on the shoulders of the fat taverner and, darting love into his eyes,—

"O my beloved," she pleaded, "thou wilt go to the fountain of which Saïd speaks. Thou canst find a neighbour or two to go with thee: and thou wilt bring hither the body of Mustafa! Saïd, as thou seest, is broken with fatigue, else he would bear thee company. I shall be very grateful to thee, O my soul, and I shall await thee here. . . . Say not 'Nay'!" she cried impetuously, discounting his scandalised stare by a pout and a girlish gesture. "I beseech thee, cross me not in this matter. He was a rich man, remember; and thou wilt not only oblige me, that am a woman and of no account, but also confer a favour upon Saïd Effendi, heir to all his wealth, who will henceforth rank with the great ones of Es-Shâm. . . . What sayest thou?"

Abu Khalîl, greatly perturbed, pushed his turban awry the better to scratch his head. He glanced furtively from Nûr to Saïd, and from Saïd back again to Nûr.

"Now, by Allah, this is no light thing you require of me. Nevertheless, since it is the case of an old friend . . . and to serve Saïd Effendi whom, I call Allah to witness, I have ever regarded as a favourite son . . . I say not that I will not go. For all that, it is a hard thing for an old man, the father of a family, to go out by night into the gardens where, as all men know, gipsies and other children of sin do abound; not to speak of those who are more than men—jin, I mean, and afârît; and the uncleanness I shall incur, and the tedious purification to follow . . ."

Said broke in coaxingly,—

"Be assured, O Abu Khalîl, O lord of kindness, thou shalt have a large reward; may Allah increase thy property!"

"Good. I go!"

Abu Khalîl shuffled to the place where the ass stood swishing its tail, and bestrode it so earnestly that he nearly fell over on the other side.   Then, remembering that his steed was tethered, he leaned over its head to untie the rope.   Nûr led the staggering beast up the steps and out into the alley, which the beams of a rising moon were beginning to silver.

"I will seek out Zeid the carpenter and Abbâs the Nubian who sells sweet stuff!" said the taverner, bowing his head to avoid contact with the lintel as he rode out.   "Both are young men, strong and fearless.   Both have donkeys belonging to them, so that we shall seem a goodly company riding together. Moreover, Abbâs has a rare whip he showed me yesterday, being a strip of the hide of a crocodile or other monster common in Masr where he bought it.   By Allah, it is a fine thong !   Two strokes of it would flay a dog. . . .   In your grace !"

"With my peace.   Allah guard thee in safety !" cried Saïd and Nûr in one breath as the doughty taverner ambled away in moonlight and shadow, thwacking his steed bravely on the hindmost part.   The clip-clap of the donkey's hoofs and its thousand mocking echoes soon died away.

Nûr stood in the doorway looking after him.   She stepped forth into the street and listened towards the Christian quarter.

"The tumult still continues," she said, returning.   "It is thin now and feeble—the shadow of that I heard during the day.   With the dawn it will revive ; and so it will be for many days till every Nazarene is either slain or escaped far away. There is a redness of fire on the sky yonder, where all day long there was a cloud of smoke.   They have slain Allah knows how many hundred Christians ; and Mustafa is dead.

"My heart is very sad, O Saïd, light of my eyes !   Hadst thou seen him as he was when first I knew him, thou wouldst grieve for the days of a man which are as steps hewn in the rock leading downward to a sepulchre.   He was a fine man, I tell thee—straight as a Bedawi's lance, strong and healthy even as thou art.   As the breath of winter tears leaves from a mulberry-tree, so does the length of years strip the beauty and the majesty from a man.   At last the tree falls and only the bitter wind remains. . . .   Allah is greatest !"

Saïd groaned aloud,—

"Allah is merciful! But, by my beard, it was a cruel word thou spakest, that I must go sleep without the city. Only let me abide here and I swear I will not go near the girl to trouble her."

"It cannot be," said Nûr, firmly. "My house is thy house, and thou art ever welcome to that which is mine. But Abu Khalîl has heard a rumour that search is made secretly for the leaders in rebellion. It is true, what I told thee, that no wise man sleeps within the city this night. To-morrow, in the day-time, thou mayst show thyself without fear; the slaves of power will then be fast within doors for terror of their lives. I will care for the girl and order all things seemly for the burial of Mustafa. Go quickly, with my peace!"

Saïd, who, for all his freedom of address, stood greatly in awe of the old woman, rose grumbling from the floor, and, holding up the pouch of his trousers like a sack, stumbled up the steps into the moonshine. His nether limbs were very sore and stiff with bruises. In walking he was careful to keep his feet wide apart. He cut such a queer figure, seen from behind, that Nûr called after him to know what ailed him.

"I am happy—in the extremity of good health!" he cried back with affected cheerfulness. "I did but trip over a stone as I ran hither. My knees are somewhat bruised from the fall."

"Stay, O my eyes, and let me rub them with a salve!" she cried again with seduction; for, contrasting his gait with the tones of his voice, she knew that he lied.

"May thy wealth increase!—there is no need," he answered, striving to quicken his step.

From a rhythmic bellying of the skirt of his long robe, as well as from the manner of his going, Nûr made a shrewd guess at the nature of his embarrassment.

"He walks like a she-goat whose udders are overfull," she thought, laughing to herself; "there is something heavy and cumbersome in the sack of his trousers."

That he was loth to linger or speak of the matter afforded her more light.

"By the Coràn, it is the treasure of Mustafa he carries thus for safety, lest one should rob him of it! He would not trust me so much as to let me know, and he bears his punishment along with him.   Allah is just ! "

And in the midst of her grief for the old beggar she chuckled most heartily out there in the moonlight, pointing the finger of scorn after him with keen and friendly relish of his avarice.

XXVIII

THAT was a ghastly night for Saïd—a night full of strange faces, of awful whisperings, and of the shadow of death. His first thought on leaving the city was to find some shelter where he might sleep within call of his fellow-men. To that end he sought the coffee-house of Rashìd, thinking to find a welcome there now that he was again on cordial terms with Selìm. But as he went, in the tremulous shadow of the trees and the moonlight between, he grew more and more afraid, until the bump of the treasure against his shins and the patter of his own footsteps were separate terrors.

It was almost within hail of the tavern, in the gloom of some apricot-trees, that he blundered upon something soft, yet tight, like a body or a full waterskin. He drew back aghast. A shapeless mass rose before him with a horrid groan. Catching up the sack of his trousers he ran for dear life. Far from allaying his terrors the lowing of a cow at his back lashed him to fresh exertions. He knew it for the angry voice of a jinni cursing him.

For hours he fled on by shadowy ways, pursued by a host of devils. Foul shapes flitted and danced behind him; dread hands were stretched out to stay him and clutch his treasure; a flapping of huge wings filled the welkin. Pale faces he had seen in death that day grinned at him from the ground, from the sky, from the gloom of the trees. Even the dwellings of men—a sleeping village half-seen between the trunks, flat-roofed hovels and pleasure-houses bosomed in foliage—were sinister, the abode of unknown fears. Fiends rollicked over the whole earth. The vista of his life was packed with them —a gruesome throng. From his youth up he had been their sport. In the hour of his prosperity, whenever wealth had seemed within his grasp, they had appeared to balk him. His flight from his native town, the loss of his donkey, the robbery

M   177

which had deprived him of the price of his horse—he saw plainly the cause of all his misfortunes. Then, as now, he had been the butt of evil spirits.

Of a sudden it occurred to him that the whole night was a procession of ghastly, pallid shapes, moving silently as one man. It seemed that he had a moment's insight into the hidden mysteries of earth, that this gliding march of a vast, fiendish army, unsuspected of men, had been going on ever since the world began, and would continue unbroken till the Last Day. The horror of it was not new to him. He had experienced it before many times, but could not remember when or under what circumstances.

Was not Abdullah himself an evil spirit? And the soldier who had lifted his donkey—was he not an afrìt in disguise? There was no doubt of it now as he recalled their faces.

In his despair he thought lovingly of Hasneh. Why—oh, why had he cast her off? To his fevered brain she seemed desirable as on the day when he had first beheld her, a young girl, at play with other maidens on the seashore. He would have given the half of this treasure which was killing him for a touch of her hand, for the sound of her voice.

Once he stood still in an open place. He had a mind to lighten his trousers by flinging all his wealth upon the ground. It was for that that the hordes of darkness were tormenting him. He cried aloud that all of them might know his purpose, and bade them swear a solemn oath that they would let him go in peace. But there came no answer; only a jackal's cry out of the distance, ending in three short yaps. It rang derisive—very like a laugh. At that Saïd grew dogged. Since not a jinni of them all would swear, it was their lookout and he would keep the treasure. For two seconds he felt courageous and knew that there were trees about him rustling peacefully in the moonlight.

Fear breathed hot on him again and he ran, a hideous whisper in his ears. The balm of the silky Eastern night had no sweetness for him. Shifting the sack of his trousers from aching hand to hand, striving to keep his mind intent upon the name of Allah, he fled on. The trees thinned about him; the gardens gave place to vineyards; the vineyards thinned in their turn with spaces of waste land between; the wide

plain rolled out before him with soft undulations to some
low hills on the horizon floating in pale haze. The boundless
silence throbbed in his ears like the pulse of a living creature.
The plain whitened in the moonshine. Here and there, as
the ground waved, there were ribs of velvet gloom. A lonely
tree, a peasant's hovel, a dark patch of cultivated land, a
square-built khan, a knoll, a jutting boulder—the least object
was distinct with a black shadow on the smooth-rolling
expanse.

With a clear view all round him and no shades to irk his
fancy, Saïd's panic subsided to a holy awe and he slackened
his pace. He was very weary, the weight of his wealth seeming more than he could bear. The howl of a wakeful dog was
wafted to him from the distance. In the quarter whence it
came black specks were discernible upon a rising ground.
It was an encampment of Bedawin or gipsies, Saïd supposed,
and instinctively turned his face thitherward. But care for
his treasure and the fear of marauders prevented him, and he
held straight on.

There was already a bite of dawn in the air when he came
to a large khan, square-built and frowning like a fort, and
caught the welcome tinkle and stamp of beasts in a stable.
There was a well before the gate, watched by a great sycamore
tree. The door was open. Saïd stole among the beasts in
the yard and found a snug nook amid a pile of bales. With
a sigh of contentment he curled himself up and fell fast
asleep.

He dreamed.

It was the last day, or he was newly dead; he knew not
which. He was lying spellbound in a place of tombs. Mustafa
lay not far from him with a great stone at his head. Veiled
women flitted to and fro like phantoms. He knew without
looking that Hasneh was among them, and his soul yearned
after her. On either side the stone stood an angel, black and
shadowy, with a mace in his hand. There was a balance
between them, hanging in the air, and they were weighing
the works of Mustafa. All that was good went into the one
scale and all that was evil into the other. The faces of the ex-
aminers were set and moody, as those of men who watch a
grave issue. Ever and anon they beat the old man's head
with their maces, so that he shrieked frightfully. Saïd sweated

cold with fear lest Mustafa should lose Paradise, and also for his own turn, which was to come.

"This soul is lost, O brother," said one, gravely. "Thy scale kicks the beam, though each deed placed there counts two of what is placed in mine. Allah is just!"

The other was thoughtful for a space. All at once his stern face brightened. A glory like moonlight emanated from it, flooding all the plain.

"See!" he cried, pointing towards the city. "There is blood—blood of the heathen!—blood of unbelievers!—blood of the enemies of our Master! There is a great pool of it, and it is counted to him for righteousness!"

At that Saïd waxed faint with relief. Hasneh bent over him and peace dropped from her like a precious ointment. The vision faded. There was sweet music of bells—a caravan passing in the distance. With a deep sigh he awoke to a deafening clangour of real camel-bells and the pungent reek of a stable.

It was quite dark and a little chilly. But the khan was astir, and through the gate he could see a white eye of dawn opening over the edge of the desert. Men with lanterns moved sleepily among the beasts. A group of camels were being laden with black mill-stones, each of which it took four men to lift and hold in position, while a fifth lashed it fast with a strong rope. The task was enlivened by a chant panted in cadence, invoking the help of a holy dervish long since in Paradise.

Another and more numerous train of camels had just arrived. They were laden with sacks of corn and seemed to have been journeying all night, for the drivers were stiff and surly. With them was a woman of wretched appearance, who stood timidly in the gate, trying to dispose her tattered veil so as to conceal her face.

A bare-legged hostler threw a coarse jest at her in passing. An idler pinched her arm and tore aside her veil, vowing he was sick for love of her. But a sturdy old man, one of the camel-drivers with whom she had come, interfered. He pushed her insulter away roughly, saying that she was a good woman and none should vex her while he was by.

In the hope of a quarrel, Saïd stole forward among the beasts and merchandise, careful to lift the sack of his trousers above contact with any of the coils of rope, halters and saddles which cumbered the ground. The other camel-drivers stopped work and gathered about the disputants. But the aggressor was a coward, or he thought the woman not worth a fight, for he slunk off, muttering that he knew not she belonged to any man there. Her champion contented himself with nodding his head after him and explaining pithily, in a long growl, how he would have punished obstinacy. Their forms moved black in the gateway; beyond them was the grey dawn upon the plain.

"The woman is thine, O sheykh?" asked one who stood by with a lantern.

"No, by Allah!" answered the champion, with a shade of defiance; "but I hold her as a dear daughter. When I cut my foot upon a stone in the neighbourhood of Mazarîb and thought to die for loss of blood, she used me tenderly and rent her veil that my wound might be softly bandaged. No, she is not my woman, but was given into my care by the men of Beyt Ammeh beside Nablûs. There is a strange story belonging to her."

At the name of Beyt Ammeh, Saïd pricked up his ears. Observing the form of the woman narrowly, his heart leapt so that it became a lump in his throat.

"The story, O sheykh! Deign to tell us the story!" urged the bystanders. Unnoticed, Saïd joined the press about the narrator.

"Know that this woman had a husband, a fisherman, whose name was Saïd. He set out on a journey to Damashc-ush-Shâm, the woman with him. In a lonely pass of the mountains between Beyt Ammeh and the sea he met a man called Farûn riding on a camel, asleep. Then Saïd, being a joker, picked up a stone from the path and flung it at Farûn so that he fell to the ground. And as he lay there, stunned and bleeding, Saïd took all the money that he had and beat him somewhat with a stick, and so left him.

"Saïd went on his way rejoicing until he came to the village of Beyt Ammeh. There, his woman being faint, he entered the house of a certain fellah, who took pity on her and let her lie on his own bed. After that, as they sat smoking and conversing, the lord of the house questioned

Saïd, saying, 'Didst meet in thy road hither one riding on a camel? Behold, my brother, Farûn by name, is gone this day to the coast with a load.' Then Saïd—a clever fellow, by Allah!—answered thoughtfully, 'Yes, it is true; I met such an one. I found him by the road in a sad plight. His blood was upon the stones of the path. He had been robbed and almost killed by wicked men. I stayed a little to bind his wounds, and gave him money—all that I had. I caught his camel and set him upon it. Then I blessed him and came on hither.'

"At that the lord of the house praised and exalted Saïd above all the sons of Adam. He besought him to abide there several days. But Saïd, pretending that his brother was dead in Damashc-ush-Shâm, said that he must hasten to claim the inheritance. Nevertheless, since his woman was sick, he entreated that kind man to take care of her until she should recover her strength. The lord of the house agreed gladly, and when he had given Saïd to eat and drink, he blessed him and let him go. He paid great honour to the woman for the sake of the mercy shown by her husband to Farûn, his brother. But after two days Farûn returned, and then, as you may guess, his mind was changed. All the men of Beyt Ammeh cursed that clever joker who, having first robbed and beaten Farûn, had then left his sick woman to the care of Farûn's brother. They kept her for two months, making her the common drudge of all, supposing that Saïd would return or send to fetch her, when they would have slain him or his messengers as the case might be. But he was too clever for that. By Allah, he is a devil! He had no care for this woman, for it seems she is barren.

"So at last, weary of her sighs and weeping, they delivered her over to us as we passed through their village, telling us her story and giving us a little money to take her to Es-Shâm. They charged us, if ever we should meet with Saïd the Fisherman, to slay him without ado for the affront put upon their village. But I admire the rogue. He is a famous joker—what say you? . . . By my beard, he is a devil!"

In the midst of the laughter at his cleverness, Saïd pushed through the group and confronted the woman. "Welcome, and thrice welcome, O Hasneh!" he cried. "Praise be to Allah, thou art alive and in health! My heart has been very sad for thee all this long time. I am rejoiced to find thee once again, O my soul!"

Throwing up her arms, with a shrill cry, she fell on his neck and wept.

"It is Saïd the Fisherman!"—"Saïd the Joker!"—"Saïd the Devil!" "How came he hither?" was whispered in tones of awe; as who should say, It is His Majesty the Sultàn—His Excellency the Basha. Men pressed forward to touch but the hem of his robe, to get but a glimpse of his face; so that Saïd began to fear lest the fulness and weight of his trousers should be remarked. He saluted the company, and circling Hasneh with his arm, led her out into the brisk air of the dawning.

At the angle of the wall which looks towards the desert they sat down on their heels side by side. He told of the awful night he had just passed, and she listened, with patient eyes devouring him.

"I am rich, O my beloved!" he cried, plucking at a dew-drenched thistle. "I will buy a fine house where we shall dwell together. Thou shalt rule over a numerous harìm. I have a sweet girl—a beauty!—the daughter of a Christian pig who is slain. She shall be thy handmaid to do thy bidding. Let us abide here to-day, for while the tumult continues there is neither buying nor selling in the city. . . ."

He paused, thoughtful, remembering the burial of Mustafa and his duty to be present. But reflecting that men would suppose him with the slayers, and excuse him for the cause of the Faith, his brow cleared directly and he continued,—

"To-morrow, or the next day, we will return thither, when thou shalt help me to choose a grand house, and shalt see the girl Ferideh of whom I spake. She is sweet, I tell thee—a perfect pearl. But thou art mistress of my fancy—that is understood. Now, in the name of Allah relieve me of some part of this treasure which bruises my legs and impedes my going."

The prospect seemed very bright to Hasneh. She ceased to grieve that her veil was torn. Gladly she opened the bosom of her robe and bestowed the half of their riches in the pouch she wore there. The transfer made, Saïd rose and took a turn to enjoy his novel lightness. The well and the sycamore tree grew rosy, casting long blue shadows. The wide plain was barred and flecked with pink.

"O Saïd, dost thou remember the fig-tree and our house among the sandhills by the sea?" murmured Ḥasneh; and then, with a blissful sigh, her eyelids closed against the sun's first ray, "Allah is Merciful!"

END OF PART I

NOTES TO PART I

TIME TABLE

A.D.				Year of the Hejra (Lunar).
622 (16th of July).	.	.	The flight of Muhammed the Prophet from Mecca to Medina. . . .	—
1831.	.	.	Ibrahim Pasha, adopted son of the Khedive Mehemed Ali, conquers Syria. Battle of Konia. . .	1256-7.
1831-1840.	.	.	A time of great prosperity for all classes, Christians and Moslems alike, under an enlightened government. . .	—
1840.	.	.	Syria signed back to the Sultan at Conference of London. . . .	—
1858.	.	.	Bombardment of Jedda by the French as a punishment for the massacre there.	1275.
1860 (March-April).			Saïd leaves his native town, his house and his fig-tree by the seashore. .	—
1860 (June).	.	.	The Maronites attack the Drûz and are slaughtered all over Lebanon. .	1277.
1860 (June-July).	.		Great massacre of Damascus. . .	1277.
1860 (September).	.		Execution of Ahmed Pasha, Waly of Damascus, for culpable incompetence shown during the massacre. . .	1278.

185

CHAPTER XIX.—"The House of Islâm and the House of War." All the territory successively annexed to the rising of the Ottoman Empire was classed either as forming part of the "dar ul Islâm," the house of Islâm, or as belonging to the "dar ul harb," or the house of war, according as it was inhabited by Mohammedans or by Christians. In the latter case the new subjects of the Sultan were called "rayahs," and they were personally assessed to ransom their lives, which were forfeited by defeat, and as an equivalent for military service from which they were exempted, or rather, which they did not enjoy the privilege of rendering. This capitation-tax received the name of "haratsh," and its payment entitled each Christian to keep his head on his shoulders for the space of one year. (Skene: *Anadol, or the Last Home of the Faithful.*)

CHAPTER XIX.—"When the first of the sevens," etc. "It was predicted in the beginning of the present century by a much-revered sheikh that when the first of the sevens falls the ruin of Islam will commence, and when the second falls it will have been completed. We are now in the year of the Hegira 1277 ; the year about to open will invert the first of the two Arabic sevens read from right to left—V becoming Λ ; that is, 7 becoming 8, and in the year 1280 of the Hegira the second 7 will also be inverted. This prophecy, supported as it is by the reality of the troubles now arising in various quarters, has naturally exercised a great influence on the fatalist tendencies of the Mussulmans and increased their ill-will towards other sects. (Skene: *Rambles in Syrian Deserts.*)

CHAPTER XXV.—"The garrison was divided into two companies" (Selim loquitur). Ahmed Pasha sent some troops under the command of two colonels into the streets. They soon applied to him for instructions, under the impossibility of keeping the peace without resorting to violence. He ordered them in writing to fire upon the people. One of the colonels in command of the *regulars* obeyed his order and dispersed the mob, proving thus that the evil might have been checked. The other colonel, who had charge of the *irregulars*, was won over by a Mussulman sheikh, who adjured him in the name of the Prophet and their common religion to join them and clear the holy city of Damascus of infidels. He went over to the insurgents with his troops. (Skene, as above.) For further particulars of the massacre, *see* Skene, already quoted, Churchill: *Druses and Maronites*, and *Ten Years in Mount Lebanon*, and the newspapers of the latter half of 1860.

CHAPTER XV.—"Jesus the Prophet, whom the faithful call Ruh' Allah." It has been told me for a fact that when the exiled Khedive Ismail Pasha (known to London street-boys of the period as old Ishmel Parker) was at Naples, one of the officers in attendance on him challenged an Italian in a *café* for having dared to insult a Prophet of his (the Egyptian's) religion. The man had been blaspheming, it appeared, as only a Neapolitan or a Tuscan knows how to blaspheme, heaping foul epithets on the name of his Saviour and the Blessed Virgin. A duel, my informant assures me, actually took place on these grounds.

GLOSSARY OF ARAB EXPRESSIONS AND NAMES OF PLACES.

Abd=A servant, a slave, much used with an epithet of the Deity in the formation of proper names, as Abdúllah, the servant of God ; Abdul Cader, the servant of the Powerful, and so forth.

Abu=Father of. A man assumes his son's name with this prefix as an honourable title, letting his own name be almost forgotten.

Afrìt=A devil, a jinni (pl. afærìt).

Ayûb=Job.

Bara=Para.
Basha=Pasha. }The Arabs have no letter "P" and cannot pronounce it.

Bedelleh askerìeh=Tax in lieu of military service, levied on unbelievers.

Cabil=Cain.

Caimmacam=A local governor, inferior to the provincial governor (Wâly or Mutesarrif) and appointed by him.

Damashc-ush-Shâm (or simply Es-Shâm)=Damascus. Shâm in this name is generally taken to mean "Left" in contrast with "Yemen" meaning "Right." But it has more likely to do with Shem (Ar. Shâm). Syria is called Es-Shâm or Birr-ush-Shâm.

Daûd=David.

Dejîl=Antichrist.

Dîn=Religion, faith—*e.g.*, dìn Muhammed=El Islâm.

Dursi=A Druze (pl. Drûz).

Ebn=Son—*e.g.*, ebn Ali=the son of Ali.

Effendi=A title of respect given generally to Mahometans.

El Ajem=Persia.

Eljizar=Algiers or Algeria (often confused with Eljezireh=Mesopotamia).

El Khaßl=An epithet of the patriarch Abraham appropriate to his city of Hebron.

Emìr=Prince, an hereditary and purely Arab title of nobility, having nothing to do with the Turkish gamut of dignities which, like the Russian, are purely official. It is given, for instance, to all the kindred of the Prophet, in addition to the epithet Sherìf (=honourable, holy).

Fellah=A husbandman, a peasant (pl. fellahìn).

Fulàn=An imaginary person (*cp.* Span. Don Fulano) as we say Mr So-and-so.

Habil=Abel.

Haleb=Aleppo, surnamed the White (Esh-Shahbah).

In sh'Allah=(lit., if God will) I hope.

Isa = Jesus (Mahometan).
Iskendería = Alexandria.
Istanbûl = Constantinople.
Jebel Târic = Gibraltar.
Jinni = A geni, a fallen angel dwelling on earth and sharing with man the chance of salvation (pl. jin or jân).
Kâfir = Infidel, heathen.
Khawaja = A title of respect given exclusively to unbelievers.
Kibleh = The point towards which the face is turned at prayers (for Jews, Jerusalem, for Mahometans, Mecca).
Lândra = London.
Marûni = A Maronite (pl. Mowarni).
Masr = Egypt.
Ma sh'Allah = (What does God wish !) the commonest exclamation of surprise.
Mehkemeh = A court of law presided over by the Câdi.
Miriam = Mary.
Mûfti = A religious judge in every city.
Mûsa = Moses.
Muslim = A Mahometan (pl. Muslimûn).
Mutesarrif = A governor of a province, less than a Wâly in dignity, but, like a Wâly, dependent directly on the Sultàn.
Nabuli = Naples.
Neby = Prophet.
Nûh = Noah.
Oäh = A cry equivalent to "Look out !"
Rûm = Greece.
Sheykh = An old man ; hence (age implying precedence) a chief, the head-man of a tribe, a village, or indeed of any community.
Suleyman = Solomon.
Tarabulus = Tripoli (Tarabulus-Esh-Shâm, Tripoli of Syria ; not Tarabulus el Gharb, Tripoli in Barbary).
The Chief of Mountains (Jebel-ush-Sheikh) = Mount Hermon.
The City of Peace (Medinat us Salam) = Baghdad.
The Mountain (El Jebel) = Lebanon.
The Sunset-Land (El Maghrib, el Gharb) = The north coast of Africa west of Egypt : The Barbary States.
Wâly = The governor-general of a province, appointed directly by the Sultàn (or at least from Constantinople) and for a period of five years.
Wilayet = The province governed by a Wâly.
Yafez = Japheth.
Y Allah ! = (O God !) the commonest of all exclamations, meaning whatever you please, oftenest with a sense of "Make haste !" or "Forward !"
Yesua = Jesus (Christian).

PART II

THE BOOK OF HIS FATE

"O ye men, it is not the great king, nor the multitude of men, neither is it wine that excelleth; who is it then that ruleth them, or hath the lordship over them? Are they not women?"—1 Esdras.

I

ABOUT the third hour of a summer's day, Saïd the merchant strolled lazily in the streets of Damashc-ush-Shâm. A bare-legged servant, whose brown heels peeped in and out of a pair of large red slippers, held a sunshade obsequiously over his head. The parasol was white with a green lining. It amounted to a badge of the highest consequence, and Saïd was faint for pride of it.

More than ten years of ease and good living had greatly increased his bulk. He had gained that appearance of mixed dignity and benevolence which the habit of a full belly imparts to a man. Many there were who louted low to him in the way; he acknowledged their presence by the slightest scooping motion of his hand. But a notable of the city riding by upon a grey horse, heralded by an outrunner with cries of "Oäh!" scattering the crowd to right and left, Saïd was foremost of all to bow his head and touch his lips and brow in token of reverence.

He entered the shelter of a roofed bazaar and the sunshade was presently put down. The cool shadow, bringing relief from the blinding glare outside, disposed all men to dawdle. Brisk movement, the hoarse cry of impatience and the peevish oath gave way all at once to sighs, murmurs of praise to Allah, and much wiping of faces. Saïd, however, thanks to the parasol, was not much heated, and he sauntered on leisurely as before. His ample form, richly clad, and his disdainful bearing wrung a salutation even from strangers. Such of the bystanders as knew his quality blessed him loudly by name. And he said in his heart,—

"Can it be that I was once Saïd the fisherman—a thing despised for all men to spit upon? Now behold, I am Saïd the merchant, in the height of prosperity and honour, so that they bow low before me in the market, and even men of family deem it no dishonour to kiss my hand.   Surely I am great and glorious, and my wealth is established upon a sure foundation. Allah is great and bountiful, and I, His servant, am much indebted to Him."

The next minute he made a rapid sign with his hand and he muttered a formula reputed potent, lest that jealous eye which is ever fixed upon the heart of man should mark his boastfulness and lay a snare for him.

The bare-legged servant, very proud of a new tarbûsh he was wearing for the first time, now walked a few steps in advance of his master to clear the way.   The shadow was inky upon the crowd.   Motes danced golden in a bar of light where a rift in the barn-like roof let in a sunbeam.   The divers hues of the multitude, and the rich array of stuffs displayed in the doorways on either hand, were cool and restful as reflections in water.

Striking into another bazaar which ran at right angles to that he had hitherto threaded, Saïd turned in at a low doorway of humble seeming, bidding the servant await him there.   He traversed a narrow passage and, crossing a filthy court in sunlight, mounted some worn stone steps.   At the top of the flight was a crazy door.   He knocked, crying,—

"Open, O Selîm!   It is I, the master!   Make haste, lazy one!   Know that I am busy to-day and have little time to spare!"

The sound of the voice had not died away ere the door swung inward with a great creaking, and Selîm appeared in the entrance.   He pounced on Saïd's hand and kissed it.

"Welcome, O my master!" he exclaimed, as he made fast the door behind his patron.   "It was in this minute that I wished to speak with thee concerning certain carpets of thine which have arrived with the caravan of Ali Effendi and now lie at the great khan awaiting thy orders.   Is it thy wish that I go there after noon? . . .   How is the health of thy son, Suleyman?   Mayst thou be blest in him!"

Saïd sat down cross-legged upon the raised platform of stone which formed a kind of daïs at one end of the room. With a look of concentration he began to roll a cigarette, leaving Selîm's questions unanswered for a minute.   The delicate tracery of the lattice at his back sifted and subdued the light while admitting what breeze there was.

It was pleasant to lounge there, in the place of honour of the large, cool room, and let his eye range over the piles of rich carpets, roll upon roll, which almost concealed the walls. It was pleasant, sitting thus, to inhale the smoke of a cigarette, or, better still, of a narghileh. The whole of his life passed before him at such times, like a tale of the Thousand and One Nights. But for evidence of the piles of carpets, and the presence of Selîm, moving to and fro among them, he would sometimes have doubted the truth of it all, so marvellous it seemed. It was pleasant to recall the old life with Hasneh in the little house among the sandhills by the seashore, to curse again the treachery of Abdullah, to review his wanderings and all the wondrous chances of the great slaughter. Even the weeks of terror which followed those days of bloodshed, when the Saving Faith seemed humbled for ever and the power of the infidels was paramount in the land, were sweet in the memory. He looked back to them as to a dream of delights, for they had passed, dream-like, in the first, full rapture of possession after long months of yearning. Engrossed by bliss, dazed with a delicious languor of soul and body, he had heard talk of executions, of shooting and hanging of true believers, only as one hears whose ears are stuffed with wool. Sad tidings had reached him in the little pleasure house he had hired among the gardens at the foot of the great brown hills. One day Hasneh had returned from her marketing, half dead for horror, with the news that Ahmed Pasha had been led out and shot that morning. In the space of a week or two, more than three hundred of the faithful were hanged, so that the Sultàn's envoy, who introduced and, as some said, invented that shameful and unclean way of death, was named of all men Father of a Rope. There were accounts of a French army in Mount Lebanon, slaying every Druze they met, were it man, woman or child. It was said they had sworn to wipe out the Druzes utterly from the face of the earth, because they had dared to be victorious over the Maronites, who were reckoned as French subjects for the nonce. But Saïd, though cursing the French and all unbelievers by rote, had, in fact, felt but little concern for the calamities of his neighbours. The death of Ahmed Pasha had been of direct benefit to him, for it set Selîm free to be his agent in those commercial enterprises on which he soon began to employ his capital.

N

Ferideh, tamed at last, and submissive to his pleasure, Hasneh re-found and willing to wait upon him hand and foot, his treasure bestowed in a safe place; he had been feverishly happy throughout that time of trouble and disgrace. The true Faith was sure to triumph in the end. Meanwhile he had not neglected to pray to Allah five times a day, had eaten no pork, and had been careful to avoid handling any unclean thing.

From the height of wealth and honour to which his native shrewdness, under Allah, and a run of the rarest good luck had conspired to raise him, he could con over his life with some of that enjoyment a traveller knows in recounting hardships past. For a long while he sat musing with a far-away look in his eyes—a look having no concern with the pile of Meccan prayer-mats on which he seemed intent. The smoke of his cigarette curled lazily upward in the tempered gloom. A little cloud of flies hung buzzing over his head. At length, the silence growing irksome, Selîm hazarded,—

"How is thy health, O Saïd?"

"Praise be to Allah! And thy health?" was the mechanical reply. Then, starting from his brown study and brushing the flies from his face,—

"We have a fine store of carpets, O father of Mûsa—none like it in all the city. For how much, thinkest thou, could we sell all that is now on our hands?"

Selîm stroked his beard and his forehead puckered thoughtfully. After some inward reckoning he named a large sum of money as a fair estimate. Saïd's face grew rapturous.

"Now listen, O Selîm," he said, bending towards his henchman and speaking in low, eager tones. "It is in my mind to buy the house of Mahmud Effendi—thou knowest it?—which is towards the Jewish quarter. He asks a vast sum for it—a fortune, by Allah! But it is known that he needs money, that his creditors harass him for payment. Wait a little, and he will be glad to accept much less. Nevertheless, it is a fine house and a costly; the price of it will amount to more than I have in my hand. I am minded to sell all these carpets and to part with this upper room. In time to come it shall be said of Suleyman: his father is a great Effendi, who dwells in a palace.

"Now, O my brother, I know thee for a wise man whose

advice it is good to take; and thou wast ever careful for my welfare. Counsel me, I pray thee, and tell me what comes to thy mind on this matter."

Selîm stared aghast at his employer. Dismay made his eyeballs dilate and his jaw drop.

"To hear is to obey," he faltered at length. "It is for thee to order and dispose of what is thine. I am but thy servant to hear and bow my head. Nevertheless, O Saïd, O my brother, O father of kindness, what is it that thou purposest? To sell a thriving business like this, which yields more and more profit with each year, were the dream of a madman! And why dost thou so covet the house of Mahmud? I fear an evil spirit prompts thee in this matter, seeking to engulf thy fortune. Hast thou not already a fine house enough—one well becoming the lord of thy wealth? Hast thou not a beautiful woman for wife, one who is mistress of thy fancy, who has already borne a son to inherit thy honour? Hast thou not also another wife who loves thee, and maidens to wait on thy harîm? Hast thou not two men-servants and a doorkeeper, without counting Selîm and all his father's house, who are ever ready to do thy behests? Sure, if ever man was happy, thou art happy; if ever Allah favoured any man, he has favoured thee. The higher a person rises, the closer do envy and ill-will and hatred beset him on every side. The more conspicuous he becomes, the more he has need of money. Hear a story, O my brother.

"Know that there was once a man who owned a she-camel, which fed him with her milk and earned money for him by her labour. But the man was not content. Going one day to the city he beheld in the shop of a certain merchant a collar of gold. And he said in his soul, 'O my soul, if I had but that collar I should certainly be happiest of all the sons of Adam.' The thought of it robbed him of sleep by night, and in the daytime it was ever present to his mind. At last he bethought him of the camel, and he said in his heart, 'A collar of gold for a camel is a famous bargain. Every poor fellah has a camel belonging to him, but only the greatest wear collars of gold.'

"On the morrow he arose and drove his beast to the city, and there sold her, together with the packsaddle and the halter, a bag of corn and a vessel of oil which happened to be

with him in the house.   Then he went straight to the
merchant's, and, having assured himself that the collar was
there, he inquired the price.   At first the trader laughed and
eyed him askance, for the poorness of his clothes.   But afterwards, finding that he had money with him, he deigned to
name a sum.   It was more than the man could pay; yet,
being an astute fellow and good at a bargain, he at length
obtained the collar.

"With it clasped round his neck he strutted about the
streets, deeming himself an Emîr.   It was not for a long
while he became aware that men were pointing after him and
laughing in their beards.   Then shame came upon him, and
he wished to hide the ornament; but he could not, it was so
big and his robe so scanty and ragged.   He tried to unclasp
it, but he knew not the trick of it, the merchant having made
it fast for him.   He sped to the shop, wishing to give it back
and receive his money again; but the merchant drove him
away with curses and threatening words.   He dared not have
recourse to any worker in metal lest the price of his release
should be more than he could afford, and, in default of payment, the collar should be taken from him.

"By the time he had eaten and drunk and had paid his
lodging for one night, he had no money left.   On the third
day he was driven to beg in the gate of the city.   But those
who passed in and out mocked him, thinking he was a joker
or one that begged for a wager or a vow.   And this became a
proverb in the land : The beggar with the collar of gold craves
a mite of thee, O muleteer.

"Full of distress he prayed Allah, if it might be, to take
away that plague from him and give him back his camel.
Soon he prayed more earnestly that Allah would cut off his
life.   His prayer was heard ; for certain wicked men of the
city had cast greedy eyes upon the collar.   They lay in wait
for him in a lonely place, and there slew him.   But being
powerless to unclasp the collar, they cut off his head and
drew it from the neck still fastened.

"Now, O my brother, the drift of my story is clear and
needs no explaining.   I think it no wise thing to sell all thy
stock-in-trade that thou mayest buy a fine palace.   Remember
that he who bartered the camel for the collar of gold had
shame and misery and a ghastly death into the bargain."

During the tale Saïd's face had become overcast. As Selîm ceased speaking his displeasure broke out. Frowning, and with a peevish gesture,—

"Thou speakest folly and thy words are far from the purpose!" he cried. "What have I got to do with thy poor man and his camel? Behold, I am rich, as thou well knowest. Even when I shall have paid the price of the house there will yet be money left in my hand wherewith to trade anew. Because I speak of selling this shop and these carpets, thou art afraid of thy own meat and drink, lest thy livelihood be taken from thee. Thou makest believe to rede me a friendly counsel, whereas thy mind is wholly set upon thy private advantage. I had thought to make thee a handsome present —enough to keep thee in comfort and honour all thy days; but now, since thou choosest to cross me, I know not what I shall do."

Stung by the accusation of self-seeking, Selîm bounded to his feet.

"Now, Allah pardon thee, O Saïd," he exclaimed in a low voice broken by emotion. "Surely thou art possessed with a devil to think this evil of me! In all the years that I have served thee in this place, hast thou ever found me wanting in my duty? Have I not ever loved thee as a dear brother, while serving thee faithfully as my lord? Hast thou ever known me to seek my own advantage to thy prejudice in the price of a single prayer-mat? Do I not bring up my children to bless thee as their father's benefactor? . . . These words which thou hast spoken wound my inmost heart. Behold, am I not thy thing, to take up or to cast aside? If I likened thee by chance to a poor fellah, who had but one camel, Allah be my witness, it was because I knew no other story to meet thy case. Fables ever deal in extremes; I meant thee no insult, as thou knowest well. I did but give thee the best advice that I had out of the little store of wisdom which is mine. O Saïd—O my dear! I have loved thee with a great affection ever since the day thou didst hire me to be thy servant, and didst give me that rich garment—the root of my honour— which I still cherish in my house. That is long ago, when Mûsa, my first-born, was yet at his mother's breast. Now Mûsa is almost a man to wear the turban, yet I love thee with the same love still. It will grieve me to forsake this upper chamber, where I have sat cool through the heat of many a day; while the bees and the flies and the wasps made a drowsy moaning, and the voice of the water-carrier came to me out of the street like a wild bird's cry. It is natural, is it not? that I should grieve somewhat at thought of leaving a place where I have spent many years in peace of mind and body. And the little room adjoining, where all my children save Mûsa have been born, is dear to me for the cries of the young ones and the voice of the anxious mother crooning soft to them. But thou gavest, and it is thine to take away. O Saïd, O my brother, seek not to quarrel with me after all these years!"

The pathos of this appeal touched some answering chord of the merchant's heart, for the lines of his face softened and his eyes filled with tears. At last, when Selîm had made an end of speaking, and stood gazing at him with eyes full of entreaty, Saïd started up and, going over to him, fell on his neck. Surely an evil spirit had prompted him to doubt for a minute the good faith of his more than brother. He asked forgiveness of the harsh words uttered in haste. But he had set his heart on purchasing the house of Mahmud Effendi, and the unlooked-for dissension had angered him.

Deeply moved by his patron's tears, Selîm gave way completely; vowing to be faithful to him in all things, whatever he should require. He called Allah to witness that he had not meant to oppose Saïd's will, but only to help him with advice, that nothing might be done rashly or without due consideration.

"What is the hour?" asked Saïd at length, with a startled glance at the tracery of light and shadow thrown from the lattice upon wall and floor.

"It is between the fourth and the fifth, O my master," Selîm pronounced, after reference to the same dial. "With thy leave, I will call for coffee, if, indeed, thou must depart so soon." At his shout of "Mûsa!" a sturdy boy, clad in a robe of striped cotton, close buttoned at the neck, and having for head-dress an ancient and weather-beaten fez, appeared from an inner room. The shrill tones of a woman scolding and the piteous howl of an infant came through the same door with him, out of the gloom on which he stood revealed.

"O Mûsa, bring coffee and that quickly, for our master has little time!" said Selîm.

The two elders took counsel together how to dispose of shop and merchandise to the best advantage. There were debts of long standing to be collected, or, where the debtor was too great and powerful, to be forgiven with as much circumstance as possible. Selìm undertook all the more tiresome business of the settlement, leaving for his master that lighter part which could be transacted over a glass of sherbet and a narghileh. Saïd thanked him, as for a matter of course, and heartily cursed the buzzing swarm of flies which infested the room. Then, when he had swallowed a cupful of coffee, he arose and set out for the house of Mahmud Effendi.

He thought of the joy Ferideh would have in that palace, and his heart beat faster; for, after more than ten years of possession, he still doted on the daughter of Yuhanna.

II

MAHMUD EFFENDI sat in the audience-hall of his great house, in the highest seat. Door and windows open on the court showed a vine-covered trellis, a few orange trees grouped about a marble basin, and the opposite wall of the quadrangle in dazzling sunshine. Draughts of lukewarm air brought the pleasant sound of leaves rustling and water trickling to freshen the deep shade of the room, which would else have been gloomy and oppressive.

Mahmud Effendi was a man of thirty summers, unhealthily white and fat, with dark creases under his eyes. He wore a long morning robe of striped silk, a high fez and a finely-embroidered turban; but a pair of Frankish boots of patent leather were most obvious as he lolled in the cushioned seat of honour. As a member of the council of notables, and one who had spent a year at Instanbûl to complete his education, he usually donned the Turkish frock-coat and dark trousers on state occasions. It was told of him that he could sit on a chair stiffly, like a Frank, for minutes together without a symptom of uneasiness, could wield a knife and fork cunningly and speak with the tongue of unbelief. But in the freedom of his own dwelling, with his kinsfolk and servants obsequious about him, he was the true Arab grandee, scornful and un-mannerly.

On the morning in question the couches of the presence-chamber were well filled. On the daïs reclined a number of the great man's relatives and cronies, grouped in order of their rank; while the body of the hall was sprinkled with the men of the household and other dependants, together with sundry persons who presented themselves every morning with praiseworthy constancy, for no other purpose than to make their names and faces familiar to one in authority.

The walls of the room were a mosaic-work of marble of

different colours, the words of the Fatiha, or opening chapter of the Coràn, running all round under the ceiling by way of frieze. At all points the name of Allah met the eye, cunningly obscured and twisted into puzzling monograms; and further veiled by such epithets as the Merciful, the Praiseworthy, the Powerful, and so forth. The pavement, too, was of mosaic, where it could be seen for rugs. A wide stone bench or divan, which ran along the foot of the walls, was cushioned upon the daïs, bare elsewhere. Before the lord of the house, on a soft carpet from Persia, stood a stool, or little table of dark-stained wood inlaid upon the top and sides with arabesque patterns of mother-of-pearl. It bore an inkstand, a reed pen, and a bulky scroll of parchment covered with close writing in a clerkly hand.

Mahmud Effendi was restless and spoke little. No sooner was one cigarette lighted for him by an attentive neighbour than he flung it away, with an oath of impatience, and began to roll another. Conversation in the room was carried on by low whispers, and eyes kept straying anxiously to the door.

"This man—what is his name?—this Saïd is late!" exclaimed the great one, fretfully, with a yawn. "Is it meet, I ask you, that my father's son should be kept waiting by the child of a dog?"

"It is true! He is late; curse his religion! May the fire, the mother of hospitality, be quenched on his hearth, and his father's grave be perfectly defiled!" Glad of the chance to lift up their voices, all present cursed the tardy one most heartily.

It was but yesterday that Nasr, the son of his mother's sister, had come to Mahmud with news that a certain merchant, reputed lord of boundless wealth, was minded to buy the palace at any price. The man, whose name was Saïd, would present himself, said the informant, betimes on the morrow. Nasr spent most of his life in the taverns of the city. He was a famous gossip and no mean liar. But in this case Mahmud, in sore straits for money, had gladly believed his tidings and had summoned all the heads of his kindred to support him at the interview. Now, seeing that the morning was fast wearing away and no one came, he began to have an inkling that his cousin had lied to him,

knowing his instant need to sell the house and wishing to
please him and gain honour for himself by bringing agreeable
news.   He bent ominous brows on the unconscious Nasr,
who sat fourth removed from him on the seat of honour;
and was on the point of upbraiding him fiercely with the
deceit, when a murmur of satisfaction, first raised by a group
of servants at the door, spread throughout the assembly.   A
man's voice was heard at the gate, crying,—

"Peace be upon this house, and the mercy of Allah, and
His blessings!"

Mahmud Effendi straightened himself in his seat.   The
elders upon the daïs composed their limbs and faces on
decorous lines.   The menials in the body of the hall fell
bowing into two rows, forming a lane for the passage of the
newcomer.

Having slipped off his shoes at the threshold, Saïd the
merchant entered the presence-chamber with a mien of the
utmost deference.   His servant followed bearing the white
parasol with the green lining, as it had been a rod of office.
Leaving his bodyguard among the folk of the household, Saïd
advanced to the daïs.   All the great ones who sat there arose
at his approach, and his humble salutation was returned
twenty-fold.   Mahmud Effendi came a little way to meet him,
and, after the brief and languid struggle enjoined by politeness, yielded his hand to be kissed.   Then he led the guest
to a vacant seat on his right, and called loudly for refresh-
ments.   With his own hand he made a cigarette for Saïd, and
insisted on lighting it for him with a match borrowed from
the uncle who sat on his left.   Then he renewed inquiries
concerning the visitor's health, scanning his face earnestly for
any sign of disorder; while all the rest of the company
put the same or like questions after him in chorus.

Quite overwhelmed by the honour paid to him, Saïd
could only bow repeatedly, murmuring blessings upon his
host and all belonging to him.   But when two serving-men
drew near barefooted, each carrying a large and curiously-
wrought brass tray laden with glasses of several kinds of
sherbet, Mahmud's attention was called away for a minute
and he found time to regain composure.

He glanced craftily round upon that numerous gathering,
whose presence there, he shrewdly guessed, was planned to

abash and outface him. But the mental resolve to prove a match for them all found no expression in face or attitude.

At length, when all the empty glasses were replaced on the trays and the servants had retired with them, a silence ensued which Saïd deemed favourable for the opening of his business. With a cringing twist of his body, he begged the ear of Mahmud Effendi, who gave heed to him with the gravest condescension.

It was noised abroad in the markets.—The common people are all gossips, scandalmongers, by Allah! and publishers of every silly rumour.—It was noised abroad that his Excellency was desirous of selling that great palace, where he had the honour to behold his Eminence in the extremity of welfare and good health. The report—which was of course an idle one, unworthy the credence of a man of sense—had at length reached the ears of his Honour's devoted servant. Though at once perceiving it to be a foolish fable, such as low people, muleteers and others who frequent the bazaars, spread abroad for love of mischief; yet it had so far carried weight with him that, being at present in search of a fine house and having by the blessing of Allah some little wealth at his disposal, he had allowed his mind to dwell on the thought of this great palace, to desire it. He had therefore ventured to wait upon his Grace, in order to make sure that the report that he had heard was groundless, and, in case there should be a measure of truth in it, to inquire what price his Worship was pleased to demand. He was aware that it ill became him, a small man and of no account in the city, thus to thrust himself forward in the presence of his Highness and of his Highness's illustrious kindred there assembled. To aspire to possess that fine house were the last presumption in one of his mean quality. As for the notion of supplanting, or in any sense replacing, his Excellency, it was far from his mind. Can the fox claim fellowship with the lion? And yet it is no sin if the fox come to dwell in the lion's den, after the noble beast has forsaken it, needing change; provided he do so meekly, with a proper sense of his own unworthiness, giving praise and thanks at all times to Allah for his great good fortune.

He (Saïd) was a merchant, whose business, by the grace

of Allah, had thriven with him; and, whereas a great one
of the city, having much property but little ready money,
would pay the price hardly and by many instalments, he
was prepared to bring the whole sum at once in his hands and
place it in the hands of his Excellency. A small sum paid
down in its entirety was worth more than the promise of great
riches. Wherefore—his voice became a coaxing whine and
his smile waxed eloquent of deprecation—wherefore he had
dared hope that his Highness would deign to abate something of the price in his favour; if he were indeed minded to
sell the house, which was most unlikely. Might Allah
preserve his Excellency's life for ever, and increase the goods
of his Excellency to the crowning point of prosperity.

Mahmud Effendi listened to all this long speech with
courteous attention, as did all who sat upon the daïs, taking
their cue from him. Having heard Saïd patiently to an end,
he raised a hand to his beard and stared round upon the faces
of his kindred with the dazed look of a man taken quite by
surprise. After a pause long enough to fully impress the
visitor with a sense of his amazement, he spoke slowly and
falteringly, as one striving to muster his wits.

"Allah pardon! It was a false report thou heardest, O
my uncle. Men are wont to speak idly in the markets, and
their tongues wag ever most glibly of those who sit in high
places. I marvel only that a man of thy penetration should
have paid any heed to their talk. The wish to sell my house
is very far from me; nay, it was but in this hour I was taking
counsel with the heads of my father's house about a plan for
adorning the women's apartments with a screen of Cairene
lattice-work, and to inlay the walls of the court with devices of
marble. At the moment of thy entering I was reading in that
scripture thou seest upon the table, which is an exact account
of all that the house contains and the value of it. If thou
doubtest the truth of what I say, inquire of any man here,
and he shall certify thee.

"By my beard, I am amazed at thy speech, for to sell this
house, which belonged to my father and my father's father
before me, was never further from my thoughts than it is to-
day.

"And yet . . . now that thou hast put it in my mind, I
know not that I should altogether refuse to sell, were one to

make me a tempting offer. As thou sayest, a large sum in the hand is better than the like sum paid in slow instalments. Moreover, a man like me has many liabilities to which one of thy condition is not subject. Thou receivest money every day, and thy wealth is with thee in the house; whereas the fortune I inherit is vested in lands and houses, which cannot be moved, and which it is tiresome to sell; and withal I must always be spending. Thou art eloquent, O my uncle, and thy talk sways my mind a little. Having no instant need of money, nor indeed any enduring wish to sell at all, I shall not certainly part with this fine house for less than its utmost value. Nevertheless, since the whim is upon me, I am curious to know what price thou wouldst offer!"

He did not wait for Saïd's answer, but very carelessly shouted an order for coffee to be served at once.

All his kindred raised hands and eyes ceilingwards, calling Allah to witness their astonishment at what they had just heard. Mahmud Effendi to think of selling his house! Surely the great man spoke in jest! If he were indeed serious, then the sun might shortly be expected to rise in the west! They murmured together in amazement and concern.

Saïd, with eyes fixed upon one of his host's Frankish boots, appeared lost in reflection. At length he faltered,—

"O my lord, know that I am a small man, wholly unworthy to compete with thee in any way. Who am I that I should presume to set a price on that which belongs to thy Highness? Deign to name such a sum as thou deemest just, and I, thy servant, will say whether I can afford to pay it. I am a small man and my wealth is limited. Notwithstanding, having a great regard for thy Grace, I shall endeavour by all means to content thee."

"Truly thou askest no easy thing of me," muttered Mahmud, with puckered forehead. "It is hard to compute the price of that which has never been sold nor valued for sale. If I were really earnest in this matter, I should say, Bring valuers, one for thee and one for me. Let them go over all the premises and make each his estimate. But, as it is, wishing only to know what thou wouldst give, I know not what to say. I would rather that some other gave an opinion in my stead, lest thou shouldst say, Of course, he extols that which is his own. Now behold, there are many honourable persons here present, who know the house perfectly and all it contains. If it please thee, let them confer together and we will abide by their judgment."

But Saïd put in humbly,—

"Nay, O my lord, I cannot engage to pay whatever price the arbiters may lay upon me. My wealth, alas! has limits. Allah keep thy Grace ever in safety; that which I ask of thee is only reasonable."

"Of course, it shall be as thou choosest," said Mahmud, carelessly.

While the coffee was being passed round, the umpires spoke earnestly together in low tones, now glancing at Saïd, now at their kinsman, with manifest impartiality. At last they resumed their seats and their former languid postures. An aged man, uncle to Mahmud on the father's side, had been chosen spokesman. He now rose to make known the verdict.

The sum he named made Saïd wince, though he was prepared for almost any extravagance. Mahmud himself could not refrain from throwing an admiring glance round upon his relations. The merchant smiled painfully and stroked his beard.

"Well, what sayest thou, O my uncle?" said Mahmud, in a voice of encouragement. "Remember, thou hast not yet seen all the house, and this is not the only fine room in it. Observe the walls a little, I pray thee, what excellent workmanship is there! By the Coràn, I think it a low estimate. What sayest thou?"

Saïd, though secretly gnawing his underlip, made shift to smile. Shrugging his shoulders and spreading his hands wide in deprecation.

"The price exceeds my fortune," he murmured. "I cannot bid more than a third of it."

"Never!" cried Mahmud, in extreme disgust, fending off the insulting offer with his hand. "Never!" cried all his kindred in chorus, eyeing Saïd as though he had done every one of them a mortal injury.

A long and chilly pause ensued, until Mahmud, having managed to bring his outraged feelings into subjection, renewed his inquiries after the visitor's health in the cause of hospitality. But there was a marked change in his manner, and Saïd, perceiving that he was no longer welcome, made haste to depart. The lofty courtesy of his company had daunted him during the whole interview. That sudden change from the sunshine of condescension to the frost of contempt sent him forth bewildered into the scorching street. But ere he had made many paces from the outer gate he was again master of his wits.

Walking in the shade of the white parasol with the green lining, he reviewed the whole scene with a chuckle. With patience, he felt sure of getting the house at very nearly his own price. He had made a not unreasonable offer. In a very few days, he foresaw, Mahmud would summon him once more to his presence; and then the haggling would begin in earnest. It might last a month, it might last a year. All depended on the temper of the great man's creditors. In any case, he felt sure of his bargain in the end; and the memory of that splendid presence-chamber made his brain swim with ambition.

III

THE house of Saïd the merchant was so set in the heart of the city that for strangers and country people, who had not the clue to the labyrinth, it was a day's work to find it. The approach from the nearest bazaar was by an archway infested with dogs and beggars, down a winding lane, and through a gate in the wall. Even after the gate was passed, callers were forced to ask their way, for one passage gave access to three several dwellings, and who, uninspired, could tell which door to choose? As one stood on its roof and looked out over the town, it seemed an easy feat to scramble thence to the minaret of Isa, half a mile distant, without once descending to the level of the streets. You would have deemed Es-Shâm hewn of a single stone, so hard it was to mark where one building ended and another began. It was on the house-top that Saïd was wont to say his prayers at nightfall, and often in the daytime, with face turned duly southward towards the kibleh. Often, too, he would cause a servant to bring an ewer of water to him upon the roof, and there, in sight of the many who sought refreshment in the evening air, he would perform the lesser washings of preparation, without which no prayer of man is acceptable to Allah.

He had a very large and precious copy of the Coràn, so exquisitely written that each word was a monogram for a learned scribe to decipher; for Saïd it was quite illegible. This manuscript, bound in finely-chased leather, was carried every Friday by a servant to the mosque, together with a cushion. It was a small place of worship frequented by poor people, to whom a merchant was a great man. As soon as Saïd was comfortably seated on the cushion, the volume was placed in his hands. Opening it at random, he would recite

208

some passage which he knew by heart, in a very loud, nasal voice, and to the edification of all who sat there on the bare stones, waiting for the coming of the preacher.

He was known to give alms of all his substance, and it was understood he would make the pilgrimage as soon as ever his house and business could be set in order. No wonder that he was reckoned a holy man, esteemed and reverenced of all his neighbours; the roof of his house being high and conspicuous, and little of his devotions done in private.

His abode consisted of a small square court, elaborately paved; three sides of which were taken up by the living rooms and offices, the fourth being filled by a blind wall of the next house, in which was the entrance door. The court was no larger than a large chamber, and the house was small to match it, but convenient and more roomy than it promised to be. Hard by the entrance was a little chamber with a vaulted ceiling, where the doorkeeper lived, and facing it, across the court, yawned the doorway of a large cellar or storehouse beneath the women's apartments, where cooking and other work of the household was done.

It was in this place that Hasneh sat on a morning, grinding with one of her maidens at the handmill; while another who, being high in favour with Ferideh, thought herself entitled to do as she pleased, sat idly looking on, burying her hand in a sackful of wheat, and letting the grains glide through her fingers. The sound of grinding was loud in room and court-yard, relieved by the voices of the women chanting shrilly at their task. Now and then one would cease singing and let go the handle, to draw her veil closer as a protection from the flies; only to burst out afresh in song, and fall again to the turning with renewed strength.

Out in the sunshine, the doorkeeper, a burly negro, could be seen dozing with head against the wall. The heat and the glare, abhorred of others, were dear to him. He basked in them languorously, with closed eyes, stretching himself like a cat and showing his white teeth.

"Our lord is late to-day," said Hasneh, excitedly, pausing to push back a fold of her robe which was in the way. "Allah grant no ill has befallen him. I have to speak with him when he returns."

"Thou hast to speak with him, sayest thou?" said the

O

maid who sat idle, in languid amazement.   "Is it thy errand,
pray, or another's?"

"There is a word from Nûr, the old woman, and something
I must add to it of my own knowledge."

"It is plain thou hast little understanding, O mother of
nothing!" said the girl, jeeringly.   "Our lord holds thee of
no more account than an old sandal, and the words of thy
mouth are as the voice of a fly in his ears.   If Nûr desired a
hearing for her message, she would surely have addressed
herself to the lady Ferideh, or to me, that am her handmaid.
This errand of which thou boastest is some slight message of
compliment such as men bandy in the streets and count not.
Or it may be"—the girl tittered—"thou hast something of
moment to tell concerning thyself.   Nûr is reputed skilful in
such matters.   How is thy health, O honoured lady?   Say,
art thou once more with child, O mother of a thousand?"

Hasneh let go the handle of the mill and sprang to her
feet.   Ever since Ferideh had borne a son her life had been
full of bitterness.   Never a day passed without some cruel jest
at her expense.   The child she would have loved for his
father's sake was trained by his mother to strike her and spit
at her.   From the time he first began to lisp, Suleyman had
been taught to call her Childless Mother, Mother of Wind, and
a host of other unkind names; and the maidens, apeing their
mistress, were for ever nettling her with the like taunts.
Anger, as she had learnt by long experience, only gave point
to their amusement; and she had schooled herself to be
patient under their gibes.   But this morning, with a biting
retort on the tip of her tongue, she gave full vent to her pent-
up spite.

"Daughter of a dog!" she screamed.   "May thy father's
grave be defiled and thy race perish utterly from off the earth!
Thou art made on the pattern of thy mistress, and she is a
harlot!   Our master is deceived when he thinks her at the
bath all the morning.   Ah, I have learnt a thing by the mouth
of Nûr—a thing which, whispered in Saïd's ear, will cause the
downfall of this fine lady who lies all day long among soft
cushions, and fears to soil the whiteness of her fingers.   Saïd
may kill her in his wrath—such deeds are common! . . .   No,
I warrant thee, the message I bear to Saïd is no vain
compliment—by Allah, no!   It is of weight to crush thy

mistress and thee, and a hundred like thee. Go tell Ferideh that I have enough of her taunts, that I will abide them no more! Give her my peace, I pray thee, and call her by the name she has earned for herself! To be childless by the will of Allah is no sin; but for a woman to be faithless to her husband is a crime in the sight of God and man. Let her despise me because I am without issue, because my hands are rough with work while she lies at ease; it is well—very well! Praise be to Allah, I am not as she is—curse her father!"

Hasneh spat at the girl, who blenched before her. Then, still trembling with the tension of her outburst, she sat down with what countenance she might, and turned her handle of the mill so furiously that her helper was obliged to expostulate.

"What is there?" cried the negro, sleepily, from his basking-place in the yard. "Allah destroy you women! A man can enjoy no length of peace for the noise of you. It seems that a warm day of summer, when it is pleasant to rest and praise Allah, is the same to you as a winter's day of rain and wind. You quarrel at all times, jabbering at the pitch of your voices. Be quiet, I say, and cease bickering, or I will throw my great staff at you!"

"Hold peace thyself, O Ibrahìm, and be more courteous in thy speech!" retorted Hasneh, highly, from her task, without looking at him or turning her head.

Conscious of having knowledge which would ruin her enemy, elated from the triumph of her late denunciation, she was inclined to be arrogant. She fondly believed that the shame of Ferideh would mean her own reinstatement; and clearly the handmaids were of a like opinion, for their bearing towards her was wholly changed. The girl, Ferideh's pet, whose ill-natured jest had called forth that storm of her wrath, sat shrinking and abashed, and seized an early occasion to slip away. Her fellow-worker at the mill was become obsequious, full of attentions.

She exulted in the thought that Saïd would be restored to her at last; forgetting that she grew old, that the day of her charm was passed and the light of youth quenched in her eye She recalled bright moments of her life; the last days of maidenhood, when Saïd led a bride to his dwelling on the seashore; her meeting with him after long separation in the gateway of the lonely khan, in the first pallor of the dawning. Then, as they sat together, the sun rising upon the desert, he had vowed that she alone was mistress of his fancy, and should rule in his harìm. His heart had warmed to her then, and she had been very happy. But Ferideh, the Christian's daughter, had cast a spell upon him, weaning his love from her. Now it was in her power to make him hate Ferideh, and, when the first mad rage of jealousy should be spent, he would surely come to his old wife for comfort. Her heart made a song of passing sweetness rhythmic with the grinding of the mill.

She was indulging in such dreams as these when the tones of her lord's voice, cursing the doorkeeper for a sleepy pig, scion of a race of dogs, caused her to start. She rose quickly and, disposing her shroud-like clothing as decently as the hurry would allow, stepped out to meet him in the sunlight. Her companion remained by the mill, gaping after her with eyes of awe.

Saïd strode aimlessly into the yard, followed by his bare-legged escort and the sunshade. Seeing Hasneh come towards him, he greeted her carelessly and straightway turned his back; but she ran and, falling on her knees, caught the skirt of his cloak.

"Allah bless thee !" he cried testily, striving to draw away. "Come to me at another time when I have leisure. For the present I am very busy. . . . O Ferideh, what wouldest thou, light of my eyes? I come to rest awhile with thee till the heat of the day be over. . . . Let go my robe, woman, lest my anger light on thee !"

In her eager haste to be heard, Hasneh had had no eyes save for Saïd only. She did not see Ferideh issue forth from the door of the women's quarters, nor the face of the favourite handmaid peeping from the projecting lattice of the upper storey. Now suddenly, as Saïd ceased speaking, she found herself face to face with her adversary; and the shock robbed her of speech. Ferideh had come forth hurriedly, unveiled. Her eyes were steely bright, her mouth was a thin line of dire rage and determination.

Hasneh still clung to the merchant's robe, but her gaze was fixed on her rival's face, fascinated with a kind of horror. Saïd strove to free himself but could not.

"If, indeed, thou hast anything to say, speak, woman, and

make an end!" he exclaimed, with rising anger. "If thou art dumb, as thou seemest to be, unhand me—dost hear?—and that speedily, or it shall be the worse for thee!"

"O Saïd, O my beloved, hear me but a minute!" she gasped, aiming to kill Ferideh with her eyes. "It is no good news that I bring thee, O my soul. Know that Nûr visited thee this morning, and, finding thee from home—"

She fared no further, for Ferideh sprang on her and closed her mouth. Though, from glaring in her rival's eyes, Hasneh had seen what was coming and was half prepared to meet it, the shock all but bore her to the ground. It forced her to quit hold of Saïd's garment, and, kneeling as she was, pressed her back and down on to her heels.

"Merciful Allah! What does this mean?" cried the lord of the house, surprised out of all countenance. "Allah destroy you both! Speak, O Ferideh! What has Hasneh done to thee that thou shouldst so misuse her?"

"Thou askest what she has done! . . . O my dear lord, she is a liar, a backbiter and a breeder of all mischief! She hates me, as thou must surely have observed, with a great hatred, because I have borne a son to thee while she is childless. She had a quarrel in this same hour with Sàadeh, my handmaid, wherein she called me every foul name and swore to poison thy mind against me, she cared not by what falsehood. Every day she does something to my hurt or annoyance, and Sàadeh tells me that she has vowed to kill Suleyman, thy son and mine. There is no safety with her in the house. . . . Do I not right to stop her mouth with my hand lest she speak a lie in thy ears? A false tongue is powerful to make mischief, and, Allah pardon! I die only to think thou mightest have believed her tale. O my beloved, hasten to my chamber, where I will explain to thee the whole matter."

One of her hands closed Hasneh's mouth while with the other she held her rival's throat in a tight clutch, forcing her backwards so that she was nearly powerless. Even when Saïd sharply bade her let go if she would not strangle the woman, she still clung to her hold.

"Speak, O Ibrahìm," quoth Saïd, turning to the doorkeeper, who, with the bare-legged henchman, stood looking on aghast. "Heardest thou aught of this quarrel of which the lady speaks?"

"Yes, surely," replied the negro, with a candid grin. "There is no doubt but that the mother of Suleyman—may she be blessed in him!—speaks truth; for I myself was disturbed a while ago by a great din, and heard with my own ears the lady Hasneh utter foul insults. But of a truth I wonder not that she grows spiteful, for she is the butt and laughing-stock of the other women. They name her Mother of Wind and jeer at her for no reason. It is no wonder, I say, if she try in her turn to hurt them a little, for to my knowledge they use her very ill. No one should laugh at a camel for his crookedness, nor at a woman because she is childless. These are as Allah Most High was pleased to make them; it is no fault of their own if they are not otherwise."

Saïd waved him off impatiently.

"Enough," he said. "I perceive clearly that the right is with thee, O Ferideh. Now leave off fighting with that woman and come with me into the house. It is a sin that thou shouldst be so unveiled in the sight of men."

Ferideh gave her enemy a final push, so that she fell heavily on her side. Exultant, with bright eyes and face aglow, she followed her lord into the gloom and coolness of the house. A reaction shook her from head to foot, inwardly, as the seeds of grass are shaken. As she crossed the threshold of an inner door, the voice of Hasneh was lifted shrill to denounce her. The words were of hatred unmeasured for bitterness. They let her know all that she had escaped. Looking soft-eyed into her lord's face, with hand caressing his arm,—

"Said I not that she had a grudge against me?" she murmured. "Hear now the words of her mouth, how evil they are. Hadst thou listened to the voice of her spite, thou hadst believed her tale, perhaps, and then, alas! I had lost thy love, O prince of my soul! Did I not well to silence her in time?"

"Thou didst well," whispered Saïd, fervently, drawing near and circling her with an arm. "But Allah have pity! thy hand bleeds. The palm of it is bitten through. Behold the blood is on my robe—and thine likewise! Thou hast great courage, O my beloved. By the Coràn, I, who am a man, and reputed no coward, had screamed for a wound like this."

Smiling tenderly, "I felt it not," she murmured, seeking

his eyes. "I care not what befalls me so that I be still mistress of thy fancy, O stream of my life!"

He tore a strip of his own clothing and swathed her hand in it. Full of care for her, he did not quit her chamber until the evening.

After a frantic attempt to pursue her rival, which was easily frustrated by the two serving-men, Hasneh returned to the storehouse. She found it empty, for the work of grinding was done and the maid was flown to join her fellow in another place, to chat over the scene and debate its meaning. For a great while she sat there heart-broken. Once Suleyman ran in upon her out of the sunlight, to kick her, spit upon her, and slap her repeatedly with his tiny hands; cursing her religion, her parentage, and calling down all evil upon her for the hurt done to his mother. But, as she seemed not to heed, the child soon wearied, and, with a last kick, trotted out again into the court. She could hear him pestering the doorkeeper, telling the tale of her misdeeds with a child's exaggeration of detail. Then he went back to his mother or to join the maids, and there was quiet once more.

At length, when the day was far spent, she drew her veil, and, gliding unobserved by the drowsy negro, bent her steps towards the cellar of Nûr.

IV

"O MY loved one, I tell thee there is no end to her hate of me; and Nûr is as her mouthpiece in this matter. Thou wouldst know the reason? That I cannot tell thee, for I myself have not ascertained it. But one thing is sure: she would fain destroy me and mine. For my life I fear her, and for the life of Suleyman, the hope of thy father's house. It may be that she cannot bear to see me preferred to her in the secret of thy love, to know that I shall rule a part of this great mansion thou art minded to buy. She would kill me, thinking to make thee all her own once more. Laugh with me, O my soul!—she thinks she yet has charms to tempt and hold thee. . . . She will say all things to turn the favour I have found in thy sight to loathing; and, if speech avail not, she will certainly compass my death and the death of Suleyman, thy darling. This day she has tried one way and failed. It is likely she will next bring Nûr hither, as it were to confirm her report, to tell thee lies of her teaching. Thou wilt not hearken to her, O my lord? Swear to give no heed to the words of her mouth—the words of my enemy, whose creature she is! O Saïd, swear this to me by the spirit of thy religion! For the sake of the son I have borne to thee, set my mind at rest! My heart grows sick for fear I should lose thy favour by which alone I live. Swear that thy understanding shall lend no weight to their calumnies, that I may know I have yet a little grace in thy sight! And ah! swear to put away this wicked woman—to cast her forth as an evil-doer from thy house. Does she not daily, hourly, plot my death and the death of thy son? Is she not therefore guilty of blood? O Saïd, O my beloved, O spring of life to me, scorn not my prayer or I shall know that thy desire is clean gone from me!"

216

Saïd fondled Ferideh's head as she lay in the crook of his arm upon the couch. He swore eagerly, as a lover swears, that he was deaf thenceforth to all that might be said against her. But with regard to Hasneh, he would ponder the matter at length and decide what was best to be done.

At that she cried out that he loved her not, and made as if to break away; but his strong arm held her fast. Pouting, with reproachful eyes,—

"What is this?" she whispered. "Art thou then weary of me and has that foul hag thy favour, that thou shakest so thy head and wilt not vouchsafe me a plain answer? Does she not plot to murder me and my child?—Ay, and it may be thee also, O sun that warms me! My prayer is for thy happiness and the lives of all who love thee. Cast her forth, I beseech thee, as thou carest for me."

She hung upon him with strained throat and bosom crushed. Her eyes languished into his, striving to cast that spell upon him which made his heart like melted wax for her will's moulding. For a brief space his purpose wavered. The faintness of strong desire came upon him as a mist confusing his brain, so that he saw things dimly. But he mastered himself; and his face took on a look of tender firmness, such as one uses to chide a well-loved daughter.

"Allah witness, I would do all things to preserve thee, O Ferideh, O garden of my delight! But this one thing I cannot; to cast out a woman who has been mine since first I wore the turban, and who has given proof of faithfulness in many trials and hardships. To do this would be a crime in the sight of Allah, and all my neighbours would cry shame upon me. It may well be that she is jealous, but thou in thy anger dost think too ill of her. Nevertheless jealousy is an evil spirit to possess man or woman. It makes a virtue of foul sin, and is mother to the lust of blood. I will have her watched narrowly, I promise, so that her malice shall not harm thee. Moreover, I swear I will never speak friendly to her from this hour forth, since she is hateful to thee, O full moon of my nights. But cast her forth I cannot, lest all good men should forsake me."

He thought directly of Selîm, that upright servant, before whose outspoken criticism and advice he had quailed more than once despite his show of assurance. Selîm was a good

Muslim, a man pious and devout both in practice and at heart. Had he been born to wealth and eminence he would have been revered of all men for a saint, even as Ismail Abbâs, the Sherîf.   Saïd, coveting above all things a reputation for sanctity, had come, almost without knowing it, to model his behaviour on that of his bailiff.   Whenever a question of conduct confronted him, he would refer it mentally to Selîm, conjuring up a bearded face, with mild eyes looking shrewdly from under a high, turbaned forehead.   This time the brow of the vision was knitted in strong disapproval and the eyes were keen of reproach.

Though far from content with his answer, Ferideh understood that it was final.   She hung back from him, and, resting her chin in her hand, sulked awhile with downcast eyes and jutting underlip.   The change from girlhood had taken nothing from her charm.   The full, round lines of bust and limbs, scarcely blurred by her under robe of silk gauze, might coarsen to fatness by-and-by, but showed as yet no more than a pleasing softness.   The skin of her face and neck were waxen white, except the cheeks, which were painted.   Paint also was responsible for the extreme redness of her lips, which made them like a wound.   Her grey eyes, artificially brightened, languished under long black lashes; and her hair was glossy with unguents.

Saïd's passion for her, instead of abating, had grown with the years.   Hasneh had given him her whole heart at one gift, and he had soon wearied of her.   But with Ferideh he was haunted by a suspicion of something withheld, of some inner shrine still barred to him.   There was a reserve in all her tenderness.   Though never felt at the moment, it struck him always in the retrospect.   Looking back upon the times when she had been most yielding and full of endearments, he recognised its presence then as ever.   And the feeling of something beyond kept his ardour alive, as the fire leaps always to fresh fuel.

The scene of their talk was an upper chamber, lighted discreetly by a deep-bayed lattice projecting over the yard. The vault of the ceiling was shaped like a sea-urchin; and from the height of its dome a curious lamp of bronze hung by a chain of the like metal.   In one corner, near the door, stood a bed, decked with a white coverlid cunningly embroidered with gold, and veiled by mosquito curtains of the finest gauze. It was a true Frankish bed—just such another as that Saïd had coveted years ago, in the house of the missionary. Its iron frame was supported on six legs, and above it at each corner stood a brass knob flanking the rail. He had bought it of a Greek merchant for the price first asked, so instant was his desire of it, and the money burning his hand. Two or three large stools inlaid with mother-of-pearl, a great chest or press of the same workmanship, a large divan, wide as the bed, and made as soft with gaily-coloured cushions—these and a number of vessels and trays of earthenware, copper, brass and even silver, set in a row beside the entry, made up the furniture of the room. The walls had once been painted in a chequered pattern, but the paint had worn or peeled off for the most part, and none had cared to renew it. The pair were alone.

"What part has Nûr in this business?" asked Saïd at length, breaking a thoughtful silence. "She has ever been most friendly to me—and to thee likewise, O my soul; since it is by her aid that I am lord of thy fancy. It cannot be that she is turned my enemy. . . . By Allah, no! it is impossible."

Ferideh slipped from the couch and knelt at his feet. She reached out her arms to draw him down to her, gazing tenderly into his face.

"O my great lord," she murmured, with a playful fondness, "thou art a man and wise, while I am but a woman and of no understanding. Yet must I be thy seer, it seems, to point out to thee the cause of many things thy wisdom cannot fathom. Know then, O breath of my life, that mightier than jealousy, more misleading than strong drink, more heady than the perfume of a fair woman, is the greed for money. Now Nûr is the very mother of avarice, and, since her lot is not as the lot of other women, she can have her will of what belongs to her. A maid or a wife may hoard money, but she is sure it will never profit her. With this old woman it is otherwise. The thirst for more grows on her with the years. I doubt not but thou didst fully requite her for her service to thee in the year of the great war, when—may Allah preserve thee for ever, O father of kindness!—thou didst stoop to rescue me, thy handmaid, from the ruin of my father's house. I say, I am

sure thou didst reward her nobly.   Yet, now that she beholds
thee rich and high in honour, she remembers it as little and
grumbles openly.

"O my beloved, the cause of all this coil is thy distrust of
me.   I am not jealous of Hasneh—Allah forbid!   Yet it
grieves me to think that thou hast a secret with her which is
concealed from me.   I mean the secret of the place where thy
store is hidden.   Nûr knows well that Hasneh is in thy confidence; it is for this that she courts her favour.   I, thy
servant, am the main obstacle in her way, wherefore she, as
well as Hasneh, schemes to remove me; well knowing that I
suspect the Mother of Wind, and keep strict watch on her and
all who visit her.   I know not what reward she holds out to
Hasneh, but it must be a great one; for Sàadeh tells me that
the eyes of the childless one brighten strangely when she
speaks apart with her, and all her bearing is of one who
clinches a rare bargain.   Now, O my lord, thou knowest all—
as much as I have been able to gather of the plot.   May Allah
preserve thy life to me for ever, and may all who hate thee
perish utterly!"

V

SAÏD'S anger burst forth like a torrent after rain. Even Ferideh's life was of less moment than his precious hoard. He called down every kind of shame and disaster upon Nûr and all her kind. Though his understanding discounted the tale of Hasneh's complicity, his savage rage of the moment made no distinctions. He had no doubt but that Nûr had beguiled his woman to let her into the secret of the hiding-place; and he cursed Hasneh with all the venom of threatened greed.

A slight hubbub arose in the court below, but he heeded it not, though Ferideh strained her ears to listen.

"By Allah, I must at once remove my treasure to some other place; and henceforth I will trust thee, and thee only, O Ferideh," he muttered in a kind of frenzy. "It may be they have filched from it already. Praise to Allah, thou hast warned me in time! At present there is but a small sum in the house; but, after a few days, when my shop and stock-in-trade shall have been sold, the whole head of my wealth must lie here for a while, until I have closed the bargain with Mahmud; for I have sworn never to trust a usurer with my fortune. Mahmud is obstinate and makes a brave show of holding out, but I know privately that his need is urgent; and he must shortly come to terms. By the Holy Coràn; by Allah Most High, I shall henceforth trust thee only, O my soul! Now listen. . . ."

She sat at his feet with veiled eyes, but her whole posture told of the keenest attention. The chatter of voices in the yard was no more to her now than the droning buzz of flies which filled the room, and which from long use was accounted silence.

"Thou knowest the roof of this chamber, how it towers above the rest of the house, and the flight of steps leading up to

it. Beside the steps, on the right of one ascending, there
is a stone like to other stones in the wall, seeming firmly set
as they.   Thou mayest know it by the mark of a chisel near
its centre.   It is a cheat, being but a thin slab—the door of
a kind of cupboard.   This night I must move my money
thither, and if thou canst contrive to join me by stealth, I will
teach thee the trick of it.   It was made by the owner of the
place for his own ends.   He showed it me as giving his
house an advantage over others; but hitherto I have not
used it, considering that Ibrahîm, the doorkeeper, had dwelt
long on the premises and might well have an inkling of its
whereabouts.   But now that my own hiding-place is discovered, I must place the money there.   Henceforth thou
and no other art in the secret.   Allah reward thee, that thou
hast warned me in time!"

Ferideh kissed his hand and fondled it, her face shadowed
by the tresses she had loosed to charm him.   A sweet perfume
rose from her, enervating him.   He stretched his hands to
raise her.

But, even as he leaned forward, the door was pushed open
and Suleyman ran in with a burst of laughter.

The little boy was arrayed as a miniature Turkish soldier—
a fancy dress Saïd had seen in the shop of a tailor, and had
brought home with him to please Ferideh.   The doorkeeper
had fashioned him a tiny wooden sword, which he wore
proudly stuck in his belt.   With a spoilt child's confidence
he flew straight to Saïd, laughing, childlike, for no cause
whatever.   Scrambling upon the couch, he seated himself
cross-legged, still laughing, ere he deigned to speak.

"O my father," he piped.   "It is Nûr, the old woman,
who is come to see thee.   She waits below with the Mother
of Wind, whom I have beaten stoutly—I promise thee, by
Allah—for making my mother's hand bleed.   She—I mean
not that wicked one, but Nûr—she bade me say that she
would speak with thee alone.   Now I love Nûr well, because
she brings me sweets from the shop of Kheyr-ud-dîn, and
Kheyr-ud-dîn, as thou thyself hast said, O my father, is the
lord of all for candies.   See, O my mother, what she has
brought me to-day!"

He opened his hand to show a sample of the sweetmeat
called "baclawi," which is a kind of pastry sandwich, filled

with spices, sugar, and a dough of sweet nuts, the whole
perfectly soaked in honey. The hand displayed was sticky,
so he licked it; rubbing his belly with the other to convey
a gluttonous joy.

"Up, O Suleyman!" cried Saïd, fiercely. "Run, bid
this old woman come hither, to this room, if she has aught
of importance to say to me. Tell her besides that I have
no secret from the mother of my delight!"

The little boy slipped down from the sofa and stood a
minute staring up at him, the half smile of his parted lips
begging but a little encouragement to become a guffaw. Then,
awed by the sternness of the eyes meeting his, he ran to do
the errand as fast as his short legs could carry him.

Ferideh snatched up a shroud-like garment and a veil
which hung over the end of the couch, and made haste to
don them. Then she knelt to Saïd and kissed his hand, pressing her forehead to it, as a servant craving protection. He fell
to stroking her head-dress, a great storm in his throat choking
speech.

They heard footfalls on the stair, and a sound of laboured
breathing. Then the tall figure of Nûr, which the years had
bowed a little, stood in the doorway; and a deep, unquavering
voice, said,—

"Peace be upon thee, O Saïd, child of my soul! and upon
thee also, O daughter of Yuhanna."

Ferideh returned the salutation mechanically; but the
wrath of her lord broke through the habit of a lifetime.
Without one word of compliment or blessing, he rushed upon
the visitor and cursed her for a thief and a liar, the mother
of all mischief. She stood aghast as one thunderstruck,
staring at him, while he heaped insult upon insult, sparing
no taunt that might wound her. He reviled her with her
way of life, calling her all the foul names his throat could
frame or his lips utter. He spat upon her for a robber, and
would have smitten her face where the eyes shone through
the veil, had not Ferideh rushed forward screaming to stay
his arm.

For long Nûr remained speechless under his abuse; but by
degrees, the lash of his tongue stinging her, she waxed furious.
The words of her mouth scarcely reached Saïd save as a
stream that strove and failed to drown the torrent of his

cursing. Yet a few of them remained with him long after as a menace. "I have loved thee ever as my own child, O Saïd, lord of ingratitude. I would have served thee with my life. And yet thou returnest me no greeting when I bless thee, neither dost thou wait to hear my tale, but assailest me suddenly with evil words, heaping dishonour upon me. Thou art a fool thus to outrage one who never drew near thee with any other purpose than to promote thy welfare. . . . Get me gone, forsooth! Yes, truly I will get me gone, and that for ever, from this house and the pig its owner. Allah witness, I wash my hands of the dirt of thee. It is well seen thou art the son of low people, O fisherman, who breakest every law of behaviour in thy own house. See how he winces, how the mean soul thinks shame that he was once poor by the will of Allah! Ah, there are many things thou didst bind me not to tell which now shall be made known in the city! How gottest thou that wealth, the root of all thy honour? Didst thou not take it from the old man, the beggar who called thee son? And did he not plunder it from the house of Yuhanna, father to this woman, whom he slew with his own hand? Was there not the Sultàn's order that restitution should be made, even to the full amount of all that was looted from the Nazarenes? and hast thou made any? Have I not been thy preserver a hundred times, when a word of my mouth could have ruined thee? Even now, when I publish the truth, thou shalt hardly escape a heavy penalty. It may be they will deprive thee of all that thou hast; for the Waly is needy and loves money, and thy name and honour stand not high enough to acquit thee. . . .

"Allah knows I loved thee as though thou hadst been my own child, and because I loved thee I have been a shield to thee these many years; but now all ties are broken betwixt me and thee. All I know concerning thee shall be noised abroad; and thou hast told me much that ill becomes a believer. Thy neighbours shall turn from thee with loathing when they learn how thou didst use thy more than father, when he lay dead; making off at once with the money, and leaving thy duty of burial and grief to be done by others. Oh, may Allah blast thy life and blind thee, thou hypocrite who wouldst be called a saint! I came hither, a friend, to warn thee of a peril threatening thee : I go hence, thy foe till death, the friend of thy haters, O dog, son of a dog !"

She was gone and the sound of her retreating steps died upon the stairs. But odd phrases of her speech, which had come to him through the thunder of his own rage, rang yet in Saïd's brain, like the catch of an evil song, and rankled there. He frowned and his eyes grew haggard. A hush seemed to have fallen upon the house; or was it only that he was deaf from the late uproar? He pictured the servants whispering together in corners, and hoped to Allah no word of Nûr's had reached them. He heard the voice of the doorkeeper raised in a farewell compliment, and the slam of the closing gate behind someone who had passed out; and he was thankful to know that she was gone.

Ferideh laughed scornfully, looking at the empty doorway as if she still saw the bowed figure filling it, wrapped in its shroud of blue with tarnished fringe of gold. Then, marking her lord's gloom, she knelt down at his feet and put up her arms to him.

"Praise be to Allah !" she murmured. "Now I surely know that I have favour in thy sight, because thou hast refused to hear the tale of this wicked woman, which is a lie even as the words she spake but now concerning thee are all lies. Seem not so sad, O my dear, for she is powerless to hurt thee seeing thou art set high in wealth and honour, and all men know thee for a good man and an upright. For the sake of the kindness thou hast shown me in this matter, and because thou hast deigned to reveal to me the secret place of thy treasure, I am now more fully thine than ever before. What thanks can I render thee, O my soul? Behold, my inmost secret heart is thine, and I have no desire apart from thee. Take me in thy arms, O sun that warms me! Kiss me, O my beloved !" . . .

Whereat Saïd became as one of no understanding.

P

VI

ON an evening Saïd went forth alone into the gardens, to the coffee-house of Rashîd, which was on the river bank. He was sure to find Selîm there at that hour; and he walked eagerly, having blithe news to tell. At last Mahmud Effendi had humbled himself, and Saïd was master of the bargain, though in no haste to conclude it. One more interview with the needy grandee and he would own the finest freehold palace in the city. Moreover, thanks to his address in beating down the price, he would have plenty of money left when it was paid. The surplus he would employ in trade and usury, to such advantage that he would soon be the richest man of the province and highest in honour. He saw himself a member of the Council of Notables, enthroned at the Waly's right hand, advising the Governor in all things.

The sometime fisherman hugged himself at the prospect. As he emerged from the eastern gate the last rays of sunlight, glanced from the dark hill-tops, were melting the leafage to amber and pale gold. A rich purple gloom gathered in the east, under a sky of amethyst melting to palest green. Down the narrow road, between stone walls more or less ruined, which led to the pleasure-groves by the riverside, men in flowing robes were sauntering by groups of two and three. Their moving shadows were long, oblique and very blue. Most of them dangled chaplets, whose beads they shifted lazily one by one. A few of the more exquisite held flowers of strong perfume to their nostrils, at which they smelt rapturously with a deep breath like a sigh.

The blaze on the hill-tops died suddenly, leaving a glow as of live coal. All things took on soft, dead tints. Shadows grew faint, ashy grey all at once. The sky basked in an afterthought of glory, growing tender for the stars.

A low doorway of the kind which is usual in walled vineyards admitted to the garden, or rather wilderness, in which was the tavern of Rashîd. Saïd bowed his head to pass the lintel, and then stood still in astonishment. In a space pretty clear of the bushes, which formed thickets on every side, there were four tents pitched. Three of them were large marquees; the fourth, a mere canvas screen about a fire, was observed closely by a gathering of curious loafers. Hobbled horses grazed where they could. In the mouth of the largest tent a party of Franks, lounging on chairs of loose structure, were enjoying the cool of the evening. The sound of their laughter reached Saïd, like the beating on a tin for emptiness. From the point of the tent where they sat drooped a small flag of red, white and blue, oddly striped. Saïd knew the pattern of it. It was the same which fluttered on the first day of every week over the dwelling of the English Consul. "Travellers from the land of the English," he thought, and marvelled at the folly of men who, having wealth and honour in their own country, and being neither merchants nor pilgrims, would thus wander forth in discomfort.

Taking stock of the encampment, he drew near to the tavern. Two or three persons who knew him rose and saluted at his approach. He returned their greeting in a preoccupied manner and passed on to Selîm, who had carried his stool apart and sat against the trunk of a walnut-tree which overhung the stream. Rashîd himself was forward to bring a seat for the merchant and to ask what he would be pleased to drink.

"What news, O my master?" asked Selîm, settling down once more to the enjoyment of his smoke.

"Good news—excellent!" rejoined the other, with a complacent purse of his lips. "Praise be to Allah, one may say that the bargain is concluded."

"Now, by my beard, I am happy with thee. May Allah make thee blest in it!"

There followed silence between them for a little while; Saïd reviewing his cleverness with a gratified smirk, Selîm gravely watching the dark swirl of the eddies in their bed of pale stones.

"I needs must call in all my money by the third day of next week," murmured Saïd, as one who thinks aloud.

Selîm knitted his forehead, calculating.

"To hear is to obey," he said ruefully. "Nevertheless, there is much business and the time is short. Two weeks would scarcely suffice for all that must be done, and behold, thou givest me but a few days. He who sells in a hurry sells at a loss. If, as thou sayest, thou hast made an easy bargain, it cannot surely be that thou wilt need the whole of thy wealth. O my brother, I counsel thee to put off the sale of thy merchandise for at least a little time!"

"It cannot be," said Saïd, peevishly. "I must know the true sum of my wealth. To buy a fine palace and not to know exactly what was left to him were the action of a fool! The man who did so would be a laughing-stock, and rightly despised. . . . By Allah, it will be sweet to behold it all before me—all the great wealth which is mine—to pass my fingers through it as one does through dry grains of corn; to reckon it over and over and know that it is with me in the house. Praise to Allah, who has made me rich!"

"Now, Allah forgive thee, O my brother, for thou settest too great store by thy money. Thy heart and thy soul are in it. At that time evil befalls a man when most he vaunts his honour and is puffed up because of it. It is not right for one to keep too close an account of his goods. A man's fortune is like his vineyard: the heart of it is his own, but every wayfarer has a share in the outlying parts which skirt the highway. Who would deny a bunch of grapes to the thirsty? And if he pluck for himself, would any be found to blame him? So the heart of thy fortune is thine by Allah's leave; yet thou shalt not take too exact an account of it, lest from always saying 'I have so-and-so much' thou set thy wealth between thee and Allah Most High. When a man has a field of corn he will suffer God's poor to glean in it at the harvest time. Likewise, when a man is blessed with riches even as thou art, it is seemly that, in taking account, he leave an undefined portion for the poor. Nothing of all a man has is his own, but he must pay a part of it in alms to God. If he omit to do this, Allah Himself shall call him niggard and shall soon strike him down, as unworthy, from his high estate. O my brother, all this while that I have been thy servant it has been in my mind that I would rather be a simple hireling, as I am, than the lord of great riches, as thou art. Many snares are in the path of the great, but—praise be to Allah!—the way of the humble is plain."

"Thou speakest vainly," said Saïd, snapping him up; "and thy words have no point for me. All this which thou tellest me so solemnly, as if it were some new piece of wisdom, I have known and observed from childhood. With what one fault canst thou tax me, I should like to know! Do I not give alms to the utmost of all that is mine? Do I not always praise Allah at the appointed hours? Have I ever omitted to purify myself according to the law? By Allah, I wish to know for what cause thou scoldest me!"

Selîm pleaded,—

"Nay, O my master, be not angry with me. Allah forbid that I should venture to chide thee at all. I know well that thou art in all things a just man, and I myself have great reason to bless thee. I call Allah to witness that, from the time thou didst bestow on me that rich garment which I still treasure in my house, I have held thee always as a dear brother. It was but as a brother that I spoke to thee, fearing lest thou shouldst make for thyself an enemy whom none may withstand. And in truth I think thou holdest too much by the outward duty of the law, which, as his Honour Ismaîl Abbâs says, is to its spirit as the word is to its meaning, or the shell of a nut to the kernel. Moreover—"

But Saïd stopped his ears.

"Enough! Enough! . . . Thou wilt provide that the goods and the shop be sold, and the money brought to me on the second day; I command thee: it is finished. And now, with thy leave, we will speak of other matters."

After that Selîm was silent a great while, while Saïd puffed defiantly at his narghileh.

The stars were bright by this time, though the sky above the western horizon was still pale green and lustrous. A single dome of the city, seen through a gap of the foliage, seemed to shine beyond the dark walls with a spiritual whiteness all its own. The moon, a thin crescent like the paring of a fingernail, hung just above it, salient as a jewel on that silky sky. A bird cried drowsily from the upper branches. The wailing voice of a singer came from some other pleasure-house down the stream. The eddies sang and murmured as they sped by.

Anon Saïd picked up his stool and drew near to the tavern.

He had remarked the grouping of those who sat there about some person in their midst, and had caught several deep-breathed "Ma sh'Allah"s, betokening amazement. Undoubtedly there was some story - teller whose fables might serve to while away an hour and dispel the gloom which Selîm's sanctimonious croaking had cast upon him. He imparted the conjecture to his henchman, who followed, nothing loth.

They set their stools within the circle of light shed by a clumsy lantern which hung from a joist of the roof; their coming hardly noticed by the other customers, so absorbed were they in listening to the words of him who sat in their midst. Those nearest them, on the outskirts, turned their heads for a second and that was all. Rashîd, grown very fat with the years, was leaning against the door-post of the inner room. His eyes ranged over the seated crowd before him and his lip curled in scorn.

Saïd beckoned him to draw near.

"Who is the narrator, O my uncle?" he whispered. "Is it anyone of whom one has heard? Are his stories worth heeding?"

"Faugh! It is no narrator, effendi, but only a braggart Nazarene who, having acquired a smattering of the learning of the Franks, is become a dragoman. It is a shame that true believers are found to flatter him by giving ear. By the Coràn, it angers me to see it! He is a great liar, as thou shalt presently hear."

Having imparted this to the merchant in an undertone, the taverner returned to his door-post. The rays of the lantern brought the faces of some of the listeners into warm relief; but the story-teller had his back to the light. He wore a fez set rakishly on one side, and for the rest was very gaily dressed in the Turkish fashion. He seemed consumedly proud of a whip of rhinoceros hide mounted and ringed with silver, for he kept it constantly before the eyes of his audience, illustrating every remark with a flourish. The man's attitude was boastful and assuming, blent, however, with pride at sitting thus on equal terms with men of the dominant creed. Without, in the blue gloom of the garden, the camp-fire and the light of a lamp within the largest tent shone bleared and ruddy. Black shapes were seen moving athwart them from one to the other; the travellers were being served with their evening meal.

"And that city—that Lûndra of which thou speakest—is it a great city like this of ours, or a small place like Hama or Zahleh?" asked an old man of poor appearance.

The dragoman laughed loud and long.

"O Allah! . . . O Lord! . . . How you make me laugh, you men who have seen no land but that you were born in! I tell you that if the city Es-Shâm were five times as great as it is, it would not amount to the half of that great city Lûndra of the English."

At that there was great outcry of wonder and unbelief. "Ma sh'Allah!" cried some and held their peace, aghast. "Allah pardon!" cried others. "Was there ever such a liar? We are simple men and unlearned—that is true—but this thing passes belief!"

"By the Holy Gospel, I speak truth," insisted the dragoman, with vehemence. "May Allah cut off my life if that which I say exceeds the truth by one tittle. I am likely to know; for I went to the city of Lûndra and sojourned there half a year by favour of an English lady—no less than a princess, by Allah!—who loved me and would have me with her in the house."

"Ah, the women! Tell us, I pray thee, O khawajah, what the women are like," said a young and handsome Muslim with a chuckle of self-conceit.

The dragoman grew rapturous.

"The women, mean you? Ah, how can I describe them! . . . And yet I promise thee it is not from want of knowledge that my tongue fails me. The girls of that nation are white and often plump. Their hair varies in colour from black to the hue of clean gold. They are cold and difficult to men of their own race, for whom they are used to care nothing; but they are warm and easy of access to foreigners, and especially to us sons of the Arab, whose blood is as fire in our veins, whose speech is impassioned poetry: so different from the men of their nation, in whom the blood is a stagnant pool and the tongue a sluggard. When I was in Lûndra, fair women followed me in the streets to beseech my company. I speak not, you understand, of the loose women of that city, who are very fine and numerous, but of the wives and daughters of men of substance. There were even some who offered me money to go with them. I tell you, any son of an Arab of an agreeable presence could have his pick of the women of that land, from the wife of the greatest Emìr to the daughter of the meanest fellah."

"By the prophet, I have a mind to visit that country," said the young Muslim with a fatuous laugh.

"Now in this party which I conduct at present"—the dragoman pointed with his whip in the direction of the tents —"there is a girl—ah! I tell you—a pearl—a delight." He held out his hand, pressing the tip of his thumb on that of the extended forefinger: the common gesture of those who would describe something too nice for words. "She loves me, and comes forth to me every night while her parents sleep. She entreats me always to marry her; but I am doubtful whether to do so or not. Her father, you must know, is rich—a great lord. It would be honourable to wed the daughter of such an one. Perhaps—Allah knows!—I shall yield at last to her prayers. Hist!" . . . He sank his voice swiftly. "Hither comes the very girl. No doubt she strays in search of me. Observe now, I pray you!"

Saïd stood up so that he could look over the intervening heads. Every neck was craned, and all eyes peered in one direction.

A young girl of about sixteen years, clad in the close-fitting garb of the Frankish women, was sauntering towards the tavern, eyeing the scene there with dreamy curiosity. She wore no head-dress save her thick fair hair, which hung free down to her shoulders, where it was gathered in and confined by a ribbon. In spite of her unveiled, undraped state, which, to the mind of the onlookers, was little better than nakedness, she moved freely, without a trace of embarrassment, until she grew aware of the gaze of so many prying eyes, when she averted her face and stepped more consciously. She passed just within the sphere of the lantern, so that a faint, warm light played on the outlines of her figure, hinting rather than revealing its slender grace. Her hands clasped behind her neck threw her bosom forward, strengthening the curve of it. Saïd had often seen Frankish women and had marvelled at their lack of modesty, but he had never beheld one so fair, so young and so perfectly shameless. Believing the tale of the Nazarene, he envied the good fortune of that son of a dog.

She was passing by with a timid glance when she caught sight of the dragoman, who to that end had thrust himself forward. She smiled and nodded graciously to him, saying something kind in her own language. The man replied in a tone of familiarity which conveyed all he meant that it should to the minds of his hearers.

"Aha!" said he, as soon as she was out of earshot. "Aha! She is a peerless gem. By-and-by, when her parents sleep, she will steal out to seek me. By Allah, her mouth overflows with honey. The taste of it makes me drunken."

The young Muslim stared after the maiden; then, turning,—

"Now, by my life, thou art in luck's way," he said. "It is well seen how fair she is! But her father is surely a man of no understanding, and her mother must be like unto him, to let her thus wander without a covering."

"There is one law for the daughter of an Arab, another for the child of a Frank," said the dragoman, sententiously. "As for me, I have dwelt so much among foreigners that a veiled woman is almost a strange thing to me. And, in truth, I know no cause why a woman should veil her face any more than a man, unless she be extremely frightful or loathsome to view."

The tavern-keeper here spoke for the first time, and severely,—

"Young man, thou speakest folly, being a stranger to the Faith that saves. It is a law from of old that every woman shall hide her face from the sight of men. Know that sinful Cabil ebn Adam did lust after his twin sister, Abdul Mughis, and for her sake slew Habil, his brother, who was a good man and dear to Allah. Wherefore it was ordained that all women should hide their shape, that mere lust of the eyes might never more induce so great a crime. Allah is just and merciful!"

At that the garrulous talker was abashed, and his audience looked strange upon him. In the interest they took in his conversation they had all but forgotten the difference of creed. A pause fraught with mutual shyness ensued. Then the dragoman called for more arak and launched forth once more, though with somewhat less of assurance, feeling lonely all at once.

Saïd abode in the little tavern until the first watch of the night was almost spent. He was unaccountably interested in all that the rascal had to tell of that distant land of the English, where the sun was seldom seen, and the women were at once so lovely and so kind to strangers. He questioned the narrator shrewdly as to the state and manner of trade in those parts, and was pleased with the answers he got. It seemed that the finer merchandise of the East—as silks and rich carpets, spices and sweet perfumes—were much prized by the Franks. The way of life there was easy, he learnt, for one who had money and was warmly clad. He felt attracted, and hoped to visit that land.

He imparted this desire to Selîm as they walked back together to the city whose walls rose black before them under a sky pale with stars. But Selîm was chary of sympathy.

"It is true what the drunkard told concerning the Frankish women, how they love men of the East," he said gravely. "Lo, is there not the English princess in our midst —she who dwells in the house called the House of the English Garden, which is beyond the Christian quarter? She submitted herself to a young man of the Bedawin, and is become his wife. It is true what the dog said. But as for thee, thou hast not yet performed the great pilgrimage; and that must be done ere thou canst think of migrating to a land of unbelief."

"Perhaps the right is with thee," rejoined Saïd, moodily. "Yet, from what the infidel said, it must be a pleasant land to dwell in—none like it under Heaven! Didst mark the girl, how sweet she was? By Allah, it is a shame that the son of a dog should have her . . .   I charge thee make all speed with the business of which we spoke. Allah keep thee in peace, and may thy night be happy!"

They kissed and parted at the city gate.

VII

EARLY on the morning of the second day of the week Saïd strode through the bazaars towards that familiar upper room which was his shop and which would soon be no longer his. His servant walked a little in advance of him, using the furled parasol as a staff to admonish such of the crowd as were slow to make way. All the ways were thronged with noisy folk. The whole city hummed of life. Rifts in the crazy roof admitted a sunbeam here and there—a bar of light, hazy with dancing motes, which transfigured wayfarers for a moment, causing the colours of their raiment to bloom, and fade as suddenly.

Many of the traders who sat cross-legged behind the stalls bordering the causeway were well-known to Saïd. He used his right hand to salute them as he passed; his left hung limp, telling the amber beads of a chaplet. Pleasant odours assailed his nostrils, for many vendors of perfumery had their shops in the lane he was threading.

He was light at heart. The full tale of his fortune was to be told into his hands that day, and on the morrow he would dazzle Mahmud with a part of it. He remembered how Selīm had ever striven to dissuade him from taking this sure path to glory; and his lip curled with the blandest scorn. Selīm was a good man and pious; he could be trusted to the utmost at all times. But he lacked the fire and enterprise which exalt one above others. Calling to mind the fable of the beggar and the collar of gold, Saïd quaked with inward laughter. It tickled him to think that such a story had been told for his instruction—to him, the wiliest of men living.

A woman, cowled and veiled, stood in the way before him, conversing with a tall Christian. The man was dressed in the Turkish fashion, with a tight vest of murrey-colour buttoned down the front, a blue zouave jacket, and a sack for trousers.

235

The woman was shrouded in dull crimson—a common choice of colour.   They blocked Saïd's path in spite of the servant's cry of "Oáh!"   He observed them pretty narrowly in passing, thinking shame that the wife of a Muslim should converse with an unbelieving pig.   When he was a little way beyond them the voice of the woman startled him.   For a moment he could have sworn that it was Ferideh speaking.   He turned sharply to look back, but the conversation was over and the woman lost to sight in the throng.

He felt uneasy.   It was the hour when Ferideh and her handmaid were wont to visit the bath.   He had sometimes remarked upon the length. of time she spent there, and had heard her excuses.   Could it be that she was deceiving him?   The more he thought of it the less likely it seemed.   She had been most docile of late, fulfilling his heart's desire gladly in all things.   Besides Ibrahìm, the doorkeeper, was there to watch her, and he at anyrate was trusty; he would never suffer her to go forth alone.   A little reflection showed his fear groundless.

A loud shout to clear the way disturbed his musing.   He looked and saw a rider drawing near, well seen above the press of foot-passengers.   The crowd parted, making way for an old man of exceeding fatness mounted upon an ass, which was kept at an ambling pace by the vigorous prods of one who walked behind, using his staff for a goad.

"May thy day be happy, O abu Khalìl!" cried Saïd, merrily.   "Whither away so early?"

The fat taverner, who of all men was used to be most friendly to Saïd, for once seemed alarmed to encounter him.   He returned the merchant's greeting falteringly, as one aghast at some sight of terror.   He neither reined in his steed nor showed the least wish to parley, but rather urged the donkey to greater speed by vicious digs with the sharp corners of the iron stirrups.

"Cut short thy life!" cried Saïd after him.   "What ails thee, old man?   Surely thou art possessed with a devil! . . . Allah keep thee, O Camr-ud-dìn; what is amiss with thy father?"

The young man stood still to scowl at the speaker.   Then, seized with sudden anger, he threatened Saïd with his stick.

"My father is a just man and honourable, and thinks

shame to speak with a murderer!" he hissed. "Who was it that slew his father shamefully for the sake of gain? Thou knowest not who it was, I warrant! The blood of Mustafa, my father's friend, is between us, O thou false saint!"

He spat on the ground for very loathing, and so ran on to catch up the donkey which, curbed only by the weak hands of Abu Khalîl, was making sad havoc of the crowd.

Saïd had shrunk back, fearing violence. For some time he strove to collect his wits. Roused at length by the servant's inquiries touching his health, he became aware that people were staring at him.

"By Allah, it is a lie!" he gasped. "May Allah strike me dead if one word of what the dog said is true!"

The bystanders thought him raving. They murmured of compassion one to another. The servant took his arm respectfully to lead him home; but Saïd, recovering his balance, shook him off and ordered him angrily to lead on. He was glad to be sure that few, if any, had observed the true cause of his discomfiture.

As he pursued his way through the shaded markets like passages in a vast house, he pondered the words of Camr-ud-dîn with mingled anger and distress. It was not hard to guess the source of the libel. Nûr had sworn to make him rue the day he flouted her, and this foul slander was undoubtedly the first-fruits of her spite. The lie was chosen with devilish cunning. He could by no means disprove it, for there had been no eye-witness to the manner of Mustafa's death. His only course was one of flat and obstinate denial, and even then many were sure to think he spoke false.

But in the very midst of gloomy forebodings a droll memory came to make him chuckle. He grinned broadly, and his eyes twinkled under brows still lowering. It had often been told him how, at the burying of Mustafa, Abu Khalîl had all but met his death through excess of mourning. The faithful have the custom to put a little soap in their mouths when attending a funeral, that the foam on their lips may vouch for the frenzy of their grief. Now Abu Khalîl, being an elderly man and wheezy, had managed to swallow his piece of soap at the very outset, before it was well melted. It had stuck in his throat, choking him; so that he flung himself on the ground, spitting, coughing and struggling in mortal terror.

All those who walked with him, ascribing these antics to respect for the deceased, looked on admiringly; until Camr-ud-dìn, divining the true cause, rolled his father over and thrust a finger down his throat, when they saw the fun of it and fell a-quaking, exaggerating the gravity of their faces to mask the untimely mirth convulsing them.

He had always felt friendly towards Abu Khalìl, and to know the old man's mind estranged from him was of itself a cruel blow. He consoled himself, however, with the reflection that on the morrow he would be the peer of princes, owning a great palace, and so out of reach of the malice of these low people.

No sooner did he arrive at the shop than all cares were drowned in the instant bliss of counting out a great sum of money all his own. His entire wealth was there before him, bestowed in leathern bags whose fulness was a joy to see. He abode in that upper room, drinking sherbet, smoking and gloating over his riches till the fall of night, when, with the help of Selìm and his son, he conveyed the treasure privately to the hiding-place prepared for it in his own house. The delight of possessing so much made him generous, and Selìm's faithfulness was suitably rewarded. Saïd sat late upon the house-top that night, looking out over the city and up at the moon, a great pride choking him and bringing tears to his eyes.

VIII

THE moon was near the full. The city, precise in clear light and velvet shadow, seemed a fantasy of carven stone with its domes great and little, graceful minarets tapering like spindles, and the jutting cubes of its upper chambers. Seen thus from above, it had no life save that which the glow from some high lattice hinted, or a group of black forms motionless upon some terraced roof. The half-circle of the hills closed the distance, as it were the dark rim of a cup filled to the brim with moonlight.

Saïd's eyes strayed from the precision of the near buildings to the floating mystery beyond. He was dreaming a fair dream, and the realism of keen outlines hurt his eyes. He sat there in the hollow of the night, and its silence talked with him ; while the city murmured weary as a shell, so faintly that it seemed a hush made audible. He was alone with Allah : the thought hallowed his selfish ecstasy. Exultant, he lifted up his heart in thanksgiving to God, who had endowed Saïd the Fisherman with sharp wits beyond his fellows, so that, by the blessing of the Most High, he was now risen to be Saïd the Merchant, lord of a great palace, and of money enough. He hugged himself for a clever one. By the Coràn, there was none like him in all the world !

A sound of weeping rose from within the house. It had long been audible, but he perceived it suddenly and with a start. It came from the chamber where, by his order, Hasneh was confined. She had been in durance except when at work ever since the day of her attack on Ferideh. Always she prayed to be allowed to speak with her lord, were it but for a minute, but Saïd had been peremptory in refusal. The voice of her distress broke jarringly upon his dream. His heart smote him so that he frowned and cursed her under his breath. The next impulse was to go down and speak kindly

239

to her, to silence the one note discordant with his happiness. But he was mindful of his promise to Ferideh, and, moreover, was loth to move lest, by so doing, he should break the spell of his lonely musing. He contented himself with a vow to treat her better in the future. The new house, which would be his on the morrow, was roomy enough to accommodate many women. Hasneh should have a separate lodging in it, and, it might be, a handmaid to wait on her.

Having given this sop to his conscience, he was falling again into his waking dream of pride, when he became conscious of a soft footfall on the roof behind him. Turning, he beheld Ferideh, her veil thrown back, coming towards him with outstretched hands.

"O father of Suleyman !—O my lord !—O my dear !" she besought him. "Thou hast taken no food since the early morning, and now it is sleep-time. Thou art surely famished and faint with the fatigue of the day. Come down, I pray thee, and partake of that which with my own hands I have made ready for thee ! Ever since the sunset Suleyman has been crying for thee—hardly could I coax him to sleep. Come now, O star of my soul, and delay not to take refreshment !"

"Good—I come !" said her lord, brushing away the last mists of reverie with the back of his hand. "Allah increase thy wealth, O mother of Suleyman ! Now, indeed, I perceive that I am hungry, though the thing had escaped my mind. I will gladly go down with thee into the house for an hour, but after I have eaten I must return hither. No sleep will seal my eyes this night for the care of my treasure which is here bestowed. Wherefore I purpose to wrap me in a cloak and abide here till daybreak."

"Now, of a truth, thy speech is not of wisdom," said Ferideh, chiding, as she followed him down the stone flight which climbed by the wall. "By watching thou wilt but weary thyself to no purpose; for who is likely to rob thee, O light of my eyes? I alone, of all in the house, am privy to the secret of thy treasure, and I shall be with thee through the night. Nay, by Allah, if thou thinkest indeed that vigil must be kept, I myself will watch instead of thee. Thou hast toiled all the day while I have been lazy; wherefore thy servant is now the better fitted for this duty."

Saïd was touched by her devotion. He blessed her, but bade her speak no more on the subject for his mind was made up.

In the best chamber of the harîm a meal was set forth on a large tray of brass, beside which was spread a square of carpet. There was a savoury mess of rice and chicken meat, another of beans fried in oil; a large earthen bowl brimmed with a syrup compounded of honey and the pressed juice of grapes, in which were whole grapes floating. Two loaves were there, as flat as pancakes, besides a little heap of figs, very tempting in their purple ripeness. At sight of these dainties Saïd's hunger strengthened apace. He took stock of them, enjoying the foretaste, while Ferideh fetched a vessel of water, a basin and a napkin from the antechamber. His washings done, he crossed his legs upon the mat, and, leaning forward, plunged a ravenous hand into the mess. Ferideh waited upon him clingingly. Her fingers had a trick of caressing whatever they touched, of dwelling lightly for a moment as if reluctant to quit hold. To watch her through the open door, bending languidly over a brazier where coffee was stewing, lifting things and setting them down with that strange touch of hers, thrilled Saïd unaccountably.

"Art thou still minded to keep lonely watch upon the house-top to-night?" she said archly, when, having cleared away the fragments of the feast, she came to nestle against him.

He answered,—

"Nay, by Allah; I have no mind to do aught save content thee. Nevertheless, after I have spent an hour at thy side and thy eyes grow heavy with sleep, it may well be I shall repair again to the terrace. Understand, O my pearl, that my mind is anxious out of all reason. And to watch upon the house-top in the cool night air seems better than to be wakeful in a narrow room."

She turned her shoulder upon him, pouting, but held her peace. His arm circled her lovingly. Of a sudden she started away and clapped her hands in childish glee.

"O my dear, I have something good for thee!" she cried, "something sweet for thee to taste. Merciful Allah! I had quite forgotten it until this minute. Wait but a little and I will bring thee a glassful hither!"

Q

She ran from the room and shortly returned, carrying in her hand a glass filled with some amber fluid. She offered it to him.

"What stuff is this?" asked Saïd, cautiously, taking the glass in his hand and holding it up between him and a candle which burned on the wooden press by the wall, so that a ray shone through it.

"Know, O lord of all my doings, that I, thy servant, was idle after noon of this day, and I grew weary of being idle. So I called Sàadeh to me and took counsel what to do. And it happened, by the grace of Allah, that there were many figs with us in the house—of the gift of Rashìd the taverner, thy friend, who sent us yesterday three basketfuls. And it came into my mind to make a new dainty—I mean a sherbet of figs. So we made careful choice of the fruit and crushed it with sugar in a little water and set it in a pan to boil. And afterwards, when the mixture was cool again, we sipped and found it very good. And I said in my soul, O soul, my idleness has been well employed for I have devised a new dainty for the mouth of my beloved. Now taste, I pray, and tell me how thou findest!"

Saïd sniffed at the contents of the glass and made a wry face.

He said,—

"The smell of it is not good. It is perhaps some trick thou wouldst put upon me for laughter's sake. Allah grant it be no unclean thing or fierce drug to madden me. It were a sin to make me drink wine who am preparing for the pilgrimage."

But Ferideh's gaze of stricken love reassured him. Once more he held the potion up to the light and looked through it.

"Sherbet of figs, saidst thou? Allah have pity! Surely it cannot be. Figs are all too fleshy to yield clear syrup like this."

Ferideh's voice quavered a little as she replied,—

"We strained it through a piece of new muslin, and when all which would run through was collected, we took the cloth with what remained therein and wrung it out over the basin. Thus we obtained much syrup. O my dear lord, it is cruel to tease me so; being as if thou didst doubt my care for thee, which Allah forbid! I beseech thee drink and tell me: Is it not good?"

Saïd sipped at the lip of the glass, then worked his tongue reflectively.

"It is not unpleasant," he admitted. "But, by my beard, I perceive no taste of figs in it, but rather of walnuts, I should say, or something of that kind. It is sweet, however, and I am fain to drink it if by so doing I may pleasure thee."

At that she drew closer, with tender looks and soft speech inflaming him. When he had emptied and set down the glass she locked her hands behind his neck. She knelt close to him upon the ground, her bosom strained to his chest so that he felt its warmth. Her head was thrown somewhat back, that her eyes might look into his. The poise of her head, with the trail of her body along the ground, suggested a snake in act to strike its prey.

He clasped her to him. "Allah is great!" he muttered; more as a convenient explosive than for any bearing the words had upon the case. He marvelled vaguely at the change which had taken place in her during the last few weeks. Formerly it had been hard to win the least endearment from her, but now she lavished tenderness upon him at all times. Once her words of love, when uttered, were spiritless, as though she had them by rote; now they were impassioned even beyond his own. Referring this new fire of hers to the circumstances attending Hasneh's disgrace, he wondered that so slight a thing should have power to change the whole nature of a woman.

She went on speaking feverishly, gazing ever into his eyes as if she expected something to appear there which was long in coming.

A strange slumber stole upon Saïd. At first it was but a pleasant languor. Then he grew dizzy. Things dilated and dwindled unaccountably. He heard himself murmur, "O garden of my delight!" . . . and then all was a blank. He knew no more until he awoke in broad daylight to find Sellm bending over him with an anxious face.

"What is the hour?" he inquired drowsily, putting a hand to his forehead. There was pain like a keen dagger in either temple.

"It is near noon, O my brother," said his henchman with

a rueful grin. "I come from the house of Mahmud, where thou hast long been expected. Merciful Allah! What ails thee? Never before have I known thee lag abed. Know, O my master, that Mahmud Effendi is furious at thy delay. He believes that thou hast a set purpose to insult him. All his father's house are gathered there to witness the sale. O my eyes, come quickly and bring the money humbly in thy hand, for they are very angry and would fain do thee dishonour; but the money will appease them. This is a strange humour of thine, to sleep on the bare floor when there is a fine bed at hand."

Saïd sprang to his feet and looked about him, searching every corner with his glance.

"Where is Ferideh?" he cried distractedly.

"Allah alone knows, if thou knowest not!" retorted Selîm in great surprise. "When I came hither it was told me that thou and she were together in this chamber, that the door was made fast with a key for a token that you would not be disturbed. Knowing what grave business awaited thee, I presumed to break open the door. Thine was a heavy sleep, O my brother, for thou heardest not the crash of it. It has taken me so long to waken thee that I began to be afraid, counting thee for dead."

Saïd did not stay to parley. Like a madman he rushed out of the room, through the antechamber, and up the flight of stone steps that led to the roof.

His hiding-place had been rifled. With brutal carelessness the robber had omitted to replace the slab of stone. The hole lay open, quite empty.

Saïd rent his clothes and shrieked for rage and despair. Then he ran down the outer steps into the court so furiously that he fell heavily at the bottom, striking his head upon the pavement. His cap and turban fell off, but he knew it not. He rose, a wild figure, with face all bruised and bleeding, with bare head close-shaven so that the ears stuck out monstrously, and ran forward shouting,—

"Where is Ferideh? I command you, tell me where the lady Ferideh is! . . ."

But the cowering servants had no tidings of her.

"Where Suleyman? Where Sàadeh?"

But there was no answer, only a cringing protestation of innocence from one and all.

His brain reeled. He stretched out his hands vaguely for support, and with a faint cry, "Allah! Allah!" fell lifeless on the pavement.

Cries of distress and horror rent the air. Selîm bent sadly over the form of his sworn brother. Ibrahîm the doorkeeper brought the turban and tarbûsh he had picked up and placed them reverently on his master's head. Hasneh, who had found freedom in the general confusion, flung herself across the body in a passion of grief.

Saïd was carried back into the chamber where he had slept so long and laid upon the Frankish bed which had been his pride. A leech was called in, who bled him freely. By the evening he was able to get up and take count of his misfortunes. He sat on the bare stones with torn raiment and ashes on his head, crying ever, "O Allah, have pity! . . . O Lord, take my life also!" so that men wept to hear him.

By the evening, too, his story was known throughout the city. Men thronged to see but the house of a man who had lost his wealth and wife and son in a single night; and Ibrahîm the doorkeeper became a person of great importance. Saïd the Merchant and Ayûb the Prophet were commonly named in the same breath together; and vows of vengeance were freely made against the man, whatsoever his quality, who had caused this great wrong to be done in the city.

IX

SELÌM, quite distraught with grief for his master's adversity, sought the Waly, the chief of the police, the Mufti, and whomsoever of the great men of the city he thought could succour him. For two days he knew no rest, but was ever on the run from his own lodging to the Serai or the castle, and back again to Saïd's house. His efforts were not in vain. Seeing that the whole city was moved by the outrage, the authorities were strenuous in their endeavours to find the culprits. A description of Ferideh and her child, with such conjectures as to the appearance of her paramour as could be formed from what Hasneh had to tell, were sent post-haste to Beyrût and Hama, to Tarabulus, to Homs, to Haleb, and to various outposts on the desert frontier. Thoughts of the great sum of money the criminals had with them turned each sleepy official to a hungry wolf. They were certain to be taken, the head of the irregular troops told Saïd; it was a question of a few days at the most. He boasted that he had made the whole country a net for them, and awaited but a sign to haul in and take them fast in its toils. His confidence was of great comfort to Saïd, the more so that he could appreciate the metaphor. He vowed the half of his wealth to those who should recover it for him; and he cried night and day upon the name of Allah, with lamentation and every kind of self-abasement, so that all men marvelled at his piety.

At first, as has been said, the Government was very eager in pursuit of the offenders, sparing no pains to ensure their capture. But by-and-by, when many days had passed and all search proved fruitless, zeal began to flag. It was said that the criminals were clean gone out of the country, or else they must surely have been taken, with the hue and cry raised everywhere. If it was Allah's will that they should escape, where was the use in further bothering about them? The man Saïd was left penniless, or nearly so; and that is an ill day's work which is done for thanks only.

The ruined merchant went from house to house, from public office to public office, exhorting, entreating, urging the need of fresh exertions. But, bringing nothing with him, he met with deafness. He found high officials dozing frankly over narghilehs, and came away disheartened, bemoaning his lot, to return on the morrow and get angry words. Doors were closed against him. Those in authority refused to see him any more, and he fared no better with the underlings, having no money to give.

Weary and heartsick, he at length gave up all hope of redress, and turned his mind to the ordering of his affairs. This was no easy matter, for the waste of the household had been great. Saïd, though shrewd and even stingy in all business concerns, was fond of display as tending to his own aggrandisement, and this passion he had of late indulged to the utmost. His infatuation, too, with Ferideh had cost him a pretty penny. Debts of long standing, which had been trifles overlooked in the day of prosperity, were heavy burdens now that there was nothing to meet them. And the creditors clamoured for their money—the whole sum of it; they would not hear of a compromise.

The house was his until the end of the year; but, empty and dismantled, it was a gloomy dwelling-place, having a dismal echo of bygone joys. He saw himself obliged to sell all that was best of the furniture, and the superfluity of rich clothing he had purchased in his grandeur. He dismissed the servants, all save Ibrahîm, the doorkeeper, who refused to leave, having grown attached to the house and taking great blame to himself for the flight of Ferideh, but stayed on without care of wages. He was reduced to beggary, without even the collar of gold of Selîm's parable to distinguish him from others in the same plight. More than once it had entered his mind to steal away to the coast and take ship, he cared not whither. But he thought himself a marked man. For aught he knew, there were spies set to watch his every movement. He dreaded that mysterious net of which the chief of police had told him, and, dreading, stayed to face his creditors.

But the tale of his distress is not all told. There would

have been some satisfaction in haunting the taverns of the
city and dinning the tale of his misfortunes into all men's ears.
The horrified "Ah!" and uplifted hands of his listeners
would have stroked his vexed soul soothingly.   But even this
dismal gratification was denied him.   A story, whose source
he guessed too surely, began to pass from mouth to mouth.
It was commonly said that Saïd—who now, for the first time
since his rise, began to be known as the Fisherman—had
obtained his money in the confusion of the great slaughter by
murdering an old man and a pious Muslim, his adopted father.
Men looked askance at him in the markets.   In vain did Selìm
speak everywhere on his master's behalf, giving the lie direct
to evil tongues ; the voice of slander was silenced only in his
presence, and the rumour gained ground until all men knew
it.   Many of Saïd's old acquaintances drew aside their raiment
and passed him with averted faces.   Mahmud Effendi, who had
paid him a formal visit of condolence in the early days of his
downfall, when all men pitied him, now rode by him in the
street with scarcely an acknowledgment of his low obeisance.
He skulked like a dog through the streets, seeing knowledge
and belief of the rumour in all eyes.

His sole resort in those days was the tavern of Rashìd
without the city walls.   There he was always welcome to what
refreshment he chose, and no word of the libel was ever
uttered in his hearing.   Selìm, too, took care that he should
want for nothing, but provided for his needs secretly, through
Hasneh, without himself appearing as the giver.

The month of Ramadan came ; and Saïd, in awe of the
strong hand which had laid him low, disposed himself to fast
as he had never fasted before.   All day long he abode in the
house, touching neither bite nor sup, praying by turns and
lamenting his evil day.   He entered willingly into conversation
with no one, lest, beguiled into a moment's forgetfulness, he
should swallow his spittle, and so break his fast according to
the vow he had taken.

One evening, towards the close of the sacred month, he sat
upon the house-top, waiting for the gun to be fired.   The sun
was set, and the light in the sky was as the fire of precious
stones—a light apart from sun, moon or stars,   The first dust
of night gathered upon the fasting city.   Saïd's heart expired
in prayer to Allah, for the stress of thirst and hunger was almost

more than he could bear. Hasneh crouched near him, watching him patiently with tender eyes. Thus she would sit all the day through, grateful for a glance, a word, though it were of anger or impatience.

The dull boom of a cannon shook the whole city, echoing like far-off thunder from the encircling hills; and immediately, as if by magic, lights appeared in the galleries of the high minarets, about the domes of the mosques, and in every window. The fast of Ramadan was ended with the day, and the feast of Ramadan would endure through the night.

"Praise be to Allah!" murmured Saïd with a mighty gulp. He took a cigarette which lay beside him on the roof, set it between his lips and lighted it, while Hasneh fetched meat and drink from within the house. He ate ravenously and drank half a pitcherful of water. With what remained he washed himself and then performed his devotions, facing south, with eyes that seemed to see the holy place of Mecca, so rapt was their look. Then, with a brief word of thanks to Hasneh, he descended to the courtyard and passed out into the streets.

On all hands there was music and laughter, the sounds of feasting and all manner of savoury smells. The illuminations of lamps and candles in every dwelling made the ways nearly as bright as in the daytime. Wherever shadow was, thither slunk the dogs which, with the vultures, keep Ramadan all the year round. In passing the open door of a tavern he heard words which staggered him.

"Where is the son of Mustafa, since thou sayest he had a son? Why does he delay to avenge his father's death? This Saïd has thriven too long by the profits of his crime. 'I mounted him behind me, and lo, he has put his hands in the saddle-bags'—thou knowest the proverb. Thanklessness is common in the world, but to slay a benefactor is surely the blackest of crimes. It is for the son of Mustafa to stand forth and claim his life or the blood-money. Where is he, O Camr-ud-dîn? He must be a coward or a scoundrel to tarry so long!"

The voice of Camr-ud-dîn was uplifted in answer, but Saïd did not wait to hear what he said. He hurried on his way, a prey to this new fear. Through all these years it had escaped his memory that Mustafa had a son, Mansûr, begotten of his

own body. He trembled. It was time that he shook the dust
of Es-Shâm from his feet for ever.

As he made his way through the crowd in a bright bazaar
he was aware of the unfriendly looks of many, and could have
sunk into the ground for shame. To avoid recognition he
crept along by the wall, yet even thus men's eyes found him
out and followed him.

Said one, "What shall be done to him who slew his
father? O lord! Shall he not be stoned to death?"

"Nay, hold thy hand!" quoth another in a tone of rebuke;
"the thing is not proven against him."

Saïd hurried on in deadly fear. If he could only win clear
of the more populous streets he might reach the gardens without
danger of molestation. He caught sight of a group of young
men whom he knew for his enemies. They were of ill repute
in all the city for their wildness. To them it were as light a
thing to stone a man to death as to pelt a dog or mob a Jew
for pastime. They stood together before the blazing stall of a
sweet merchant, barring his way. He turned with intent to
flee, and, in doing so, ran against an old man, richly apparelled,
who had that moment issued from a doorway. In great confusion, Saïd blurted out a form of apology. The sheykh's
green turban proclaimed him a holy man, and his dress bespoke
him some great one high in honour. He turned swiftly to
look at Saïd, and revealed the white beard and kindly face of
Ismaïl Abbâs, the Sherîf. He smiled at the encounter.

"Peace on thee, O fisherman," he said courteously.
"How is thy health? And how do thy nets fare all this long
time that thou hast neglected them? Whither goest thou?"

Saïd was bowed almost to the ground.

"Allah keep thee in safety, O Emîr! I was going to the
tavern of Rashîd, which is on the river bank, but I have many
enemies—Allah witness, they have no cause to hate me!—and
the way is hardly safe for me to go thither. It was in the act
to turn back that I ran against thy Worship, may Allah pardon
me the rudeness!"

Ismaïl Abbâs cast a shrewd glance round upon the bystanders. Many had stayed to observe this meeting of saint
and sinner in the public street, and amazement, not unmixed
with concern, was written on their faces. The holy man took
Saïd's hand to lead him, saying loudly,—

"Now, by my beard, thou goest not to the tavern of Rashìd, nor anywhere else, but home with me to partake of the feast which I have caused to be spread for my friends."

It was as if the Prophet himself had taken Saïd by the hand and said, "This is a friend of mine: vex him at your peril." All whom they passed in the way made low reverence to the great and saintly man, and Saïd had a part in their greetings. Of all the dwellers in Damashc-ush-Shâm, Ismaìl Abbâs was esteemed most highly, both on account of his great learning and righteousness, and for his family, which was among the noblest of the city. To be seen walking with him, holding his hand as a bosom friend, did more to establish Saïd's innocence in the minds of the populace than any number of witnesses in a court of law. When at length they gained a quiet place, Saïd burst out weeping, and would have prostrated himself to kiss his saviour's feet had not that good man prevented him.

"Nay, Allah forbid that thou shouldst fall down before me!" said Ismaìl Abbâs, a little testily. "If thou hast anything to be thankful for, give praise where praise is due. I have done no more for thee than I would have done for a dog in distress; for the very dogs have living souls, as some have said."

He led Saïd on by quiet ways, and, as they went, he asked him strange questions out of all reason; as,—

"Hast thou a wife left to thee in the day of thy misfortune?"

"There remains to me my old woman, O Emìr—she who was with me from the beginning, the first that ever I had."

"Then be kind to her, as thou regardest thy salvation. Remember that, in the last day, the weak shall take their vengeance upon the strong, the unarmed upon the armed, the unhorned cattle upon the horned cattle. For Allah is just, and in the end he will make the balance level."

And again,—

"Thou that art a fisherman, and knowest the ways of the sea, tell me, What does a mariner when shipwrecked on the coast of his own country?"

Saïd reflected a minute, supposing it had been a riddle.

"By my beard, I suppose that he will praise Allah, and then he will return with speed to his own place."

"Good," replied the great man; "the case is thine. A while ago thou didst set out in the hope to gain honour; but now behold thou art shipwrecked. Out of thy mouth I counsel thee, Take thy woman with thee and go home, return to thy native place and to thy fishing, and perchance we shall find thee money wherewith to buy nets and a house."

This advice did not please Saïd. He dreaded the triumph of Abdullah, who must by this time be among the greatest of his native town. However, he said nothing openly to his benefactor, but feigned to fall in gladly with the plan.

At the house of Ismaïl Abbâs there was much company, for the host was renowned for hospitality, and many loved him. All present used Saïd friendly, wishing him a blessed feast, and not scorning to sit at meat with him. Throughout the night there was good cheer and the wisest discourse; for above all things save piety, Ismaïl Abbâs prized wisdom and learning, and his friends were chosen for their qualities rather than wealth or rank. Towards morning, when men rose to go, the Sherîf took Saïd apart to speak with him alone. He advised him strongly to go back to his first trade of a fisherman. Es-Shâm was full of his enemies, an evil story being current there concerning him. He (Ismaïl) had judged it false from the first; and yet many were found to put faith in it. It behoved Saïd to leave the city as soon as the sacred month should expire.

This last counsel fell in timely with the fisherman's own wishes, and he promised humbly to follow it. Then, having received his host's blessing, and a handsome present of money wherewith to buy nets and a house, Saïd took his leave, kissing his patron's hand repeatedly, and calling upon Allah to reward his kindness.

It wanted but four hours of daybreak and the sounds of revelry were growing faint and rare. Many of the candles had guttered and gone out, and those which remained burned dimly and awry. The stars resumed their sway and a slumbrous calm wrapped the city. There would be peace now until an hour before sunrise, when most men would rise and eat again, to fortify themselves against the long day's fast. Saïd met several parties wending homeward from carousals. He himself went not home, but to the dwelling of Selîm, where there were lights burning. The mother of Mûsa opened to his knocking. She peered hard at him. "Praise be to Allah!" she cried, flinging up her hands. "Deign to enter, O my lord! It is indeed the master! Come, O Selîm! Behold, his Eminence is restored to us in safety. Know, O Effendi, that Selîm has been greatly troubled this night on thy account, because thou camest not to the tavern of Rashîd though he sat there long awaiting thee. He feared some evil had befallen thee; but now we behold thee safe, thanks to Allah!"

Selîm rushed forward with the like expressions of joy and gratitude. It was some time before Saïd could make himself heard, for the stir of his entrance had awakened the children, who screamed and roared in chorus. But at last, by the exertions of Mûsa and his mother, the din subsided, and he said,—

"After five days I leave Es-Shâm for ever, and Hasneh with me. By the grace of Allah, I have now a little money with which we shall journey to the sea-coast, and there take ship, I care not whither, so that it be far from this city of falsehood."

Selîm received the news with a cheerful face.

"It is but a minute since I spoke to the same purpose," he said; "is it not so, O mother of Mûsa? Of a truth, since thy ruin this city displeases me and, thanks to thee under Allah, I am well provided with money, which can serve us both. I thought to go into Masr—what sayest thou? I have a brother who migrated thither in the time of Ibrahîm Basha, when Masr was as one country with Es-Shâm. He is well established in the city of Iskenderia, and from time to time he sends a word to me by travelling merchants. He declares it to be a pleasant land, favourable for every kind of trade. We will journey together, by thy leave; Allah grant us a safe voyage and prosperity in the end!"

At that Saïd seized both hands of his friend and kissed them, blessing Selîm for a good man and a faithful—none like him in all the world!

So it came to pass, one early morning, that Saïd and Hasneh left the great city, in the company of Selîm and all his family, by the same road which Saïd had followed at his coming, nearly twelve years before. At the brow of the hill, beside the shrine which is there, they turned to look their last upon that place of gardens. Saïd's eyes brooded long and lovingly over it, as though it had been indeed the earthly paradise he was leaving; and it was with a choking voice that at last he bade Selîm lead on.

X

THE little company journeyed but slowly, for the sake of the women and children. The weather was hot and breathless, as it often is at the extreme end of summer, when the air begins to grow heavy with the first storm. Selîm had provided two donkeys to carry the baggage, and also to give a spell of rest to anyone who grew weary. One bore the weight of his household treasures, and his wife with her young baby rode upon it when she chose. Saïd generally bestrode the other, which was laden with his goods, while Hasneh walked meekly beside; though sometimes, feeling the need to stretch his legs, he would alight and bid her take his place for a time. Often he would take up one of Selîm's children to ride with him; and Selîm himself, with Mûsa, made shift to carry the others when they tired.

At first their way lay through mountains, barren and tree-less, except for certain favoured nooks, where there was water and deep shade of fruit-trees. Through the heat of the day the landscape seemed of bronze, so massive it was and sullen under the burning sky. A rare terebinth, growing high up among the cliffs, was rusty black, and cast a shadow uncouth as the rocks themselves. But in the early morning, what with the young sunlight and the dewy shade, every boulder had a charm and freshness of its own, so that the little band sang blithely at setting out. And towards sundown, when the peaks were all purple and gold, and the level spaces coloured like flower-beds, they drank in the coolness of the evening with sighs of relief.

They crossed the plain called El Bica'a, with its scattered villages, and all through one afternoon they moved along in the growing shadow of Lebanon. Ere noon of the next day they paused on the crest of the mountain and beheld the coast-plain far below them languishing in a haze of heat. The

255

sea beyond was like a burnished sheet of silver. Saïd's heart leapt at the familiar sheen of it, but the sight brought no enduring pleasure. His native land was very dear to his soul now that the time drew near when he must quit it. They were now on the Sultàn's highway—a great white coach-road, the work of a Frankish company, whose zigzag windings could be traced as a wan and crumpled ribbon down all the mountainside. Carriages dashed past them, filled for the most part with Christians in semi-Frankish dress, forcing the group of wayfarers to the roadside, blinding and choking them with a cloud of dust.

The sun was near his setting when they reached the level of the plain. On all sides there were gardens plumed with date-palms, and fine stone dwellings bosomed in leafage. Seaward, across the plantations, loomed a dark belt of pines. A flight of bee-eaters wheeling in the flush of sunset seemed like dead leaves the sport of a wind. The road lay straight before them, stained with sunset light. There was much people in carriages and on horseback—townsfolk of Beyrut—come forth to taste the sweets of evening. Shadows were long and grey-blue to eastward.

The sight of the palm-trees and the diffused fragrance moved Saïd deeply. He knew that the sea was at hand—the sea which he had known from babyhood, whose voice was a home voice to him. Yet at that time he loathed the thought of it, his heart yearning to the sweet gardens and the peaceful life of a husbandman.

Weary and footsore they entered the city of Beyrut, and it seemed to Saïd that he was already in a strange land. The Frankish garb was almost as common in the streets as the dress of the country, and four men out of every five he saw were Christians. He had been there once before on an errand of commerce, but the foreign character of the town had not struck him then as now. Nearly all the houses had red-tiled roofs, and the shops were of a pattern unfamiliar to him. The streets were wide and ablaze with lights. Wheeled carriages, each drawn by a pair of horses and driven by one who sat aloft with frenzied shouting and cracking of a whip, were frequent here though in the capital they were still esteemed a fine rarity. He began to be afraid for the future. If he felt thus lonely in a seaport town of his own country, how could he bear to dwell in a foreign land? He made his uneasiness known to Selîm, who bade him be of good cheer, for that Beyrût stood alone, the lord of all the world for iniquity and unbelief. In Masr he would find it quite otherwise; there the faithful outnumbered the infidels as ten to one.

Selîm was well acquainted with the city, having often visited it in the days when he was a muleteer. He led his company by quiet and tortuous ways to the Muslim quarter, where there was less of a foreign appearance to trouble Saïd. They took their lodging at a khan which overlooked an ancient burying-ground tufted with black cypresses. Hard by was a mosque whose squat, ungainly minaret stood up against the last green of evening. An owl hooted in some bush of the graveyard. The place had a wistful sadness in the gathering night.

After they had washed and prayed, Saïd and Selîm took Mûsa with them to the guest-chamber, where they ate apart, the women being entertained elsewhere in the house by their own kind. The room was filled with men of all conditions, from the rich merchant with his saddle-bags beside him to the servant who sat or rose at his master's nod, and the muleteer squatting shamefaced by the door. A portly man of middle age sat with his back against the wall, sucking luxuriously at a narghileh. His bright, shifty eyes were keenly observant of all that went on. He looked earnestly at Saïd and watched him all the while he was eating. At length, when the coffee was brought, he coiled the tube and mouthpiece about the vessel of his pipe and crossed the room.

"Peace be upon thee, O Saïd, O my dear!" he said heartily. "Allah be praised that I behold thy face once more! How is thy health? If Allah will, it is the best possible!"

Surprised by the warmth of this greeting in a place where he was a stranger, Saïd eyed the man narrowly as he rose in acknowledgment. Surely it could not be!—And yet, who else? . . . In dismay and amazement he recognised his sometime friend and partner, Abdullah the fisherman. He stepped aside with him.

"How goes thy business all this long time, O father of Azîz?" he asked, when the perfunctory compliments had given him time to recover from the shock of the encounter.

R

"Praise be to Allah, not ill; I cannot complain, for I am now high in honour in our city. It is a small city—that is true—but what eminence may be attained therein I have attained. There is talk of recommending me to the Mutesarrif to be Caimmacam, when the time comes to make a change. Of a truth, if they choose me not I know not of whom they will make choice, for there is none in all those parts to vie with me in wealth and consequence."

He bragged with assurance, but his dress belied his words, for he was meanly clad.

"As for thee, O my soul, how fares it with thee?" he inquired in his turn.

"By the grace of Allah, I thrive," said Saïd, casting up his eyes fervently. "By the Coràn, I am happiest of men. All that belongs to wealth and honour and prosperity is mine, and I am risen to the supreme height of my desire. And behold all this is come to me because of that foul trick thou didst play me years ago, O sly robber that thou art!"

"Whoever robbed thee it was not I—Allah be my witness! No, by my beard, it was some other, and that a devil in all likelihood," murmured Abdullah, blandly, as if disclaiming an honour one would thrust on him. "But say, where dwellest thou, O my eyes?"

"In Es-Shâm—in the great city, O my dear, where I own a fine house such as a prince might envy. By Allah, I am become a great one in that city, which is the first of all cities in the world. All the notables are my friends, and the Wâly himself disdains not to seek my advice in the affairs of state. Allah is bountiful!"

"Allah is bountiful indeed," said Abdullah, regarding Saïd with a new interest. "But tell me, art thou that Saïd the Merchant whose name is in all men's mouths?"

"I am in truth that great one," was the reply; "but I know not what thing thou hast heard, for many lies are spoken concerning me."

"Listen, and thou shalt hear all I know. It is but a few hours since I met one who was just returned from the country of Rûm. And in that country he heard the story of Saïd, a merchant of Damashc-ush-Shâm, who was robbed by the woman whom most he favoured. She caused him to drink a potion wherein was a strong drug, pretending that it was a sherbet of figs. Her lover, a young Nazarene of the same city, is cunning in pharmacy, having studied here in Beyrût and also among the Franks to become a chemist. It is he who gave her the drug and taught her how to administer it. Her lord trusted her in all things, and she was in the secret of his wealth, so she robbed him easily of all that he had, and took her little son and fled away with that Nazarene while he slept. The cunning of the Christian—may Allah destroy him !— had caused him to make himself a French subject long ago, in the year of the great slaughter when all was confusion. He had a passport and Frankish clothes in waiting. To make more sure, the dragoman of the consulate—who was the son of his aunt on the mother's side—journeyed with them in the public coach to this city, where the people of the custom-house, supposing them to be Franks, let them pass un-questioned, the child with them. They tell me this Nazarene hates the child, which is natural, being the work of another than himself. He would fain be rid of the burden, but the woman will not part with it. So they took ship and came at last to the country of Rûm, where they now dwell in the largest city, in the best manner, with all luxury. Their story is known to all men, and the laugh is ever against Saïd the Merchant of Damashc-ush-Shâm. . . . The Christians are all wild beasts, by Allah—foul and wicked things, unclean and accurst. But surely thou art not the man they tell of ? Allah forbid ! It is impossible ! "

All this was bitter as death to Saïd. His teeth and hands clenched. For a moment he thought of nothing but to pursue those two who had wronged him over sea and land, to slay them, if it might be, in each other's arms. He saw his son attired as a Christian, despised and ill-treated by the pig, his enemy. He gnashed his teeth with the knowledge that men made mock of him, that his name was become a byword of scoffing to unbelievers in distant lands. But he swallowed the gall of his anguish as best he could. When he spoke it was with a scornful countenance.

"O my eyes, a part of thy tale is true, but not all. That son of a pig, that Christian of whom thou tellest did certainly carry off a woman of mine, but what is that ?—I can afford to replace her. As for the child, I have been concerned for him, but now that I know whither they are gone I will inform the

Government, and it shall go ill with me but I will recover him. The woman did in truth rob me of a sum of money; but she was not fully in my confidence. There were two hoards, thou understandest, hidden in two separate places. She mistook the lesser for the greater, and so, far from being ruined, as she fondly supposed, I am now, by the blessing of Allah, even more prosperous and higher in honour than I was before. Allah is just!"

"Praise be to Allah!" said Abdullah, feelingly. "I rejoice with thee;" and upon that he wished Saïd a happy night and withdrew, saying that he must hie to bed, as he was to start betimes on the morrow on his journey home. So these two, so long asunder, met once more on friendly terms and lied freely one to the other, neither doubting his fellow's words.

Saïd slept ill that night. Divers projects turned in his brain, distracting him. Every forward course seemed grievous, fraught with danger. There was but one bright point in all his weary musings as he tossed to and fro upon his pallet—the face of a girl he had seen once in a garden—an English girl and mistress to the son of a pig, a dragoman. He recalled all that he had heard of the land of the English, and ever he swore, with Allah's leave, he would contrive to go there ere he died.

Selîm was abroad early in the morning, for there was much to be done, and in his loving care for his former master he took all charge of it upon himself. First, he visited sundry taverns and places of resort, publishing the news that he had two fine donkeys for sale. By the third hour there was a small crowd gathered at the stable, and the sale, when it took place, was in the nature of an auction, one man bidding above another. When that was done and the beasts had been led away by their purchasers, Selîm betook himself to the Seraï to get permission to leave the country, and have the passports put in order. He was so long absent on this business that Saïd, who awaited him at the khan, began to be uneasy. When at last he did return, the expression of his face was woebegone in the extreme. Saïd cried out in alarm to know what was amiss. Whereupon the faithful fellow wrung his hands, and tears rolled down his cheeks.

"O Saïd! O my brother! Allah be my witness, I have

striven long with prayer and argument to turn their hearts; but in vain. Ah, woe is me, to be the bearer of such ill tidings! Know, O my beloved, that the men of the Government gave me free leave to depart with my family; as thou knowest, I have a letter which Ismaïl Abbâs — may Allah requite his honour!—procured for me from the Wâly. But thee they will by no means suffer to quit the land, both because thou hast no such letter, and for some other cause which is hid from me. All my entreaties, all my reasons were unavailing; thou art forbidden to travel further by order of the Government."

Fear came into Saïd's eyes as he heard. Heretofore the Government had seemed to him remote as the sky is, something impassive, neither friend nor foe. He had stood in the same vague awe of it that a simple man has of some mighty engine whose working is a mystery to him. Now that he suddenly found it his enemy, the shock was like an earthquake destroying old landmarks. He remembered the dark net of which the Chief of Police had spoken, and felt himself already caught in its meshes.

"I must leave the country, and that at once!" he muttered fearfully. "In the old days I was known for a strong swimmer. Say, O Selîm, is there no ship far out in the bay, beyond call of the Custom House, to which I can swim by night?"

"There is an English ship, O my brother—a steamer which comes hither at times with merchandise. She will depart, they tell me, to-morrow after sunrise. She lies to-night in the bay, but far out; thou couldst hardly swim so far. If thou trustest indeed to escape by swimming, wait two days, I pray thee, until our steamer arrives, so we may yet journey together."

Saïd caught at the words "an English ship." In a flash he had a vision of fair forms, and faces full of love, in a light subdued and gentle — the light, as he conceived it, of cloudy Lûndra. The next moment he was reminded of the woman who was a clog upon him, and he broke out fretfully,—

"There is Hasneh, . . . O Lord! . . . How may I be rid of Hasneh? I must escape at once; this very night I must swim out to the English steamer, and she alone hinders me."

Selîm heard him with mild surprise.

"She will go with me to Masr, as was at first arranged," he said soothingly. "Let thy mind have rest concerning her. My passport is so worded that she may journey with us unquestioned. The mother of Mûsa will be glad to have her company in a strange land, for they love one another, and Hasneh is very skilful in all housework. Be assured, O my brother! By Allah's leave, thou shalt find her safe when thou rejoinest us yonder. But alas! how can I part from thee, O my soul! As long as I live I am thy servant, for the sake of the kindness thou hast ever shown me, from the day thou didst give me that rich garment, the root of my honour, to this hour. Couldst thou not swim as well to one ship as to another? and what are two days that they should have power to ruin thee? I will find out some private place where thou mayest be snugly hid. Allah forbid that ever I should part from thee!"

But a great unreasoning fear possessed Saïd, and nothing which Selîm could say might change his purpose. The father of Mûsa blubbered like a baby. Saïd himself was deeply moved, but otherwise, the dread of this instant peril swaying him. Moreover, a thought of the fair ones awaiting him in that distant land of the English helped somewhat to soften the parting on his side. He spent the rest of daylight in preparing for his venture. By the agency of Selîm he procured a stout leathern bag of handy size, wherein he stowed all such of his belongings as seemed indispensable. Of the things which remained over he gave some to Hasneh and some to Selîm, according to their nature and use. Towards evening Selîm went forth to make inquiries, whilst Saïd did somewhat to comfort Hasneh. After a very little while he came back in a hurry, and with a face full of concern.

"It may not be, O my brother," he said, "thou canst by no means win to the steamer. Know that there has lately been much emigration—of Christians for the most part, and Drûz out of the mountain. It is their custom to do even as thou purposedst; and to check the tide of them, a watch is set upon the beach at night with orders to fire on all who take the water. Allah have pity! I know not what is to be done."

Saïd paced the paved yard of the khan, raging like a

hunted beast at bay, while Hasneh, in hopes that she might not lose him after all, sobbed with relief. At length he stopped short in his prowl, and, lifting hands and eyes to heaven, "Allah succour me!" he muttered fiercely. "I will take the risk of it."

XI

ABOUT an hour after sundown Saïd took a sad farewell
of his friends, and, all alone, went forth to the shore.
He wore an ample cloak of haircloth to conceal the leathern
sack he carried. As he made his way through the concourse
of the streets his heart thumped so loudly against his ribs that
he thought all men deaf not to hear it. On the sea-beach,
where the din of the city mingled as a distant murmur with
the sigh of the ripples, the clamour of it filled his brain.

The wide bay lay smooth and glassy, fringed along the
shore with points of yellow light shining among dark forms of
trees and bushes. The mountains rose in outline beyond,
ending seaward in a bluff promontory, the lights of many
villages plainly seen upon the nearer slopes. A dusky bloom
was on all the land—the velvet of a moth's wings. The lamps
of the shipping had dancing pendants in the water.

Saïd tried to seem careless, as if he strolled for pleasure.
It was dark and he met no one after he had won clear of the
town; but his fancy peopled every wall and garden, every
shrub of tamarisk to landward, with soldiers on the lookout;
and in spite of all his endeavours the manner of his going
betrayed uneasiness. The cry of a mariner wafted across
the still water was startling, as if one had called him by
name.

He could see the English steamer, a dark mass, with a
funnel and three masts, lying motionless a good way out. A
red light in the bows shed a sparkle of rubies in the near
water. He strove to judge of the distance, seeking that part
of the shore which would most favour his project.

A ruined wall ran out a little way on to the sand. On the
side remote from the town he sat down and strove to think.
A great pulse throbbed in his brain, so that his whole frame
was shaken with it. The sea and the lights and the mountains

swam before his eyes; the very wall seemed to rock as he leaned against it. The sharp yelp of a dog among the gardens rang bewilderingly in his ears.

At length, his mind growing clearer, he lighted a cigarette and smoked it to the end. Then he got up and took off his garments one by one, throwing some away, and binding others with a sash to the well-filled leather bag. When he was naked he sat down again, and, holding the bundle pressed on his cap and turban, set to work to lash it to his head with strips torn from his cast-off raiment. By vigorous shaking he made sure it was quite firm, then he stole to the end of the wall and peered cautiously forth.

Two men were approaching—soldiers with rifles on their shoulders. The wall alone had prevented him from hearing their voices. The place he had chosen was sheltered and convenient for keeping watch upon the shore to northward. It was most likely that they were making for it. There was not a second to be lost.

With a bound he ran swiftly across the sand and splashed in the water, dropping at once on his hands and knees. He heard a shout, followed in the same minute by the report of a gun. A shot whizzed past him; it played duck and drake along the surface, striking up little plumes of spray. A second followed, but it was wider of the mark, and by that time Saïd was out of his depth, swimming strongly. He ducked frequently to baffle the marksmen. A bullet, the last which was fired, hit the bundle and remained bedded in it.

At first he struck out blindly, thinking only of his life; but afterwards, when the bullets ceased to whirr, he made boldly for the steamer, which might then have been three-quarters of a mile distant in a straight line. He could hear the soldiers yelling and hallooing on the beach, but had little fear that a boat would put out to intercept him, for the harbour was a long way off on the left and he had passed few craft in his walk along the sands. Even supposing that those in the guardhouse on the quay heard the cries of their comrades and understood them, it would take them some time to get afloat; and a man's head, though with a bundle lashed to it, was no easy thing to mark on all the wide expanse of darkling water.

With the joy of his narrow escape yet full upon him he revelled in the freedom of the cool water The little waves smote him friendly and the stars twinkled at him out of the pale sky. As a boy, it had been his delight to swim out, whenever a ship came to anchor off his native town, and perform all kinds of antics in the sea, diving for the coins that voyagers threw to him and catching them in his mouth as they sank. In those days people had marvelled at his prowess in the water, accounting him half a fish ; and it pleased him, now that he was middle-aged and bulky, to know that he had still the trick of it. He frolicked, swimming now frogwise, now on this side, now on that. He turned over on his back and paddled along for a few strokes in that position. Then, righting himself, he splashed forward, hand over hand, like a dog. But ere long he grew weary of such fancies and settled down to a steady and enduring stroke which should carry him to his goal.

The steamer was yet a pretty long way off when he began to doubt if he would ever reach it. The smart of the brine blurred his eyes. The surface of the sea seemed now all starlight, anon black as pitch. He was sadly out of condition and had spent the flower of his energy in wantoning. Wishing to husband what strength remained to him, he slackened speed somewhat. He grew numb. His eyes were blind to everything except the steamer ; and that seemed very big, ten times its natural size, filling all the horizon. His limbs lost feeling ; stern resolve alone upheld him and kept him moving. The ship loomed nearer all of a sudden. He plunged forward, floundering rather than swimming, his mouth and nose full of salt water at every stroke. It towered above him very near indeed ; but all his life was gone. He knew in his heart that he could never reach it. The veins of his forehead were bursting, his eyes were very dim. All kinds of incongruous memories thronged his brain. "Allah is just," he thought, "and this is the end of me." But, a second later, he had caught hold of a rope which fell from the steamer's prow, and hung by it, clinging for dear life.

"Praise be to Allah !" he murmured, quaking from head to foot. Presently he raised a feeble shout. A face looked down at him, then more faces—a crowd of them. Questions were shouted, but he could make nothing of the jargon spoken. "There is much money with me !" he cried in Arabic. "I would go to the great city, Lûndra of the English !"

At that there was a great shout of laughter, and another rope was flung to him, which he caught, and with which he was hauled on board. Queer Frankish faces grinned at him, grotesque as masks, all red and many quite devoid of hair. The light of a fixed lantern sufficed to show them to him. Rough hands smote his dripping shoulders hard in applause, their owners roaring with laughter. In truth, he cut an odd figure as he stood there stark naked and streaming wet, a great bundle bound to his head with strips of calico. But to Saïd it was no laughing matter. He sprang to anger under their blows, glaring round on them with curses, and showing his teeth. But they laughed all the more at his resentment, slapping their knees and hugging themselves for glee.

The press about him gave way suddenly. A man came forward, clad in some sort of a uniform, with a gold badge on his cap. He spoke in a stern voice to the sailors and they fell back sheepishly. It seemed they made excuses, pointing to Saïd where he stood naked and shivering, his feet very conscious of the smooth planks. This man, whom Saïd took to be the lord of the ship, then addressed him in a childish sort of Arabic, asking to know what he wanted; whereupon Saïd told a grievous tale of tyranny and wrong, such as might justify any man in flight from his native land. He repeated his statement that he had plenty of money, adding that he would gladly pay the price of his passage to Lûndra. The officer eyed him doubtfully for a minute. Then, with a face of compassion, he gave a gruff order to one who stood near, and Saïd was led away to a small chamber, dim with the savoury fumes of cooking, where was a fire burning.

XII

NEXT morning there was a great bustle on board the steamer. Saïd awoke in his narrow bunk to a noise of splashing and scrubbing overhead. The door of the sort of cupboard where he lay stood open ; now and then a man's shadow darkened it in passing.

It did not take long to remember where he was. The adventure of the previous night recurred vividly to his mind, seeming a madman's to the sanity of early morning. He marvelled at the daring of it, and then, looking forward, his heart grew sick with forebodings. What future awaited him in the land of the English? It was a country favourable for all manner of trade, but he carried no merchandise with him. He had money, it was true, but when the price of his journey had been deducted from it only a small sum would be left. The fair women and girls, so easy to conquer, the chief attraction of that distant shore, seemed not so very desirable after all.

The great red face of a mariner looked in upon him with the roar of some savage beast. Its grin was friendly and its appearance cheered Saïd somewhat, so that, when it was withdrawn, he shook off his listlessness and got up. As he did so, his clothes and the leathern bag which held his treasure fell on the floor, covering it almost completely, so little space was there. Being naked, he had been hurried to bed over-night and had quite forgotten his bundle. Someone must have brought the things and laid them upon him while he slept. The garments had the crispness of linen dried at the fire.

An agony of fear seized him lest the sack should have been rifled and his money taken out. Naked save for his skull cap and turban, he knelt down in the narrow space between wall and bunk, and with trembling hands loosened the mouth of

268

the bag; but a little groping reassured him. He smiled,
drawing forth a small but heavy pouch with a string attached,
which he made haste to hang as an amulet about his neck;
first shutting the door so that no one passing by could
observe him. " Allah is bountiful! " he murmured.

By the time he reached the deck the engines were panting
like some huge beast held in leash that frets to go free. A
crowd of little boats clung to the steamer's side, waiting to see
the last of her. Already the sun stood high above the ridge
of Lebanon, and his beams made a dazzle on the dancing blue
sea. The whiteness of the town, relieved by high red roofs,
drew the eye to the southern horn of the bay, where the waves
lapped its walls. Suburbs half hidden in foliage stretched all
along the shore at the foot of the hills. Palm-trees rose
conspicuous, singly and by clumps of two and three. The
huge mountains, as yet in shadow, filled all the background,
seeming very near indeed. Snow gleamed on the high, long
crest of Jebel Sunnìn. The balm of the land and its murmur
were wafted on the breeze.

Saïd's heart went out to his native country. The sing-song
shouting of the sailors, the clank of a chain, the creaking
swing of a windlass—all the noise attendant on weighing
anchor sounded cruel and callous in his ears. It jeered him
as the voice of fate made audible. His past was slipping from
him irrevocably with every pant of the mighty engines, with
every puff of the funnel, which began to belch forth dense
clouds of whitish smoke that tossed seaward before it like the
blown mane of a horse.

The hiss and roar of the safety-valve ceased of a sudden.
In place of panting there was a dull, strong throb which was
felt in every plank and plate of the ship. The smoke from
the funnel wavered a moment, as if doubtful which direction
to take, then streamed out steadily over the stern, casting a
ribbon of shadow on the churned-up waters in the wake. The
little boats fell away from the side with men standing up in
them, waving good-bye. They dwindled, were left far behind,
and ever the throbbing grew to fuller purpose, as though the
ship had a soul, an imprisoned jinni toiling with bitter sobs.

Saïd was shortly led below to a breakfast of weird bread in
which was no sustenance, of butter whose exceeding yellowness
and bitter, saltish flavour filled him with distrust, of coffee

such as he had never tasted and hoped to Allah he might never taste again.   There was meat also, but that he would not touch, believing it to be pig's flesh or something unclean. He did not dwell long upon the meal, but when he returned on deck the city and the shore-line had already sunk out of sight ; only the crests of Lebanon stood up sheer out of the sea with white streaks of snow among them, the wake of the ship stretching, an ever-widening path, to their feet.

For hours Saïd sat crosslegged in the lee of a cabin, watching those summits dwindle and grow dreamy in the distance, till at last they were no more than a thin cloud on the horizon.   The sailors smiled and spoke friendly to him as they went about their work.   He sat in the shade, with hot sunshine all about him, and the eternal lapping of a sea, dead blue as lapis lazuli, sounded pleasant in his ears.   "O Allah! O Lord, have mercy!" was his soul's bitter cry as the coasts of Es-Shâm sank beneath the sea-line.   And yet he felt not half so wretched as he had expected.

That night a heavy thunderstorm burst, and all the next day the sky was overcast with rain driving in torrents before a cold wind.   It was the beginning of winter, and Saïd shunned the bleakness of the upper deck.   Having paid an instalment of his passage-money in advance, he was looked upon with unmixed liking by the crew as an honest fellow and a queer customer.   Yet Saïd resented the rough kindness of the sailors, as touching his dignity.   When they smote him, as their manner was, in all goodwill, he would sometimes round upon them with a snarl, making them laugh as if their hearts would break, and seeming only to increase their kindness for him. They used his word, "Lûndra," against him as a nickname ; and at first he would nod and grin when they uttered it, repeating it after them until they roared.   But afterwards, hearing it everywhere and at all hours of the day, he grew sick of the sound of it.

There were two other passengers on board—men of consequence, with whom he had nothing to do.   But one of them, a young man, with flaxen hair and moustache, and the bloom of a ripe peach on either cheek, had a smattering of Arabic and was fain to air it a little.   After the storm was passed and the fine weather had resumed its sway, he often joined Saïd as he sat upon the deck and struggled to converse with him. It was a little hard sometimes to understand what he said, for all his verbs were in the imperative mood.

One morning when the steamer rode at anchor off a seaport of the kingdom of Rûm, Saïd ventured to ask this person how long it would be before they reached that great city, Lûndra of the English. Looking out over the crisp, blue waves to a white town at the foot of violet mountains, with cypresses rising gaunt among its buildings and olives silvering all the slope behind, it seemed to him that they were yet a long way distant from that sunless land of which the dragoman had spoken.

"Two weeks and more," was the answer, "but know, O effendi, that this ship goes not to Lûndra but to Liverpool, which is distant from it a day's journey on the iron road."

"Merciful Allah!" Saïd exclaimed. "Hear now my story, O khawajah, and judge between these men and me. When I asked them they told me that the steamer went to Lûndra, and I gave them much money on that understanding. Of a truth the people of this ship are all liars; there is no vestige of truth found in them. May their house be destroyed and the fire quenched on their father's hearth!"

"Nay, O effendi, they meant not to deceive thee. The country of the English is a small country, and the iron road brings distant places close together. Liverpool is reckoned the haven of Lûndra almost as Beyrût is the port of Damascus, and the journey takes not so long. It was no lie they told thee."

"Without doubt the right is with thee, O khawajah," said Saïd with a semblance of conviction; but in his heart he felt bitterly that he had been beguiled. Lûndra was the city of his dreams, the abode of wealth and luxury, the paradise of fair women partial to strangers. "Lifferbûl" was quite a different place. He had heard the name of it before, but baldly, as of a town like another, without splendour or charm. Thenceforth, aware of a plot to inveigle him thither, he saw something sinister in the jovial comradeship of the sailors, though cunning made him seem their friend. At length, when one morning he awoke to find the steamer at anchor in a fair bay whose shores were clothed with a city and its suburbs, his airy scheme became an instant purpose. The name of the place, he knew, was Nabuli. To southward rose a lonely peak which smoked at the top like a heap of ashes smouldering. Ships were there of every sort and size, a great multitude of them, dotting the sparkling waters. Surely, among them all, there must be one that was bound for the greatest city of the earth. When he had prayed and broken his fast he took his leathern sack privily under his robe and went on deck.

A boat manned by certain of the crew was just putting off for land. Saïd shouted to the men in it, explaining by eloquent signs and grimaces that he had a mind to view the town. They laughed up at him, roaring and beckoning to him to make haste; so without more ado he climbed down among them and was rowed ashore.

In the confusion of landing, amid the busy throng upon the quays, he contrived to escape from his fellowship. For some time he dodged hither and thither, taking advantage of every turning to put more walls between himself and those he supposed in pursuit. His outlandish garb and the hurry he was in turned many heads of the passers-by to look after him. At last, finding himself again by the seaside, but at a point remote from his landing-place, he fell to scanning the faces of all he met, seeking someone to question.

Seeing a man of peaceful demeanour stand alone by a pile of bales he inquired of him in Arabic how he might best get to Lûndra. "Lûndra?" repeated the other after him with a vacant look and a shake of the head. He smiled, however, showing white teeth, and, motioning Saïd to stay, called to a knot of men who lounged hard by. They turned their faces at the call, and, seeing one so strangely clad, drew near out of curiosity. One of them, who at first sight appeared a Frankish sailor, shouted a salutation in pure Arabic spoken with the accent of Masr.

Saïd ran to him eagerly, his question on his lips. He told a fine story, how he was a great merchant bound for Lûndra whither his wares were gone before, how an unforeseen accident, which he was at pains to specify, had forced him to leave his ship, and how he would be deeply obliged to any-one who would direct him to another. His hearer, taken with the narrative, made ready offer of his service.

From this new friend Saïd learnt that there were at least two vessels in the harbour on the eve of departing for Lûndra.

The Egyptian pointed out a huge steamer in the offing, and, upon Saïd shaking his head at that, showed him a sailing-ship moored to the quay close by. The great merchant stroked his beard and thought a minute. Then he nodded with deliberation, and begged the sailor to bear him company and support him at the bargain.

At first the lord of the ship looked askance at them and spoke roughly to the interpreter. But by dint of long parley and a little earnest-money he at last changed his tone and agreed to take a passenger. Saïd thought him an evil man to look at, for he had only one eye and his face was red, inflamed with boils and spots. His voice, too, was harsh and rasping, and he spoke to men as one speaks to a dog. Saïd confided his feelings to his new friend, who only shrugged his shoulders, declaring that the Franks were all like that, unmannerly, possessed with the foulest of devils. As for the man's appearance, it was from the hand of Allah, and so no blame attached to him.

The ship was not to sail till the evening, so Saïd had some time on his hands. The Egyptian led him to a tavern in a narrow street, where high houses all but shut out the sky. The place was kept by the son of an Arab, and most of the customers were Orientals. Saïd, on his friend's introduction, was treated with much honour; and he sat there, drinking cup after cup of the coffee he loved, enjoying a narghileh, until the afternoon was far spent, when the Egyptian led him back to the ship. Before he slept that night he could hear the waves lapping against the vessel's side, and knew that he was speeding on his way to Lûndra. His dreams were all of fair women languishing in a chastened gloom.

XIII

IT was not long ere Saïd regretted the step he had so blindly taken and wished himself back on board the steamer, let it bear him to Lifferbûl or to the world's end. Skipper and crew of his new transport were altogether of a coarser type. Though the men grinned as they passed him in their work, the laugh was at him, not to him, and it filled him with distrust.

Day by day the ship leapt or glided with full sails on an endless waste of waters. To Saïd, as he squatted on the deck smoking cigarettes bought from the captain at what seemed to him a ruinous price, it occurred sometimes that the vessel was not moving at all, but was still with the waves racing past her. The fancy amused him and he would indulge it for minutes at a time until he was almost persuaded that it was so; it needed a glance at the strained canvas overhead, and another at the passing water, to dispel the illusion. He thought if Allah would grant a man wings like the birds he saw, how pleasant it would be to make long voyages, swooping down when weary to close wings and rest, letting the sea rock him for a little space. He considered the fishes of the deep, how they swim ever under water, yet, by the great mercy of Allah, are not drowned. "Allah is great!" was the outcome of all his musings.

But, as the days wore on, he grew very tired of sitting alone. He would keep near the sailors and try to ingratiate himself with them; even their unfailing rudeness and the horse-tricks they played him seemed better than sheer loneliness. The shifts he was forced to make in order to say his prayers undisturbed were a heavy burden on his conscience. Very earnestly he besought Allah to pardon any omissions in a place where clean water was hard to come by, where there was no sand and but little dust to serve for a substitute.

Allah was merciful, he reflected, and would forgive his short-comings, taking the circumstances into account.

Day by day the world grew sadder and less familiar. Skies lost their lustre, the sea darkened and waxed fierce, the very sun shone pale. Coasts, when sighted, were black and low-lying on the edge of leaden waters heaving in eternal unrest. It turned cold—more bleak than any winter. Saïd rubbed his eyes, supposing that there was a film on them which made the world seem dim. He realised that the land of the English was near, the land of cloud of which the dragoman had spoken; but the knowledge brought no gladness. He grew homesick, longing for a known face, for the sight of a palm-tree, for a train of camels passing in the blinding sunshine with sweet jangle of bells, for a word in his native tongue.

The very welkin lowered unfriendly, like a menace. The wind howled as a hungry beast of prey; the waves ravened as they leapt against the ship. All things, animate and inanimate, were hostile, and he saw their fury personal to himself. To make matters worse, a gale arose, and he became helpless through sickness. Utter despair got hold of him; he prayed ever that Allah might take his life ere he should retch again. He could take no food, but a little drink. The sailors came and mocked his wretchedness; but he was too prostrate to care for their jeers, only begging them to kill him where he lay.

After the illness he was feeble and shaky for a day or two, and felt the cold more keenly than before, though every garment he possessed was upon him, and a tarpaulin, which a sailor in savage pity flung to him, wrapped over all like a great shawl. The queer figure he cut as he tottered about shivering was the butt and derision of the whole crew.

The wind abated and the sea calmed. The sun, a mere ghost, looked down through worn places of the cloud-rack, like a pale face pressed to a rain-smeared pane. A long, wavy line of cliffs, dirty-white, blurred and indistinct in a perpetual mist, was pointed out to him as the land of the English. He saw it vaguely as one sees whose sight is dim with tears. All his hope centred in the little money-bag at his chest; there was comfort in thinking that he had enough to pay the price of a return voyage to the land of sunlight. Not for a day would he sojourn in this region of eternal gloaming, but would seek out a ship at once and take passage in her.   There was sure to be some good Muslim at the landing-place who would direct him for the love of Allah and the Faith that saves.

The cliffs were gone and the ship moved along by a low, marshy coast.   Here and there a group of dwellings, a light-house, a lonely hut broke the sullen monotony of the shore-line blackly.   There was land on both sides now—flat and dreary, shadowed, grim and inhuman as Jehennum itself. Saïd wondered what kind of men could dwell in that wilderness meant for the damned.   The water-way was dotted with ships great and small.   The sun was shining, but so faintly that he hardly knew it.   A few wan snakes at play upon the ripples were all the brightness it gave.

Anon the gloom deepened in spite of the feeble sun and became of a dull, yellowish brown.   The shore drew nearer on either hand.   They entered a great river, populous with all manner of craft—by far the greatest Saïd had ever seen.   After noon, as they still glided on, the face of the sun took on a reddish hue, and the water glinted cold and coppery to its lifeless rays. The world seemed dead, and the stir of human life upon it loathsome as the foul brood of corruption.   The river wound between two banks of fog, on which strange shapes of roof and chimney, tower and steeple, and the masts of ships appeared carven or painted by a tremulous hand.   From all sides clouds of smoke arose, feeding the gloom and blending with it perpetually.   It was as if the whole land smouldered.   Ships were moored along the wharves, at the foot of huge buildings frowning like precipices.   Here and there a large steamer, lying out towards mid-stream, had a swarm of small craft — lighters, wherries and row boats—about her, clinging to her, trailing from her like driftwood: a floating island, long and black upon the burnished water.

A mighty clamour filled all the gloom and seemed a part of it.   The beat of hammers rang out so thunderous that Saïd trembled to guess what made it.   There was a constant hiss of escaping steam, the throbbing of huge engines, the creak and rattle of cranes culminating now and then in a long roar, the whistle and hoot of steamers, sounds of puffing and the swish of paddle-wheels, shouts and cries of human kind. Smells found their way out on to the river and dwelt there, in spite of a light breeze blowing up from the sea—smells of the furnace and the tan-yard, of pitch and resin, and the prevailing pungent smoke. The taste in Saïd's mouth was a mixture of smoke and brine. He was choked, deafened, wholly bewildered.

One of the sailors, the most villanous-looking of all, who had of late made friendly overtures to him in the shape of devilish grins and murderous digs in the ribs, drew near and smote the tarpaulin.

"Lûndra!" he said, leering into Saïd's face.

"Lûndra!" echoed the passenger with a series of nods and a bright display of teeth, explaining that he understood. At that the mariner laughed hoarsely and began a lively pantomime, twitching Saïd's robe, pointing to the shore, slapping his own chest, and then making as if he would embrace the fisherman. Saïd was slow to see the drift of all this; the whole show had to be repeated a second time. But at last he gathered that this sailor of the evil countenance was his sincere wellwisher and would take charge of him when the time came to disembark.

The sun, swathed in smoke-wreaths, was already setting in crimson when, amid hoarse shouts of greeting and command, the frenzied blowing of a whistle and much flinging about of ropes and chains, the ship drew up to a wharf-side. The river flowed as turbid blood, parting a dark wilderness of masts and rigging, of endless, shapeless buildings. Here and there a pane of glass or other polished surface caught a beam and sprang to lurid flame. Westward, over against the sun, a great black dome brooded over the misty roofs. The din of the city had a note of weariness, like the sighing of a great multitude.

He shrank from landing. At least the ship was known to him, familiar in its every part; whereas this boundless, black city, whose sweat was filthy smoke, frightened him as a living monster lying in wait to devour. Surely it was the realm of Eblis, the abode of evil spirits and of souls in torment. For a long while he watched the business of the wharf, his brain ahum with doubt and bewilderment, so that he could not read or unravel his thoughts.

The skipper came and spoke gruffly to him, pointing to the gangway. He dragged the tarpaulin from Saïd's shoulders and flung it aside upon a heap of cordage. The Arab saw plainly that there was no choice left for him. Trembling and shrinking, in his flowing Eastern dress of many colours, he hurried across the plank, looking back to the ship, the scene of so much anguish for him, with longing as to a well-loved home.

The quay on which he found himself was a narrow one, oppressed and shadowed by a great warehouse. It reminded him faintly of a strip of beach at the foot of a steep cliff. He could see no way from it except through the great doors which yawned like caverns, showing bales of merchandise piled within. He felt quite helpless, imprisoned, cut off from everywhere yet within sound of a multitude. Yellow light streamed from every aperture of the building before him, making shapes of men fiendish as they moved in black outline across it. The lapping of the ripples against the piles, which is the same song all the world over, sounded more friendly than the voices of his kind speaking sternly and abruptly in a foreign tongue. Worst of all, no one heeded him. A chance look, a grin, a shrug of the shoulders, and he was passed by, dismissed from the minds of those busy workers. There was something very sinister in such absorption. Feeling dazed, he stood still, not knowing which way to look, the voice of the city in his ears— the sullen roar of a vast, unfriendly throng.

A mighty stroke on the back roused him from torpor. The sailor, who some two hours before had accosted him on the deck, stood at his side, speaking rapidly in a scolding tone. Then he laughed, and smote him once more between the shoulders. Linking arms, he led him away by a little passage Saïd had not perceived at the extreme end of the quay.

The streets were broad and open to the sky; they were lighted by lanterns set on high poles. The houses were tiny compared with the big warehouses of the river-bank, and were separated by spaces of blank wall, over which the masts and spars of ships rose ghostly. The sailor led Saïd to a house which stood, a blaze of light, at a place where three roads met. Pushing open a swing-door, he dragged him into a room full of men.

The brightness almost blinded Saïd, coming, as he did, out of the dark, and the noise deafened him. A number of red-faced Franks, seated on benches at wooden tables, were laughing and talking at the top of their voices. In his dazed condition he saw them vaguely as a multitude of strangers hostile to him. The atmosphere of the room, charged with the fumes of tobacco and strong drink, was hard to breathe; only the warmth and the light pleased him. Full of distrust of that noisy company, he would fain have drawn back, but his friend restrained him, forcing him to a seat at one of the tables.

He was aware of a crowd of faces close to his, of hands tweaking his raiment, of a buzz of curiosity ending in a mighty burst of laughter. Then a glass was set before him, full of some amber fluid. It had an evil smell and he loathed it. Remembering the potion given him by Ferideh, he had no doubt but that this was in the same nature. At best it was wine, a forbidden thing. They made instant signs to him to drink, but he pushed it from him, shaking his head vehemently and calling out that it was a sin. At that they laughed the more, and he began to fear, reading mischief in their eyes. A man of giant build caught hold of him and kept his hands, while another flung his head back and forced open his mouth. Saïd kicked with all his might, but his feet were powerless between the legs of the table. While he was yet struggling, the liquor was poured down his throat, and one held his mouth shut until he had swallowed every drop, although he came nigh to choking. Then he was released amid a roar of merriment.

A second glass was presently set before him and, sooner than submit to further violence, he made shift to empty it with a wry face. The stuff, though nasty in the mouth, had a pleasant effect, diffusing unhoped-for warmth through all his body. Soon he was joining in the general laugh against himself. Just as he finished one glass there was another full to his hand.

Instead of enemies he found himself among friends. He could have wept for the joy he had in beholding them. In a broken voice he told them all his troubles, about Ferideh and his love for her, about her elopement and the evil days he had known in Damashc-ush-Shâm, where he had been a great merchant, none like him in all that city—no, by Allah, nor in any city of the earth! It was the bald truth he was telling them—by the beard of the Prophet, he was an honest man, a man of consequence, and no liar! Whatever he said, they laughed madly; he thought it so kind of them to laugh. His eyes filled with tears as he thought on all their kindness.

His head swam queerly, and his eyes grew somewhat dim. He fancied he saw a woman somewhere in the room and, with a hazy remembrance of his purpose in coming to Lûndra, held out his arms to her enticingly. The laughter grew ever more boisterous. It was very rude of them to laugh, he considered. The Franks were fools, every one of them—accursed unbelievers having no knowledge of Allah or of Muhammed his apostle. He stood up, balancing himself with difficulty, and rated them soundly, cursing them for a lot of pigs and adjuring Allah Most High to destroy their houses and slay their parents. The next minute, he knew not how, he was sprawling face downwards on the floor, and his hands and clothing were coated with sawdust. They crowded about him, slapping their thighs and hallooing with glee. He cursed them again, declaring that they were bad men full of strong drink, and thereupon endeavoured to recite to them a passage of the Coràn. But one caught hold of his leg and proceeded to drag him round the room, while another sat on him, using him as a sort of carriage. He had no breath to resent the horse-play, but could only pant beneath the weight of the man on his back, emitting from time to time a feeble chuckle.

By-and-by they lifted him to a sitting posture and gave him more of the burning fluid to drink. He sat for a little while swaying too and fro, an insane grin on his swarthy face. Seeing his cap and turban lie at some distance upon the floor, he conceived an indistinct notion of trying to reach them upon his hands and knees; but they were so far off he fell asleep on the way.

XIV

SAÏD awoke to a headache and violent sickness. Supposing himself on the sea in a tempest, he marvelled at the quiet all about him. Presently he sat up and essayed to rub his eyes, but sudden dizziness caused him to fall back again with a groan. His couch was hard and wooden, like the planked deck of a ship, strewn, however, with something soft and powdery, like sand or sawdust. The place where he lay was dark and had a nauseous smell. He was distressed with thirst. "Water!—Water!" he moaned. "In the name of Allah, bring me a little water!—"

But the tones of his voice rang lonely in an empty room.

Events of the previous night loomed on his mind, as forms seen gigantic through mist. Sore shame and anguish fell upon him, illumined in a moment by a sudden terror. His money, his last ray of hope—where was it? He felt in the bosom of his robe, fingering his hairy chest frantically. The pouch and the string which held it were gone—stolen! He fumbled in every part of his clothing and scoured the floor with his hands; but in vain. "O Allah, All-merciful!—" He beat his breast with hoarse cries of rage and despair.

From a trance of grief, embittered by feverish thirst, he was roused by the noise of footsteps in an adjoining room. A light shone yellow through a glass hatch in the wall of partition, throwing long shadows of bottles upon the pane. He could hear a swishing noise, as of someone sweeping diligently with a broom. His eyes, sharpened by the habit of darkness, saw every part of the chamber in which he lay. It was the same to which the sailor had brought him. At sight of the tables and benches his shame redoubled so that he wept aloud. He picked up his tarbûsh and turban, which had been kicked under a trestle, and made haste to put them on. It degraded him to

know that he had played the buffoon, bare-headed, in the sight
of unbelievers. The sound of his lamentation filled the room.

A door opened and a woman looked in upon him. She
held a candle aloft in one hand, while with the other she
screened her eyes from the flame. The light reddened between
her fingers and shed a warm glow on her dirty face. She
yawned as one not yet wide awake, and spoke crossly to him.
He stretched out his hands, beseeching her by gestures to give
him to drink; but she only grew angry, and setting down the
candlestick upon a bench, shook her fist in his face and nodded
significantly towards the door. Saïd strove to reason with her,
craving only a little water to quench the thirst ravaging him;
but she cried out and pushed him from her. The noise of
approaching footsteps and a man's voice came to second her
endeavours. Hearing those sounds and dreading fresh violence
at the hands of the lord of the house, Saïd suffered the dirty
woman to unbar the door for him, and fled out precipitately
into the sharp air of the morning.

Having made a few paces, he turned with a shiver to look
back at the place he was leaving. It was a two-storeyed house,
flanked with two chimneys. A board upon the face of it
seemed to be painted with characters or symbols, but he could
not see much in the dark with only a distant lamp to help him.
It stood in a region of blind walls and scattered dwellings of
dilapidated appearance. There was a flagstaff on the roof,
which made Saïd think it was a consulate. Beyond, the masts
and rigging of great ships seemed drawn with a pencil upon the
first pale mist of dawn. In the gloom of the door by which
he had come forth he descried the form of a big man in act to
watch him; and he shuffled hurriedly away, his face pinched
with the cold.

He walked aimlessly forward, not knowing which way to
take, desirous only to escape from that wicked quarter to some
part of the city where men of honour dwelt, where he might
happen on a Muslim in the streets. More than once he found
his way blocked by a dingy wall and had to retrace his steps.
Many men passed him, clad in soiled garments and carrying
tools or sacks. They stared, turning their faces after him;
but, being sleepy for the most part, they did not hinder or
molest him. Day broke at his back, suffusing the dun mist
wanly. It showed a thin dust like salt whitening the ground,

the house-tops, and along the coping of the walls. The air was biting; it stung his nostrils so that he smelt blood. To get a little warmth, he tucked his hands beneath his robe and stamped his slippered feet hard upon the pavement.

In the shelter of an entry he found a little dry dust, with which he rubbed his face, hands and feet preparatory to saying his prayers. In the midst of his devotions, however, heavy footfalls sounded in the street, and a tall man, darkly-clad, with a strange form of hat and a cudgel stuck in his belt, spoke roughly and hit him on the back. He rose to his feet, expostulating, but the man made urgent signs to him to move on, and his mien was so full of authority that Saïd dared not disregard the bidding of his outstretched hand. "Allah pardon!" he muttered as he went his way, feeling that the day had begun badly.

Presently he came into a spacious street, so long that he could not see the end of it. The sun, just risen, looking sickly through the wreathing vapours, shed a milky stain on the road-way and parts of the buildings, casting the faintest of grey shadows. But for gilt signs on some of the houses, Saïd would scarcely have known that it shone at all. He strode on with his back to the light, wrapped close in his long robe, trembling with cold, very conscious of the inquisitive gaze of other way-farers. The road was thronged with carriages, great and small, of shapes unknown to him. Some were like wheeled houses, crowded with people inside and upon the roof. These queer conveyances pleased him by their gay colours, which he admired, as he did also certain hoardings decked with painted paper—as much as a hopeless and utterly destitute man can admire anything.

Suddenly hoots and yells of derision struck his ears, and he became aware of a horde of ragged urchins following him, capering, grimacing, and howling with all the strength of their lungs. They picked things out of the gutter to throw at him, bespattering his raiment with filthy refuse. He rounded upon them with a snarl, showing white eyes and teeth; whereat they fled helter-shelter, only to return again and pester him the moment his back was turned. He looked appealingly at the passers-by for help; but they laughed for the most part, though some of the women had eyes of pity, and a man who seemed of rank superior to the multitude stopped and spoke sternly to the pursuers. Saïd was beginning to despair of ever getting rid of them, when the rabble suddenly dispersed of its own accord, flying this way and that like small fry at the approach of some big fish of prey. Looking in astonishment for the cause of his deliverance, he beheld a man in a tall, dome-shaped hat and dark clothing, having a bludgeon in his belt, so like the party who had cut short his orisons, that Saïd believed it was the same. He saw in this individual, drawing near with deliberate tread and solemn bearing, a high officer of the irregular troops charged with the maintenance of peace and order. He bowed low to the personage and invoked blessings on him in passing.

In the relief of being unmolested for a while, his spirits rose, and he felt almost happy. The streets grew ever more crowded as he advanced. The road was filled with two streams of wheeled vehicles, going in opposite directions. The throng on the footway jostled and elbowed him roughly, giving no more heed than the sea gives to a piece of driftwood. It surprised him to see no horsemen nor pack-animals, not so much as a train of mules. All was busy, yet orderly. Though the press of the traffic was so great that the wheels of one vehicle grated those of another, and the nose of a carriage-horse was in the back of a cart in front, there was no frenzied shouting, such as might have been expected, no gesticulation on the part of drivers, but only a dull rumble and roar akin to thunder.

A display of familiar dainties in a vast window caught his eyes and held them for a while. He flattened his nose against the pane, gloating on oranges and lemons, bananas and pomegranates, dried figs and dates and raisins, with grins of delighted recognition. He stood a long time gazing at them, shouldered impatiently by wayfarers. It was with a sigh that at last he turned away and pursued his endless walk.

Many women and girls passed him, clad in the immodest fashion of the Franks, which excites a man by its cunning suggestion of the form beneath. They wore strange headgear, such as never man saw. Some were young and beautiful, so that Saïd leered at them meaningly. One fair girl of provoking charm, who was walking with an elder woman, laughed at him and touched her companion's arm. At that Saïd tingled in every vein, believing that she wished for him. All that the dragoman had told concerning the beauties of Lûndra surged gladly in his brain. His pulse quickened; he forgot that it was cold. Turning, he overtook the two women and walked at the young one's side, grinning into her face, and speaking words of love in Arabic. She shrank from him, pale with fright, and clung to the older woman's arm; but he kept close to her, wooing her hotly with every term of endearment. They hastened their steps, so that he had to run to keep up with them. All at once they stopped short, and the old woman, who wore a fine cloak of fur and a head-dress of many colours, spoke earnestly with a tall man clad in the sombre uniform already known to Saïd, having a high, dome-shaped hat and a leather truncheon in his belt. He stepped forward and seized the fisherman by the shoulders, shaking him and speaking sternly to him in a tone there was no gainsaying. Then, as the women made their escape, he pointed imperiously up the street and gave Saïd a push in that direction. The Muslim, completely taken aback, obeyed mechanically, the policeman following him a little way to mark his behaviour.

All day long he strayed on purposeless, growing more and more weary, a prey to thirst, and hunger, and intense cold. After noon the gloom deepened, the puny sun becoming quite obscured in cloud. He found a large piece of Frankish bread in a gutter, which he ate ravenously; and a little later, by good luck came to a drinking-fountain with a cup fixed to a chain for the service of poor wayfarers. Feeling refreshed, he prepared to face the night, and looked about for some sheltered place where he might sleep undisturbed. In a square court surrounded by high houses there was a sort of garden planted with sorry trees and shrubs, black with the prevailing soot, having seats and paved walks, and in the midst a great idol upon a pedestal. He stretched himself on one of the benches and composed his limbs to rest. But the cold was so great that he dared not fall asleep, but was fain to get up and walk again lest he should stiffen and die.

The streets by night were even more bewildering than in the daytime. The long vistas of yellow lamps, branching endlessly one out of another, confused his brain. Every wheeled vehicle had monstrous bright eyes to frighten him. The mist of light was blinding—the eternal mist of cloud by day, of fire by night, from which the dull roar of traffic seemed inseparable. The crowd where no man saluted other, no one looked friendly at his neighbour, but every face was grim with a set purpose, seemed awful to him. He feared it with the fear of evil spirits. The cries which assailed his ears were mournful as a wailing for the dead.

At length, after hours of wandering, he found an archway giving access to a quiet court and flung himself down in its gloom, too weary to know or care that the stones were icy cold. But it seemed that he had scarcely fallen asleep ere he was awakened by the flash of a lantern in his face. A gruff voice made a humming in his ears, and the form of a policeman loomed tremendous in his heavy eyes—a dark form holding the light which dazed him. He struggled to his feet, and seeing the enemy in the act to step forward and seize him, made off through the archway and down the sounding street as fast as his stiff limbs would carry him.

After that he dared not lie down again, but wandered on, sometimes resting on a doorstep, sometimes leaning against a wall or some railings, until a pallor of dawn appeared in the east. He found a quiet place where he said his prayers undisturbed, and soon after, by the grace of Allah, lighted on another crust of bread—a huge chunk on which he broke his fast. Then, when the day was fully come, he entered a public garden enclosed with palings and lay down upon the first seat he came to.

How long he slept he could not tell, for when he awoke the sky was completely overcast, and the brown fog had no point of brightness to indicate the sun's whereabouts. But the place where he lay was noisy with the play of ragged children, some of whom fled pell-mell as his eyes opened on them. His limbs were numbed so that, setting foot to the ground, he had to support himself by the back of the seat; and it was long ere he could walk safely.

As he issued from the garden he espied a well-known object amid the hurrying crowd on the footway of a great thoroughfare—a scarlet tarbûsh. With the strength of hope renewed, he ran as fast as he could to overtake its wearer. He came up with him, panting a salutation. But the face turned to him was not the face of the son of an Arab, but darker and of an olive tint not far removed from mouse-colour, the eyes set closer together. The reply to his salutation was in an unknown language; it was the speech of an unbeliever, in which the name of Allah did not occur. With a gesture of apology, expressive also of the deepest despair, Saïd fell back from him.

He got little heart-breaking reminders of the East from the form of a building here and there, and from homely objects in the shop windows. The sullen roar of the city was terrible in his ears, seeming now the voice of a cruel monster, now the growl of thunder—always hostile and inhuman. His eyes, unused to the subdued light, unable to appreciate its half tints, met a grey-brown horror everywhere. The women, too, dressed to provoke desire, had a share in his loathing of the scene. He would have liked to kill them for the involuntary thrill they gave.

Men and women with great baskets crouched by the edge of the roadway, selling flowers. Some of the foot-passengers stopped to buy of them. Saïd met people with nosegays in their hands, and it surprised him that they did not smell at them as folks use in the East; but on reflection it seemed likely that in this land of gloom and disappointment the blossoms had no smell or, if any, a foul one. He saw the sign of the cross often in all sorts of places, and spat on the ground for hatred of it, cursing the religion of the country secretly under his breath.

His brain grew confused. He was hunting for the sunlight which was lost. Little patches of colour drew his eyes and caused him a moment's rejoicing as for a treasure found at last. But each disillusion left him more despairing. Of a sudden, at the turning of a street, a blare of trumpets smote his ears, together with the rhythmic beat of a drum. In the heart of an eager, hurrying crowd, of like hue with the houses, the fog and the mud of the roadway, marched a company of soldiers clad in gorgeous scarlet—a hundred of them moving as one man. Their brightness and the marvel of their going attracted Saïd. He followed them spell-bound, yet with a kind of horror such as one has of jin in the night-season. He knew nothing of the crowd's roughness. The moving streak of red glowed like a flower-bed in that sombre street—like a bed of wild anemones amid the dull rocks of his native land. He battled to get near to them, but could not. To his mind, unhinged by fatigue and exposure, it was clear that, if only he could win to walk with them he would be saved. They were his life, his destiny, and they were slipping from him.

At length he lost sight of them altogether and the blackest despair took hold of him. He wandered into a region of quiet streets. The air had grown perceptibly warmer since the morning, and now a fine rain began to fall. Of a sudden, as it seemed to him, lamps were lighted; it was night. The sky lowered as a vast cloud; it was like a close lid oppressing him. Here was a maze in a box, shut out from sun, moon and stars, and he was doomed to roam in it for ever. All at once he felt deadly cold; the next minute he was burning from head to foot. It occurred to him to pray to Allah; but where was the use of prayer when he was already condemned and in torment? He ceased to fight against his lot.

A host of evil spirits beset him, gibbering, snapping their fingers, grinning, and mocking his wretched plight. Things faded and grew dim. He knew the horror of a great army coloured like blood, thousands moving in silence as one man. Shrieking, he clung to some railings for protection, vaguely aware that a crowd was gathering about him in a place which, a minute before, had been quite deserted. Then he was back again in his native land.

XV

SAÏD raved of palm-trees and gardens, the great sunshine and the inky shadows. He saw again the little house among the sandhills beside a calm blue sea. There were his nets spread to dry upon the beach. There was his fig-tree with the gnarled boughs and trunk, and the big leaves wide apart. There was the fringe of tamarisks along the shore, and the little city with its dome and minaret, clear-cut upon the vivid sky. He heard the distant music of bells, as some train of camels or mules passed slowing among the landward gardens. . . .

Suddenly there was a dun fog, effacing the vision and wrapping him in its gloom. Lamps without number shone blurred through the darkness. There was a sullen roar. He cried aloud in fear, but the sound of his voice was strange to him— a new terror. He grew aware of a bright and silent army, streaming ever out of darkness into darkness across the narrow range of his sight; tens of thousands moving as one man. Their colour entranced Saïd, but the order of their going chilled him with an eerie dread. He was awe-stricken, in the presence of a force beyond man's control. He felt that, if he could only draw near and walk with them, he would be informed of all things concerning his lot; but his limbs were frozen where he stood. He cried out upon the name of Allah. . . .

The fog melted away, the throng with it.

"Dìn! Dìn! Dìn Muhammed!" . . . He was in the streets of Damashc-ush-Shâm, frenzied with the sunlight and the shouting. He slew and slew, until he waded in the blood of unbelievers. All at once he was confronted with an old man whose name was known to him. Unthinking, he flew at his throat and strangled him, flinging the body aside into an entry. Then he fell a prey to the bitterest anguish, perceiving that he had killed Mustafa, his adopted father. His wail tore the blue

T 289

sky, as it had been a curtain, and dun fog poured in through the rent.   Again he was beset with darkness, and the shiver of the silent host was upon him.   He saw well-known faces in the ranks:—Abdullah, Selìm, Hasneh, Ibrahìm the doorkeeper, Ferideh, Ismaïl Abbâs, Mustafa, Nûr, Mahmûd Effendi.   All the people he had ever known passed in endless review before him.   They were changed to the likeness of devils, and moved. in silence all together, as though one will actuated them. . . .

Presently he was sitting alone on the deck of a ship.   Anon, he was drowning in the sea.   Then he led a bride to his house on the sands, but ere he could reach it the fog came upon him.   Once more there was brown twilight and that nameless horror. . . .

It was late afternoon.   Wintry sunlight, enfeebled by the smoke-clouds, made lurid ripples on the bare white walls of a spacious room lined with sick-beds.   At one end there was a comfortable fire burning in a recess of the wall, before which three women in white caps and aprons sat at a table, conversing in low tones.   The ward was full of tossings, groans and sobs of pain, relieved by the subdued laughter of the nurses at their table; the roar of the city coming as a murmur from without.

Saïd opened his eyes upon the scene, but there was no light of understanding in them.   He strove to raise himself on his elbows, but fell back upon the pillows with a moan.   When next he looked there was a woman at his bedside watching him.   She held a steaming bowl whose contents she kept stirring with a spoon.   Her face showed neither pity nor sympathy, but all her movements were deft and gentle.

While she was busy feeding him, propping his back upon a heap of pillows, two men entered the room together and came straight to where he lay.   One of them, who was dressed all in black, his face smooth save for a great tuft of hair on either jaw, hailed Saïd courteously in Arabic, inquiring after his health and commending him warmly to the mercy of Allah.   Sitting down on a chair by the bed he informed the invalid that he had been for many years a missionary among the Arabs, and wished to know if he could serve him in any way.   The sound of his native language seemed to gladden the sick man, for he listened intently, a dreamy smile on his face; but he answered nothing to the purpose, though his lips formed words. After many fruitless efforts to chain his attention, the visitor sighed and departed. He returned on the following days to meet with the same disappointment. Saïd always listened eagerly, sometimes his face wore a puzzled look, sometimes he smiled; but he never answered a word articulate. His silence was the more surprising that the nurses declared him to be very talkative when left alone, often muttering and exclaiming to himself for minutes together.

As the days wore on his strength came slowly back to him. He was able to sit up, then to walk a little way with the arm of a nurse. But he took no delight in anything, seeming bewildered, as if stunned from a blow. His eyes dwelt long and puzzled on every object, as though they would fathom its meaning and could not. The doctor, going his round one morning, took him by the shoulder and gazed searchingly into his eyes. He made as if he would strike Saïd's face, watching the patient carefully.

"An idiot," he pronounced. "The man's mind is gone."

When next the person in black came to the hospital, he sat not with Saïd, but with the doctor. The Arab was gaining strength with every day. He could not remain much longer in a place devoted to sick people. It seemed desirable that the poor fellow should be sent back to the East, where there was just a chance that he might recover his wits. The missionary undertook to lay the case before the society whose minister he was. He had little doubt but that the matter could be easily arranged. At shaking hands, the doctor begged that he might be informed if the sea-voyage and return to familiar scenes wrought any noteworthy change in his patient. The case was a rare one, and its peculiar circumstances interested him.

Ten days later, Saïd left the hospital, supported by the man in black and another man, and was driven in a close carriage to the docks. There was a film on his eyes so that he could see nothing clearly. His companions talked much by the way, but a dull roar in his ears made their speech seem remote. He muttered often to himself; but whenever the missionary addressed him, he became intent at once, listening with strained attention, a faint smile on his face.

His brain was still full of visions, of scenes slowly changing. But from being an actor in them he was become a peaceful spectator, regarding them with the interest one has in a pageant. They were pleasant for the most part, succeeding one another with a dream's inconsequence. Sometimes they were even funny, making him laugh aloud. But there were times when a cloud shadowed him suddenly and he shuddered, conscious of a vast army moving evenly and in silence, held together as one man by some mysterious force beyond his ken.

XVI

DAY by day the air grew warmer. Sky and sea put off their gloom, shining ever bluer and more lustrous as the sun gained in strength. Day by day, as he sat on the deck of a great steamer, looking out over the restless waves, Saïd had glimpses of remembered things, at first dimly, growing clearer as time went on. Once more he knew the difference of day and night, could tell when it was morning, or high noon, or evening ; and he observed the hours appointed for prayer and thanksgiving to Allah. Scales seemed to fall from his eyes so that he saw distinctly, and sought the meaning of what he saw. The roaring in his ears dwindled to stray murmurs, letting him hear the voices and sounds about him as something more than mere senseless jabber.

Much of his past life came back, as a tale heard long ago ; but it had no significance for him. Knowing that it concerned him nearly, it distressed him that he could not guess its import. He had the same trouble with regard to all that passed on board the steamer. Everything was very hard to understand. He would puzzle for hours over some trivial detail of the scene, knowing it familiar, yet powerless to grasp its meaning. The outer shell of form and colour held his mind and prevented it from penetrating any deeper. Worst of all, he was conscious of this flaw in his vision, though he strove in vain to better it.

Yet, in spite of drawbacks, his heart was glad because of the great sunlight and its dazzle on the sea. He would smile and laugh for no reason, and would croon old songs to himself where he sat apart in the lee of a cabin. Words came to his lips, which somehow suited his frame of mind ; and he was pleased, recognising their fitness, but the words, like everything else, had no meaning for him.

Sometimes, glancing down at his clothing, he was almost

293

convinced that it was not himself at all, but someone else whom he had never known. The close-fitting trousers which strained at the knees when he sat cross-legged, the loose-hanging black coat with needless buttons upon the sleeves, the Frankish boots so tiresome to put off and on, the hat of plaited straw, bound about the crown with a black ribbon—all were strange, and vexed him with misty doubts of his identity. He would turn from the contemplation of them with a sigh, content simply to bask in the warmth and the brightness, leaving the riddle of his existence unsolved for the present.

The people of the ship were very kind to him. On all sides he saw smiling, friendly faces. One man in particular came often to sit with him; who always wore black clothes and dwelt in a part of the steamer whither Saïd was not allowed to go. He spoke in a familiar tongue, and the fisherman returned his greetings naturally, as an echo answers; but when he talked at any length his speech became mere words, having form and even colour, but no sense. One early morning this person came to the place where Saïd slept, and awoke him. He led him up on to the deck and showed a city resting on the dimpled bosom of the sea, with minarets and domes and a lighthouse, and great buildings dark beside the rising sun. And Saïd laughed for joy, he knew not why.

The vessel entered a fine harbour, where there was much shipping. As the sun got higher, the sea grew vivid blue and the sands of the coast had the colour of a ripe orange. There was green of foliage beyond the houses, the sky towards the horizon was soft and pearly. Hundreds of little boats plied upon the dancing water between large vessels which lay inert and supine, like sleeping monsters. The men and boys in them were gaily clad, with red caps, light turbans and clothing of divers colours. Homely shouts were in the air.

Saïd's heart went out to the brightness of that merry scene. He hated his companion all at once with a fierce and unreasoning hatred. He would gladly have slain him where he stood smiling indulgently at the idiot's glee. He loathed the steamer and all on board. He longed to be free of them, to escape on shore and mix with those men in bright apparel, who were his own people.

The noise of the engines ceased with the pulse of the screw; and almost directly there was a swarm of rowing-boats to the steamer's side. In one of these, Saïd discerned a Frank sitting, dressed all in black on the pattern of the man at his side, of the man he hated. He scowled at this new blot in the sunlight; and his eyes chose that boat out of all others, following it closely. He saw the Frank step out and mount the ladder to the deck. A minute later he shrank back with a snarl. The evil one had come near, and was staring at him, grasping the hand of the other man in black and speaking with him as an old friend. Presently he essayed to take Saïd's arm to lead him, but the latter sprang aside and, scrambling hot-foot down the ladder, was first in the boat.

During the brief passage to the shore, his new enemy strove to engage him in conversation; but Saïd, absorbed in watching the boatmen and listening greedily to their talk, had a deaf ear for him. Arrived at the landing-place, however, he submitted to be led through the lively crowd. He was as one demented, laughing for no apparent reason and shouting salutations to all he met. His excitement made no distinction between true believers and infidels, but beamed alike upon all who wore bright clothing. People turned in astonishment to look after one, who, though clad in all respects like a poor Frank, and walking with a well-known missionary, yet swore by the Coràn and accosted everyone in Arabic with a marked Syrian intonation.

Feasting his eyes on the warm hues of the crowd and its animation, Saïd felt that he was at home again. Great joy engrossed him to the exclusion of all else in the world. He forgot the existence of the man in black, ignored even his own existence; content to wander on through the merry, noisy streets, no matter who his guide. But at a point where several ways met, the missionary tried to draw him out of the sunshine, and the colours, and the shouting, into a shadowed, silent street, where the houses were large and of Frankish build, with big glass windows. He pulled Saïd's sleeve and spoke earnestly to him. The fisherman stared at him without comprehension, a fool's laugh dying in his throat. His glance followed the guide's stretched-out hand. Something in the aspect of the houses made him shiver. In a flash he had the vision of a vast dun cloud and a devilish blood-coloured throng moving silently through its heart. That road led somehow to it, and the man in black, the false guide, was suborned to drag him thither.

With the cry of a wild beast, he sprang upon the astonished missionary and gripped his throat, forcing him to the ground. It was in his mind to strangle him there and then, and so make an end of the gloom, the silent horror and all the hideous nightmare he personified. But a concourse of people clothed in bright colours diverting his eyes, he quitted his hold and stood up.

"Dìn Muhammed!" he said, and burst out laughing.

At that the faces of the crowd changed their looks of menace for those of concern.

"Run, O my uncle!" . . . "Make haste!" . . . "By this way!" . . . "Save thyself!" . . .

Friendly cries came from all hands. And Saïd, without knowing why, leapt forward with a shout of exultation, and ran he cared not whither.

His Frankish hat had fallen and was forgotten. His head, which had not known the razor for many weeks, bristled with a shock of white hair. His beard, white also, was long and unkempt. Women in shrouds of indigo, with queer cylinders between their eyes, ran from him with screams of terror. Brown-limbed children tumbled headlong into doorways, yelling for their lives. Men in flowing robes flattened themselves against the wall as he passed, and stood to stare after him, exclaiming together. Soldiers, set to keep order in the streets, retired trembling to their hutches, and asked a blessing on that awful runner. An old man with white hair and beard bounding forward like a boy, shouting and laughing as he ran . . . The apparition was new to the men of Iskenderia, and they wondered what it might portend. Surely, thought they, it is a madman, or some true prophet sent from Allah! Did ever man see the like? Verily the end of all things draws nigh!" . . .

Saïd sped on, laughing in pure joy of the sunshine and the shadows, the bright hues and merry sounds of a life familiar to him. Swarthy faces looked out at him from dark thresholds of taverns and shops. There were donkeys, mules, camels, laden with sacks and bales and panniers. There was nothing sad, nothing to recall the cloud and its fear, save only a few Franks here and there; and even they failed to anger him, being clad not in dull raiment but in white. The sunshine on the multi-coloured crowd, the chattering and gesticulation, the blue sky, the air, the very smells were friendly, redolent of home.

In a place where there was less traffic he slackened his pace, panting, and found himself bathed in sweat. For the first time he grew aware of the sun's beams scorching his uncovered head, and instinctively he sought the shade of a wall, near the shop of a petty trader.

His own cries and laughter rang yet in his ears, but hollow and senseless. In the plum-coloured shade he sat down to rest, his eyes dwelling on the sunlit buildings opposite. Their tint against the sapphire sky made him think of barren, stony hills—the sunburnt hills of Es-Shâm. Of a sudden, there was a swimming in his head. Sickness seized him, forcing him to vomit. He groaned aloud, calling heart-broken on the name of Allah and bewailing his evil day. The merchant reclining at ease in the coolness of his shop hard by, hearing the sound of lamentation, came forth to see who made it. He was a tall, bearded man of middle life, wearing a high fez and embroidered turban ; and his robe of mixed silk and cotton was green and crimson striped. Seeing an old man sit there bare-headed, he reproved him gravely for his folly, vowing by Allah that if he got a sunstroke he could blame no one but himself.

Saïd raised despairing eyes to the speaker—eyes which saw nothing but his own immediate wretchedness. He heard the voice of Selîm cry,—

"Merciful Allah ! . . . O my master ! . . . O my eyes ! O my dear ! Is it indeed thyself, and in this shameful plight ? . . . O mother of Mûsa, get food and drink ! Let Hasneh make ready a pleasant bed ! Behold Saïd, my beloved, is returned to us at the point of death, having white hair and the clothes of a Frank. Praise be to Allah that he is returned to us ! May Allah spare him to us, and grant him peace and good health once more ! " . . .

Saïd heard Selîm's voice and was glad to hear it. It sounded familiar, and he knew it friendly. "Praise be to Allah ! " he murmured naturally. But his mind had no real knowledge of Selîm, and the words were but empty sound.

XVII

WHEN Saïd recovered of his sunstroke, he was the
honoured guest of the little household. Selîm's love
for him, born years before of gratitude for the gift of a stolen
garment, was now doubled with the respect for one of unsound
mind. The whole house was Saïd's, the shop also and all it
contained. Selîm or his wife would have waited on him all
day long had Hasneh not forestalled them. Mûsa was told off
to shadow him when he walked abroad, lest any evil should
befall him. His head and the hair of his body were shorn
duly according to the law, and he was arrayed in good clothes,
which the master of the house bought for him at no small
cost.

At the hour of the evening meal, when men are sociable in
the relief of the day's task done, Selîm would often tell his
children and any chance guest the story of his acquaintance
with Saïd. He would lift the brown dressing-gown with the
red braiding out of the chest where it was kept, and tears would
stand in his eyes as he showed it to the little circle, handling it
reverently as a precious relic. He would glance ruefully at the
fisherman where he sat cross-legged, muttering often to himself
and making strange play with his hands.

The young ones loved better to hear of the great slaughter
and how bravely Ahmed Pasha met his death. They would
clamour for their father to act the scene for them, showing
where the Sultàn's envoy stood, where the Wâly, where the file
of soldiers who shot him down. Mûsa clenched teeth and
hands at the point where the soldiers shirked their work, and
for a time doggedly refused to fire. He vowed that he would
rather be killed himself than slay an old man and a pious
Muslim to pleasure infidels. They loved that story best for
the fighting and bloodshed that were in it; but Selîm liked
most to tell of Saïd the Fisherman and his great goodness.

298

Every morning, having broken his fast, Saïd roamed forth out of the city to a place he had discovered, where there were palm-trees beside a sandy road, and whence, through the dusty leaves of a garden, he got a glimpse of yellow sands and the dark blue sea. There, sitting cross-legged in the shade, he was happy all day long, laughing and crooning to himself, receiving homage from the poorer class of wayfarers—camel-drivers and muleteers, beggars and gipsies, snake-charmers and itinerant merchants—who respected the fine robe and the embroidered turban with which Selîm had invested him.

He loved to watch the long trains of camels winding with the road, and would strain his ears to hold the music of their bells when it grew faint and died in the distance. It pleased him to see big men and fat go jogging by upon small donkeys, their legs distended because of full saddle-bags, their feet not far from the ground. The blue-robed peasant women made eyes at him as they walked with swaying bodies, sleek brown arms raised like twin handles of a vase to steady the burdens on their heads. Sometimes rich men on prancing horses, sometimes a carriage dashed past him, heralded by an out-runner with girt-up loins. He took a childish pleasure in saluting these great ones, prizing a chance smile from one of them more than the effusion of humbler passengers. All was passionate, highly-coloured of the East. Every wayfarer was merry or furious, laughing or cursing, sullen or smiling, in the depth of despair or the height of glee, hot and heady as the sunlight itself. But sometimes, in a minute, a deep gloom would fall on him, isolating him so that he seemed to sit alone, aware of the silent march of a great bright army. At such moments he knew that the mystery was eternal, that it had been going on unguessed through all the time he had forgotten, and must go on irrevocably until the last day. He shuddered when the fit left him, and it was long ere he could shake off the horror of it.

Sometimes Hasneh would accompany him to his favourite spot and sit near him in the shade, delighting in his childlike gladness. But the wife of Selîm could seldom spare her from the house; more often it was Mûsa who dogged Saïd's foot-steps and lay hid in the garden close to where he sat. The lad got amusement out of his allotted task by imagining great perils for his father's guest, seeing himself as rescuer dashing like a young hurricane to save him, scattering a hundred well-armed men like chaff.   When the sun was set and the smoke from hidden dwellings curled blue upon the delicate flush of evening or yellowish on the dove-grey which followed, Saïd would rise and turn his face homeward ; he loved to spend the livelong day in the open, detesting the imprisonment of four walls.

For months, for years, he led this peaceful kind of life, without care or thought, conscious only of the appearance of things, their outward shape and colour, troubled only at long intervals by the ghost of a memory.   But there came a time of disturbance, when the crowd in the streets wore anxious looks, and men formed knots together, speaking excitedly with fierce eyes.   Selîm, fearing a tumult, thought it wise to confine his guest within doors lest he should come to harm.   His loving care would not trust the fisherman out of his sight.   This imprisonment fretted Saïd, to whom the sunshine and the fresh air of the gardens were become as daily food.   He grew very cross and irritable, and Hasneh, into whose charge he was given, had to bear the brunt of all ill-humour which could hear no reason.

Once when a great uproar arose in the city, Saïd's eyes flamed suddenly and he sprang to his feet.   For a moment there was understanding in his face ; but the fire died as suddenly as it leapt up, and he fell back into the old, listless bad temper.   For more than a month he was constrained by Selîm's order, going out only occasionally, when the master of the house had leisure to accompany him.   He was kept in the house in deep shadow, with nothing bright to look at, and time hung very heavy on his hands.

One day Selîm closed his shop and came to sit in the room with his family.   He spoke seldom, and was very grave.   A neighbour with a scared face looked in on them from time to time, bringing tidings or feeling the need of company. Through long hours there was booming of cannon, followed by explosions near at hand, the crash and roar of falling masonry. Saïd strained ears to hearken, and his face wore a puzzled expression, such as is often seen on faces of the blind.   The firing ceased towards evening, and Selîm, praising Allah, went out to gather tidings, but refused to take Saïd with him.

The next day there was no more booming, but towards

noon the city was filled with shouting and tumult. The whole household running out to learn the cause of the din, Saïd was left unguarded for a few minutes. They had hidden away his outer garments, thinking that his love of finery would prevent him from going abroad without it. But he was a match for them. He knew where to find a robe—an old garment of outlandish fashion, prettily bound with soiled red braid, which had often been spread out before his eyes of evenings, when there were guests present. He opened the chest and took it out, smoothing it lovingly with a furtive glance to make sure that no one saw. Then he put it on, chuckling.

Thus attired, he stole to the door and peeped out. Hasneh and the mother of Mûsa were talking with some other women a good way off. Selîm himself was nowhere to be seen. Girding up his loins, Saïd took to his heels, laughing as he ran. Clouds of smoke blurred the sky before him above the roofs; his eyes dwelt on them curiously as they did always on a new thing. There was a noise of shouting in the air.

Suddenly on turning a corner he found himself in a yelling, furious mob, all rushing in one direction. Fierce eyes, brandished weapons, curses and a roar of shouting. It was as though a door swung open in Saïd's brain, admitting light into a chamber long shut up. Understanding flashed in his eyes.

"Dîn Muhammed!" he cried, and rushed forward with the rest, only more fiercely, with more of frenzy. Even in that turmoil men looked at him and, looking, made way for him to pass. There was something awful in his face, a light of madness or inspiration beyond their ken. He was a prophet and would bring them good fortune. They pressed on behind him, shouting louder than before. On he ran, tearing a way through the crowd. At length he led them, was at their head, still rushing on.

All at once cries of warning and terror arose. The crowd surged backward, forsaking him. A sudden fear came upon him, a shudder . . . the noiseless horror! . . . A bright host, moving together as one man, appeared out of a side street, and formed a wall before him. He pressed both hands to his temples, staring wildly. There was a word of command, short and incisive as a pistol-shot. All the sunlight was filled with yells of rage and fright. Again the word of command, followed by a line of flashes and a loud report which burst his head.

"Dìn! Dìn! Dìn! . . ."

He flung up his arms. His eyes seemed to turn over in their sockets, as he fell backwards on the ground.

So the garment of the Christian missionary became the death-robe of a martyr for El Islâm, and the sunlight swam blood-red at the last.

TIME-TABLE

1871 (end of October).		Saïd left Damascus.
1882 (11th of June).	.	Riot and Massacre of Europeans at Alexandria.
1882 (11th of July).	.	Bombardment of Alexandria.
1882 (12th of July).	.	Egyptian forces under Arabi evacuated the town, setting fire to European quarter and letting loose upon it gangs of plunderers. Saïd met his death in this riot.

EDINBURGH
COLSTON AND COY. LIMITED
PRINTERS

CPSIA information can be obtained
at www.ICGtesting.com
Printed in the USA
LVHW082141010320
648664LV00009B/98